CAMBRIDGE

CW01643340

First TRAINER

SIX PRACTICE TESTS WITH ANSWERS

2

Cambridge University Press
www.cambridge.org/elt

Cambridge Assessment English
www.cambridgeenglish.org

Information on this title: www.cambridge.org/9781009212359

First published 2018
This edition published 2022

20 19 18 17 16 15 14 13 12 11 10 9 8 7 6

Printed in Poland by Opolgraf

A catalogue record for this publication is available from the British Library

ISBN 978-1-009-21235-9 Six Practice Tests with Answers with eBook
ISBN 978-1-009-21236-6 Six Practice Tests without Answers with eBook

Contents

Introduction

Who is *First Trainer 2* for?

This book is suitable for anyone who is preparing to take the *Cambridge English: First (FCE)* exam. You can use *First Trainer 2* in class with your teacher, or on your own at home.

What is *First Trainer 2*?

First Trainer 2 contains six practice tests for *Cambridge English: First*, each covering the Reading and Use of English, Writing, Listening and Speaking papers. Guided Tests 1 and 2 consist of both training and practice for the exam, while Tests 3–6 are entirely practice. All six tests are at exam level and are of *Cambridge English: First* standard.

Test 1 contains information about each part of each paper, plus step-by-step guidance to take you through each kind of *Cambridge English: First* task type, with examples and tips clearly linked to the questions. In the Reading and Use of English, Writing and Speaking papers, it also presents and practises grammar, vocabulary and functional language directly relevant to particular task types. This is supported by work on correcting common grammar mistakes made by *Cambridge English: First* candidates in the exam as shown by the **Cambridge Learner Corpus**. For more information on the Cambridge Learner Corpus see page 6. The **Keys** tell you which answers are correct and why, and explains why other answers are wrong.

Test 2 also contains training for the exam, in addition to revision from Test 1. Here too there is language input, as well as some step-by-step guidance to task types with further examples, advice and tips. In Writing, there is a full focus on the task types not covered in Test 1.

Tests 3–6 contain a wide range of topics, text types and exam items, enabling you to practise the skills you have developed and the language you have learnt in Tests 1 and 2.

How to use *First Trainer 2*

Test 1 Training

- For each part of each paper, you should begin by studying **Task information**, which tells you the facts you need to know, such as what the task type tests and the kinds of questions it uses.
- Throughout Test 1, you will see information marked **Tip!** These tips give you practical advice on how to tackle each task type.
- In all papers, training exercises help you develop the skills you need, e.g. reading for gist, by working through example items of a particular task type.
- For Parts 1–4 of **Reading and Use of English**, both parts of **Writing** and all parts of **Speaking**, **Useful language** presents and practises grammatical structures, vocabulary or functional expressions that are often tested by particular task types.
- Many exercises involve focusing on and correcting common language mistakes made by actual *Cambridge English: First* candidates, as shown by the **Cambridge Learner Corpus** (www.cambridge.org/corpus).

- In **Listening**, you are prompted to use the downloadable audio, e.g. 1. If you are working on your own, you will need to be able to access the downloadable audio files.
- In **Writing**, Test 1 covers Part 1 (essay), as well as the article, review and email tasks in Part 2. You study some **examples** to help you perfect your skills. The **Keys** contain answers to the exercises, plus **sample answers**. You finish each part by writing your own text, bringing in what you have learnt in **Useful language**.
- In **Speaking**, you are prompted to use one of the downloadable audio files, e.g. 18, and complete tasks while you listen to examples of each part of the paper. You can practise speaking on your own or with a partner, using what you have learnt in **Useful language**.
- In all papers, an **Action plan** gives you clear step-by-step guidance on how to approach each task type.
- You then work through an exam-style task, often doing exercises based on the guidance in the **Action plan** and then following the exam instructions. As you do so, **Advice** boxes suggest ways of dealing with particular exam items.
- Answers to all items are in the **Keys**.

Test 2 Training

- Test 2 contains many of the same features as Test 1, including exercises that focus on exam instructions, texts and tasks, **Tip!** information, **Advice** boxes for many exam items, **Useful language** and **Keys**.
- There is further work based on mistakes frequently made by *Cambridge English: First* candidates as shown by the **Cambridge Learner Corpus**.
- There is also an emphasis on revision, with cross-references for each task type to the relevant **Task information** and **Action plan** in Test 1. You should refer back to these before you begin working through each part.
- Test 2 **Writing** covers Part 1 (essay) plus the report, letter and article tasks in Part 2, along with **sample answers** for some of the tasks.
- You should try to do the exam tasks under exam conditions where possible.

Tests 3–6 Exam practice

- In Tests 3, 4, 5 and 6, you can apply the skills and language you have learnt in guided Tests 1 and 2.
- You can do these tests and the four papers within them in any order, but you should always try to keep to the time recommended for each paper. For the Listening paper, you must **listen to each recording twice only**.
- It will be easier to keep to the exam instructions if you can find somewhere quiet to work, and ensure there are no interruptions.
- For the Speaking paper, it is better if you can work with a partner, but if not, you can follow the instructions and do all four parts on your own.
- You can check your answers for yourself, and also study the Listening audioscripts after you have completed the tasks.

Other features of *First Trainer 2*

- Full-colour **visual materials** for the Speaking paper of all six tests in the Speaking visuals section (pages C1–C22).
- For Tests 1 and 2, the **Keys** tells you which answers are correct, and why. In some cases, it also explains why the other options are wrong. The answers to Tests 3–6 are also provided.
- **Photocopiable sample answer sheets** for the Reading and Use of English, Listening, and Speaking are at the back of the book. Before you take the exam, you should study these so that you know how to mark or write your answers correctly. In Writing, the question paper has plenty of lined space for you to write your answers.
- The **downloadable audio files** contain recordings for the Listening papers of the six *First* tests plus recordings from different parts of the Speaking in Tests 1 and 2 to serve as examples.

The *Cambridge English: First* examination

Level of the *Cambridge English: First* examination

Cambridge English: First is at level B2 on the Common European Framework (CEFR). When you reach this level, these are some of the things you should be able to do:

- You can scan written texts for the information you need, and understand detailed instructions or advice.
- You can understand or give a talk on a familiar subject, and keep a conversation going on quite a wide range of subjects.
- You can make notes while someone is talking, and write a letter that includes different kinds of requests.

Grading

- The overall *Cambridge English: First* grade that you receive is based on the total score you achieve in all four papers.
- The Reading and Use of English paper carries 40% of the possible marks, while each of Writing, Listening and Speaking carry 20% of the possible marks.
- There is no minimum score for each paper, so you don't have to 'pass' all four in order to pass the exam.
- You receive a certificate if you pass the exam with grade A (the highest grade), B or C. Grades D and E are fails.
- Whatever your grade, you will receive a Statement of Results. This includes a graphical profile of how well you did in each paper and shows your relative performance in each one.

Content of the *Cambridge English: First* examination

The *Cambridge English: First* examination has four papers, each consisting of a number of parts. For details on each part, see the page reference under the *Task information* heading in these tables.

Reading and Use of English 1 hour 15 minutes

Parts 1 and 3 mainly test your vocabulary; Part 2 mainly tests your grammar. Part 4 often tests both. There is one mark for each correct answer in Parts 1, 2 and 3, but two marks for a correct answer in Part 4. You can write on the question paper, but you must remember to transfer your answers to the separate answer sheet before the end of the test.

The total length of texts in Parts 5–7 is about 2,200 words in total. They are taken from newspaper and magazine articles, fiction, reports, advertisements, correspondence, messages and informational material such as brochures, guides or manuals. There are two marks for each correct answer in Parts 5 and 6; there is one mark for every correct answer in Part 7.

Part	Task type	No. of questions	Format	Task information
1	Multiple-choice cloze	8	You choose from words A, B, C or D to fill in each gap in a text.	page 10
2	Open cloze	8	You think of the correct word to fill in each of the gaps in a text.	page 16
3	Word formation	8	You think of the correct form of a prompt word to fill in each gap in a text.	page 20
4	Key word transformations	6	You have to complete a sentence using a given key word so that it means the same as another sentence.	page 23
5	Multiple choice	6	You read a text followed by questions with four options: A, B, C or D.	page 26
6	Gapped text	6	You read a text with some missing paragraphs, then fill in the gaps by choosing paragraphs from a jumbled list.	page 31
7	Multiple matching	10	You read a text divided into sections (or several short texts) and match the relevant sections to statements.	page 34

Writing 1 hour 20 minutes

You have to do Part 1 (question 1) plus any **one** of the Part 2 tasks. In Part 2, you can choose one of questions 2–4. The possible marks for Part 1 and Part 2 are the same. In all tasks you are told who you are writing to and why.

Part	Task type	No. of words	Format	Task information
1	Question 1: essay	140–190	You give your opinion on a topic using the two ideas given, plus an idea of your own.	page 37
2	Questions 2–4 possible tasks: article, email/ letter, report or review	140–190	You write one text, from a choice of three text types, based on a situation.	pages 41, 45, 49

Listening about 40 minutes

You will both hear and see the instructions for each task, and you will hear each of the four parts twice. You will hear pauses announced, and you can use this time to look at the task and the questions. At the end of the test, you will have five minutes to copy your answers onto the answer sheet.

If one person is speaking, you may hear information, news, instructions, a commentary, a documentary, a lecture, a message, a public announcement, a report, a speech, a talk or an advertisement. If two people are talking, you might hear a conversation, a discussion, an interview, part of a radio play, etc.

Part	Task type	No. of questions	Format	Task information
1	Multiple choice	8	You listen to monologues or conversations between interacting speakers, and you choose from answers A, B or C.	page 52
2	Sentence completion	10	You listen to a monologue lasting about three minutes, and you complete the sentences with the missing information.	page 55
3	Multiple matching	5	You listen to five themed monologues of about 30 seconds each, and you select five correct options from a list of eight possible answers.	page 57
4	Multiple choice	7	You listen to a conversation between two or more speakers, for about three to four minutes, and you choose from options A, B or C.	page 59

Speaking 14 minutes per pair of candidates

You will probably do the Speaking test with one other candidate, though sometimes it is necessary to form groups of three. There will be two examiners, but one of them does not take part in the conversation. The examiner will indicate who you should talk to in each part of the test.

Part	Task type	Minutes	Format	Task information
1	Interview	2	The examiner asks you some questions and you give information about yourself.	page 61
2	Long turn	1 minute per candidate	You talk on your own (for about one minute) about two photographs the examiner gives you. Then the examiner asks the other candidate to comment on the same photographs (for about 30 seconds). The examiner then gives the other candidate a different set of two photographs and the process is repeated.	page 63
3	Collaborative task	3 minutes (a 2-minute discussion followed by a 1-minute decision-making task)	You have a conversation with the other candidate. The examiner gives you some material and a task to complete together.	page 66
4	Discussion	4	You have a discussion with the other candidate, guided by questions from the examiner, about the topics in Part 3.	page 69

Further information

The information about *Cambridge English: First* contained in *First Trainer 2* is designed to be an overview of the exam. For a full description of the *Cambridge English: First* examination, including information about task types, testing focus and preparation for the exam, please see the *Cambridge English: First* Handbook, which can be obtained from http://www.cambridgeenglish.org/teaching-english/resources-for-teachers/

Cambridge Assessment

The Triangle Building

Shaftesbury Road

Cambridge

CB2 8EA

Test 1 Training Reading and Use of English Part 1

Task information

- In Part 1, you have to read a text with eight gaps, and choose the correct word from four options (A, B, C or D) to fill each gap.
- The words in the options will all be the same part of speech, e.g. nouns, adjectives, etc.
- Part 1 mainly tests vocabulary, and words which go together (collocations). It may also test how ideas in the text are connected.
- Knowing the meaning of the words in the options may not be enough. You will need to know how the words in the options are used in sentences in order to choose the correct one.
- You will need to understand the text as a whole to do the task. Study the words on either side of each gap and make sure the word you choose makes sense.

Useful language Verbs + prepositions

1 **Complete the sentences with prepositions from the box. Some of the prepositions can be used more than once.**

of	for	on	in	to	with	from

1 He recovered .... his illness very quickly.
2 Does anybody object .... this idea?
3 Hundreds of people participated .... the race.
4 My grandmother used to care .... me while my mother was at work.
5 They adapted .... the weather conditions without too much difficulty.
6 My aunt doesn't approve .... people eating in the street.
7 I know I can depend .... Tom when I need him.
8 I'm always competing .... my sister, but we get on very well.
9 The students all benefited .... the interesting lectures they attended.
10 How did she react .... the news?

Tip! In your vocabulary notebook, record how the verb is used as well as its meaning, e.g. *recover*: 'become completely well again' – *She's recovered from the bicycle accident now*.

2 **Correct the sentences by changing the prepositions.**

1 Why don't you apply to the job?
2 I don't believe of telling lies – it's always wrong.
3 The football match resulted with a draw.
4 Mary dealt from the problem really well.
5 What can you contribute for the discussion?

Useful language Verbs followed by either nouns or infinitives

3 **Match the verbs in the box with the correct label.**

assist	manage	accept	appreciate	imagine
agree	pretend	support	struggle	achieve

verbs followed by nouns: ....

verbs followed by infinitive with *to*: ....

4 **For sentences 1–8, decide which answer (A, B, C or D) best fits each gap.**

1 I don't know how I .... to get here on time!

A achieved **B** struggled **C** resulted **D** managed

2 The football coach has .... to run an extra practice session before the match.

A accepted **B** agreed **C** achieved **D** assisted

3 All the children laughed when Kim .... to be a lion.

A adapted **B** imagined **C** believed **D** pretended

4 Sally is an experienced violinist, so has a lot to .... to the success of the orchestra.

A contribute **B** support **C** assist **D** benefit

5 I wasn't really sure whether Mark .... to my idea or not.

A disapproved **B** complained **C** objected **D** disliked

6 The college principal doesn't .... of students shouting in the corridors.

A appreciate **B** agree **C** approve **D** accept

7 The job was difficult, but I think Greg .... with the challenges extremely well.

A dealt **B** struggled **C** managed **D** adapted

8 Larry .... all his colleagues' help when he started working with them.

A benefited **B** appreciated **C** depended **D** approved

Tip! Sometimes, a word doesn't fit in the gap for grammatical reasons, e.g. 5A: *disapproved* is followed by *of*, not *to*. Sometimes, it doesn't fit because it has the wrong meaning, e.g. 3A: *adapt* means 'become familiar with a new situation'.

Useful language Verb collocations

5 **Match the verbs in the table with the nouns and phrases in the box. Some can be placed in more than one column.**

make	take	put	hold	keep	have

into account	an eye on	responsibility	use of	a risk	your way
advantage of	your breath	pressure on	an interest	a word	charge/control
the most of	the opportunity	someone waiting	something seriously	an end to	

6 **Complete the sentences with the correct form of one of the phrases from Exercise 5.**

1 Sally managed .... under water for two minutes.

2 It's important .... all the participants' points of view before reaching a decision.

3 They .... very carefully through the dense jungle.

4 Julian never seems to .... ; he's always laughing.

5 I can't believe I was .... outside his office for half an hour!

6 Could I .... with you about the plans for next week?

7 I don't want to take the job, but my boss is .... me to do so.

8 Could you .... my little brother for a minute, please?

Useful language Adjectives + prepositions

7 **For questions 1–10, read the text below and decide which answer (A, B, C, or D) best fits each gap.**

In many countries, very young children are given soft furry toys as presents. Bears are particularly popular, and children can often become very **(1)** .... of their 'teddy bears'. I remember my younger brother had a teddy bear called Fred. He was so **(2)** .... about this toy bear that he couldn't tolerate being **(3)** .... from Fred for even a few minutes. He was always extremely **(4)** .... of anyone who tried it. I was only a few years older than him and used to feel quite **(5)** .... by this.

Of course, Fred needed washing from time to time. My little brother was **(6)** .... of the fact that only my mother was **(7)** .... to do this. As my brother grew up, he remained very fond of Fred, but the toy bear was no longer **(8)** .... to his well-being.

	A	B	C	D
1	**A** careful	**B** responsible	**C** anxious	**D** protective
2	**A** devoted	**B** passionate	**C** attached	**D** sympathetic
3	**A** split	**B** isolated	**C** separated	**D** divided
4	**A** suspicious	**B** offensive	**C** dissatisfied	**D** sensitive
5	**A** furious	**B** unsympathetic	**C** impatient	**D** irritated
6	**A** definite	**B** convinced	**C** specific	**D** evident
7	**A** skilled	**B** qualified	**C** satisfactory	**D** capable
8	**A** crucial	**B** outstanding	**C** compulsory	**D** remarkable

Useful language Words which are often confused

Tip! Words which are similar in meaning, but cannot be used in the same way, are often confused. Learn the meaning as well as the use of each new word.

8 **Complete the sentences with the correct option from each pair of words in the box.**

raise / rise	assist / support	error / fault	definitely / absolutely	valued / valuable

1 When the flight was cancelled, the airline admitted that they were at .... and compensated all the passengers.
2 It may be difficult to .... the money to set up a community theatre.
3 Some of the paintings in this museum are so .... that they have been insured for millions of dollars.
4 My boss .... told me I could leave early tomorrow.
5 Few people .... the proposal to build a road here.
6 The price of vegetables will probably .... after this bad weather.
7 The power supply was cut off in .... by the electricity company.
8 Anna is a much .... member of staff.
9 Can I .... you with your bags, madam?
10 I thought that film was .... brilliant.

Useful language Phrasal verbs

9 **Match the phrasal verbs with the meanings.**

1 catch up with something	a) manage not to be caught doing something wrong
2 give something away	b) find or meet by chance
3 fall through	c) solve
4 come across something or someone	d) be or look like an older family member
5 sort something out	e) fail to happen
6 take after someone	f) do what you didn't have time to do earlier
7 live up to something	g) be as good as hoped
8 get away with something	h) reveal a secret

Tip! Phrasal verbs are often tested in the exam. Learn their meaning, whether they are transitive or intransitive, and whether an object can go between the verb and the adverb/preposition.

10 **Complete the sentences with the correct form of a phrasal verb from Exercise 9.**

1 Nick .... his father – he's never on time!
2 I'm trying to .... all my emails before I leave the office.
3 Last year, all our plans for the summer holidays .... because of the bad weather.
4 Some criminals tried to hack into my account, but luckily they didn't .... it.
5 I .... some old family photo albums in a box in the attic.
6 The concert was wonderful and .... all my expectations!
7 Please don't .... our hiding place!
8 There were a lot of problems to .... when she took over the failing company.

Test 1 Exam practice   Reading and Use of English • Part 1

Action plan

1 Read the title, and the first sentence with the example.
2 Without filling in any gaps, read the text quickly to get an idea of what it's about.
3 Read the text again more slowly and fill each gap with one of its four options.
4 Don't forget to keep in mind the meaning of the text as it develops.
5 Look at the words on either side of each gap, as the missing word may be part of a collocation or fixed phrase.
6 Check that the completed sentence makes sense.
7 Check that the missing word fits with any prepositions before or after the gap.

Follow the exam instructions, using the advice to help you.

For questions **1–8**, read the text below and decide which answer (**A, B, C** or **D**) best fits each gap. There is an example at the beginning (**0**).

Mark your answers **on the separate answer sheet.**

Tip! First, complete the gaps that you are confident about. Then complete the rest.

Tip! If you're not sure of an answer, cross out any you are confident are wrong and then choose from the remaining options.

Example:

0 **A** turned **B** become **C** developed **D** changed

0	A	B	C	D
	▭	▬	▭	▭

Street pianos

In recent years, public or 'street' pianos have **(0)** .... increasingly popular in cities in many countries. They are typically **(1)** .... in train stations and airports, but also in markets, parks and other locations. In **(2)** .... anybody can go and play them, but it tends to be pianists who are very capable and accustomed to performing in public, often playing from **(3)** ....

The idea is that the sound of the piano being played will **(4)** .... a small crowd. These passers-by will be given something beautiful or inspiring in their day, a quiet thoughtful **(5)** .... amid the noisy hustle and bustle of daily life in a big city. It's hoped that the spontaneous music will also **(6)** .... people coming together and communicating with each other in **(7)** .... of what they're hearing.

Videos on social media websites show how street pianos can bring together people from different communities and backgrounds, people who would **(8)** .... not normally mix.

	A	B	C	D
1	**A** settled	**B** laid	**C** ordered	**D** placed
2	**A** theory	**B** consequence	**C** addition	**D** particular
3	**A** heart	**B** mind	**C** memory	**D** feeling
4	**A** attract	**B** result	**C** invite	**D** welcome
5	**A** course	**B** moment	**C** chance	**D** event
6	**A** get	**B** make	**C** pull	**D** draw
7	**A** pleasure	**B** appreciation	**C** happiness	**D** satisfaction
8	**A** alternatively	**B** instead	**C** otherwise	**D** else

Advice

1 *Which word means **put** or **installed**?*

2 *There is a contrast later on with capable pianists.*

3 *Only one of these words goes with the preposition 'from'…*

4 *Which word means **interest**?*

5 *The word you need refers to a short period of time.*

6 *Only one of these words fits grammatically with 'coming'.*

7 *Which word completes a fixed phrase with 'in' and 'of'?*

8 *Which word means **in different circumstances**?*

Test 1 Training Reading and Use of English Part 2

Task information

- In Part 2, you have to read a text with eight gaps, and write one word only to fill each gap.
- Part 2 can test grammar, for example, articles, prepositions, auxiliary verbs and pronouns.
- It can also test linking words, phrasal verbs and fixed phrases.
- In some cases, there might be more than one possible answer. You must only write one answer in this case.
- The spelling must be correct.

Tip! Make sure you know how to use words and phrases like *much/many*, *(a) little/(a) few*, *a lot of/lots of*, etc.

Useful language Articles, quantifiers and determiners

1 **Complete the sentences with words from the box where necessary.**

a	the	this	these	an

1 My two brothers are .... good chess players, and .... eldest won .... competition .... last week.

2 Steven's very happy because he's found .... amazing job at .... language school in .... Japan. .... head teacher is .... friend of his cousin's.

3 .... people I work with love going to .... seaside at .... weekend.

4 Look at .... vase. It would be .... nice present for Mum. Or do you think she'd prefer .... slippers?

5 I went to .... shops yesterday and bought .... new phone. When I got .... home, ... box for .... phone was empty!

6 .... is such .... exciting book! I know they've made .... film of it and I'm really looking forward to seeing it in .... cinema. I think it opens on .... Thursday.

2 **Complete the text with words from the box. You may need to use some of the words more than once. Capital letters may be needed.**

most	lots	the	every	some	both	more	a	none	lot	an	few	any	one	no	many

It was my sister Louisa's birthday last week, and she invited a **(1)** .... of people to her party. I only knew a **(2)** .... of her friends, so it was actually **(3)** .... food I was looking forward to **(4)** .... than anything. **(5)** .... guest had been asked to bring a dish, and I knew I'd enjoy tasting as **(6)** .... of them as possible, the desserts **(7)** .... of all.

As the guests started to arrive, I began to get **(8)** .... bit worried, as **(9)** .... of them seemed to have brought **(10)** .... sweet food or cake. There was **(11)** .... of food, but every single dish was a main course. There were **(12)** .... desserts!

Then **(13)** .... of Louisa's friends, **(14)** .... girl called Julia, arrived. She was carrying **(15)** .... interesting-looking large white cardboard box. I was sure it contained Louisa's birthday cake. As I rushed forward to help Julia carry it into the kitchen, I tripped and bumped into her. **(16)** .... of us nearly fell over, and Julia dropped the box. At this point, **(17)** .... of the other guests arrived, carrying **(18)** .... large box too. 'Here's Louisa's cake!' they said.

'So what's in your box?' I asked Julia. 'Louisa's present,' she replied. 'I can't cook, but I did make her **(19)** .... amazing hat!'

Useful language Relative pronouns

3 **Complete the sentences with relative pronouns. Sometimes there is more than one correct answer.**

1 The woman .... showed me the way to the station was very friendly.
2 I think this is the book .... has influenced me the most.
3 Jane, ... I think you've met, is my neighbour.
4 The area .... I live is very noisy at night.
5 My boss, ... has worked here for 20 years, is retiring next month.
6 The town in .... I grew up is quite small.
7 I'll try and find out .... bag this is, so I can return it to them.
8 Harry's flat, ... I helped him move into, is very small.

Tip! Read the whole text first. Then look at each gap. Check your answers by reading the whole sentence when you have completed the gap.

4 **Some of the sentences below have mistakes in them and some do not. Correct the sentences with mistakes.**

1 Let me introduce you to Barbara, her mother you know quite well.
2 The train, that was five hours late, finally arrived at its destination.
3 This is the restaurant that was recommended to me by my neighbour.
4 My cousin, that lives in America, is coming to visit me next month.
5 Do you remember Mary, whose flat I once stayed in?
6 I went back to the café which I thought I'd left my umbrella.
7 Rita was the colleague which helped me the most when I started here.
8 There aren't many people have worked here as long as I have.

Useful language Prepositions at the beginning of phrases

5 **Match the incomplete phrases in the box with the prepositions.**

behalf of	least	any case	heart	all costs	doubt
balance	a way	the sake of	risk	view of	first sight
average	theory	a daily basis	condition that	due course	real
the first place	respect to	need of	far	conclusion	

at	on	for	in	with	by

6 **Complete the sentences with phrases from Exercise 5.**

1 Thank you for coming to the job interview, we'll contact you ....
2 We need to look after the planet, ... everyone's future.
3 Are you .... any help with this project?
4 Some people are very good at reciting poetry ....
5 I didn't like the hotel very much, but .... it was near the station.
6 Do you have any questions .... your application?
7 It was an amazing experience – I could hardly believe it was .... !
8 Laura was asked to speak at the conference .... the whole team.

Useful language Linking expressions

7 **Match the linking expressions with their meanings.**

linking expression	**how it is used**
1 as long as	**a)** to give a reason for an action / decision
2 no matter how / what / where	**b)** to emphasise the importance of the final thing in a list
3 not only	**c)** to refer to something which seems unlikely if something else is true too
4 so as to	**d)** to say one thing can only happen if another thing happens too
5 despite the fact that	**e)** to emphasise that something cannot be changed
6 on top of	**f)** to say there is more than one problem
7 nevertheless	**g)** to say that more than one (good or bad) thing is true
8 not to mention	**h)** to emphasise that something may be surprising after what has just been said

8 **Use one word only to complete each gap.**

(1) .... the fact that the classes Mark enjoyed most at school were the art classes, he chose to study physics at university so **(2)** .... to have a career in science. **(3)** .... only did he do well in his studies, he also found a job in a research laboratory which he found interesting and satisfying. It looked as if all his dreams had come true.

(4) .... , Mark was not completely happy. He still dreamt of being an artist. And **(5)** .... matter how hard he tried, he couldn't get the idea out of his head. After work, he would go home and paint, and he spent most of his weekends painting too, but he never felt he had enough time to create something he was really proud of. On **(6)** .... of that, he was becoming exhausted because he worked in the lab for so many hours every day.

In the end, Mark spoke to his boss, and they agreed he could take six months off work, as **(7)** .... as he promised to return to work after that. Mark devoted himself to his painting for six wonderful months, producing a series of beautiful pictures. However, he began to miss his colleagues, **(8)** .... to mention the interesting work he did at the lab, so he didn't mind returning to work when the time came. Mark's paintings still hang on his walls at home, and he continues to combine his work and his art as best he can.

Test 1 Exam practice Reading and Use of English • Part 2

Action plan

1 Read the title, and the first sentence(s) with the example.
2 Without filling in any gaps, read the text quickly to get an idea of what it's about.
3 Read the text again more slowly and fill any gaps that you know.
4 Don't forget to keep in mind the meaning of the text as it develops.
5 Concentrate on the linking words, so that you can follow the argument of the text.
6 Look at the words on either side of each gap, as the missing word may be part of a fixed phrase.
7 When you have filled in all the gaps, read your text to check it makes sense.

1 **What is this text about?**

A It explains what happens on the chef's TV programme.
B It informs us about the chef's life.
C It presents the chef's views on cooking.

Tip! Gaps may have more than one possible answer, but you must only write one.

Tip! Don't leave any gaps blank – every gap requires an answer.

2 **Follow the exam instructions, using the advice to help you.**

For questions **9–16**, read the text below and think of the word which best fits each gap. Use only **one** word in each gap. There is an example at the beginning (**0**).

Write your answers **IN CAPITAL LETTERS on the separate answer sheet.**

Example: | 0 | | H | A | S |

The Master Chef

The Italian chef, Andrea Devoto owns restaurants in several European cities. He believes in simple, family-style Italian recipes, and **(0)** .... a particular interest in seafood. He has written two cookery books and appeared in a number of television programmes.

Andrea is famous **(9)** .... an innovative documentary-style cookery programme – an idea that he **(10)** .... up with himself. As presenter and narrator of the programme, he visits a well-known TV personality each week in **their** home. He gets to know them through their interests in and attitudes towards food, and reflects on how these have changed over the course **(11)** .... their lives. Then he introduces them to **(12)** .... of his recipes and sees how they cope with preparing it at a dinner party. He says the programme has provided **(13)** .... with fascinating insights into how people react to his recipes and how people see food **(14)** .... general. With this knowledge, he has **(15)** .... able to improve his own restaurants, for example, by making them more family-friendly, with recipes that appeal to children **(16)** .... much as adults.

Advice

9 *What preposition follows 'famous' here?*

10 *Use a phrasal verb meaning* ***invented.***

11 *Use a preposition to complete a phrase meaning* ***throughout.***

12 *The word you need refers to 'it' later in the sentence.*

13 *Use a personal pronoun here.*

14 *You can either say 'generally' or this phrase completed by a preposition.*

15 *Think of the full infinitive form of this verb.*

16 *The meaning is that the recipes appeal in the same amount to children and adults.*

Task information

- In Part 3, you have to read a text with eight gaps, and make a word from a word given in capital letters at the end of the line to fill each gap.
- Part 3 mainly tests vocabulary, but grammar and spelling are tested, too. You will need to know what kind of word goes in each gap (noun, verb, adjective, etc.) and you need to know how to spell all the words correctly.
- You need to understand how you can change words, e.g. by adding a prefix or a suffix, by making changes within the word or by forming compound words.

Useful language Word families

1 **Write the part of speech next to each word, like the example.**

1 imagine ....verb..........
2 imagination ....
3 imaginative ....
4 imaginatively ....
5 imaginable ....
6 unimaginable ....
7 unimaginatively ....

2 **Decide which part of speech is needed in each gap. Complete the sentences using words formed from the base word 'impress'.**

1 My .... was that he was enthusiastic about his work.
2 They were .... by the quality of her work and offered her a job.
3 He always .... his friends when he does a new magic trick.
4 It's not a good idea to rely on first .... as they can be wrong.
5 You performed that jump very .... !
6 Many critics thought the theatre production was .... and gave it poor reviews.

Tip! Remember that if the gap should be filled by a noun, it might need to be a plural noun. Sometimes the word will be in a negative form. Read the text around the gap to help you decide.

3 **Form between one and three words from the base words in the table using the suffixes in the box. Try to use each suffix at least once.**

-able	-al	-ance	-ent	-ful	-ion
-ment	-ous	-ness	-ly	-ive	-ity
-ic	-ify	-ed	-less	-ing	-ise

noun(s)			mystery			care	energy
verb(s)	create	add		enjoy	appear		
adjective(s)							
adverb(s)							

4 **Complete the sentences using the base word at the end of each sentence. You can refer to the table above.**

1 There was a .... light in the sky. **MYSTERY**
2 Henry has lost his keys again – I wish he wasn't so .... ! **CARE**
3 When trying to solve a problem, it's a good idea to think .... **CREATE**
4 It soon became .... that nobody had understood the instructions they'd been given. **APPEAR**
5 We have high expectations of the two latest .... to the basketball team. **ADD**
6 I haven't spent such an .... evening for a long time! **ENJOY**

Tip! Read the whole sentence to help you decide what kind of word is missing.

5 **Correct the spelling mistakes in these sentences.**

1 The skaters performed beautifuly on the ice.
2 Do you like watching advertisments on TV?
3 There are many similaritys between the two paintings.
4 That's a very convinceing argument!
5 My sister accidentaly broke my favourite vase.

6 **Complete the sentences with a word using the base word IN CAPITALS and a prefix from the box.**

Tip! One of the changes you make to the base word may be adding a prefix.

im-	ir-	mis-	un-	dis-

1 The documents were hard to find because the office was so .... **ORGANISE**
2 The argument was all a result of a .... **UNDERSTAND**
3 She tried to hide her .... , but she was annoyed that her cousin was so late. **PATIENT**
4 When the actor had put on all his make-up, he was completely .... **RECOGNISE**
5 Their .... behaviour means that we can no longer trust them. **RESPONSIBLE**

Test 1 Exam practice Reading and Use of English • Part 3

Action plan

1 Look at each word in CAPITALS and the words before and after each gap.
2 Decide which part of speech the missing word is.
3 If it's a noun, is it singular or plural, countable or uncountable?
4 If it's an adjective, is it positive or negative?
5 If it's a verb, what form and tense is it?
6 Does the word in CAPITALS need more than one change?
7 Check the word you have chosen fits the context and is spelt correctly.

For questions **17–24**, read the text below. Use the word given in capitals at the end of some of the lines to form a word that fits in the gap **in the same line**. There is an example at the beginning (**0**).

Write your answers **IN CAPITAL LETTERS on the separate answer sheet.**

Example: | 0 | | W | A | R | R | I | O | R | S |

Tip! You **always** need to change the word given in CAPITALS.

Tip! Sometimes, you may need *both* a prefix *and* a suffix.

Tip! Sometimes, you may need to make a major change to the word, such as *HIGH* → *height*.

The Amazons

The Amazons, a tribe of fierce female **(0)** .... , feature in Ancient **WAR**
Greek mythology from 2,000 years ago. The Ancient Greeks believed them to inhabit an area called Scythia, covering present-day Ukraine, southern Russia and western Kazakhstan. They were fascinated by the Amazons, writing stories
about their heroic and **(17)** .... deeds, and displaying them on **COURAGE**
pots and items of **(18)** .... They were tall and beautiful but also **JEWEL**
completely **(19)** .... , and as strong as the men they fought. **FEAR**

The Amazons lived in an all-female society. According to which story one reads, they either abandoned their male babies, sent them to live with their
fathers from another tribe, or else gave them away at **(20)** .... **BORN**

There may be some **(21)** .... in the Amazon myth, because **TRUE**
archaeologists have discovered burial sites in Ukraine and **(22)** .... **NEIGHBOUR**
countries dating from 2,000 to 3,000 years ago. The women were buried with
weapons and some display **(23)** .... of wounds. Their bones **EVIDENT**
suggest they would have been **(24)** .... tall for women of this time. **USUAL**

Advice

17 Choose from: 'encouraging', 'discouraging', 'encouragement', 'discouragement', 'courageous'.

18 You will see that a noun is needed here to go with 'pots'.

*19 You need a suffix here, and the meaning is **without fear**.*

20 You need the noun form here, and the spelling is very different from the given word.

21 The word you need occurs commonly in phrases like 'Tell me the .... .'

22 You need the adjective here and not the noun!

23 What needs to happen to the 't' at the end?

24 There are two changes to make here, and look hard at the meaning of the sentence.

Test 1 Training Reading and Use of English Part 4

Task information

- In Part 4, there are six sentences. Each sentence is followed by a key word, and a second sentence with some words missing.
- Part 4 tests grammar, vocabulary and collocation.
- The key word must not be changed.
- You must use between two and five words, including the key word.
- You have to use the key word and any other necessary words to complete the second sentence so it means the same as the first sentence.

Useful language Comparative forms

1 Use comparative expressions from the box to complete the second sentence so it has a similar meaning to the first sentence.

more / -er (...) than	less (...) than	as ... as	the most / the -est

1 Olga is a better tennis player than Ben.
Ben doesn't .... Olga does.

2 Taking the bus is much cheaper than taking the train.
Taking the bus costs a great .... taking the train.

3 I was more bored by that film than any other film I've seen!
That's .... I've ever seen.

4 Jane spoke with less confidence than she used to.
Jane didn't .... as she had before.

Tip! Don't change the vocabulary in the sentence unless it is actually necessary – e.g. don't change *big* to *large* or *finish* to *complete*. Most of the changes you have to make are grammatical changes.

Useful language Verbs followed by a gerund or an infinitive.

2 Choose the correct form of the verb in *italics*.

On the morning of the dance competition, Marian was in such a hurry when she left home that she forgot **(1)** *to take / taking* her purse with her. She had planned **(2)** *to catch / catching* the bus to the theatre, but she had to go on foot instead. She didn't usually mind **(3)** *to walk / walking*, but she was upset because she didn't want to risk **(4)** *to miss / missing* the beginning of the competition, and it was raining.

As she was rushing along the pavement, a car pulled up beside her. It was her neighbour Anne, offering **(5)** *to give / giving* Marian a lift. Marian accepted gratefully, and managed **(6)** *to get / getting* to the theatre just in time.

Tip! Make a list in your vocabulary notebook of verbs followed by a gerund and those followed by an infinitive.

3 Match the meanings (a or b) with each pair of sentences.

1 I tried editing my photos with this new software. ....
2 I tried to use this new software to edit my photos. ....
a) I edited my photos.
b) I didn't manage to edit my photos.

3 They stopped talking. ....
4 They stopped to talk. ....
a) They stopped, and then they talked.
b) They were talking, then they stopped.

5 I remember picking up my bag. ....
6 I must remember to pick up my bag. ....
a) I need to make sure that I don't leave my bag behind.
b) I can remember that I picked up my bag.

Useful language Reported speech

4 **Read the dialogue then complete the sentences below using the past tense of the reporting verbs in the box.**

> **Tip!** Do not write alternative answers (e.g. *go / going*) as you will lose marks even if one of the words is correct.

deny	admit	agree	refuse	persuade	demand	advise

David: I really need to do a bit more exercise. I'm feeling so unfit!
Mary: I think you're right. But did you ever go to the new swimming pool I told you about?
David: No actually, I didn't. I know I should have. But it's so far away.
Mary: You really must! You could go on your bike, you know.
David: I'm not sure I want to. I mean, it's always raining at the moment.
Mary: That doesn't matter – you'll get wet at the swimming pool anyway.
David: Yes, that's true. But you'll have to give me my bike helmet back first.
Mary: I never took it – It doesn't fit!
David: Let me have a look in your hall cupboard now.
Mary: Absolutely not! It's a mess!
David: That's OK, I don't mind. And you should get yourself a helmet, too, then you could come with me.
Mary: I suppose I could.

1 Mary .... with David that he needed more exercise.
2 David .... that he hadn't been to the new swimming pool.
3 Mary .... David that he should go to the new swimming pool on his bike.
4 Mary .... that she had taken David's bike helmet.
5 David .... to look in Mary's hall cupboard.
6 Mary .... to let David look in her hall cupboard.
7 David .... Mary to get a bike helmet.

Useful language Conditional sentences and *wish*

5 **Complete the second sentence so that it has a similar meaning to the first sentence, using the word given. Use between two and five words.**

> **Tip!** Two marks are given for each answer, so never leave a blank – write what you can.

> **Tip!** Contractions (e.g. *she'll*, *couldn't*) count as two words in the exam.

1 Richard's always saying he'd like to live somewhere warmer.
WISHES
Richard .... warmer place.

2 I want to call him, but I don't know his number.
KNEW
If I .... call him.

3 Gina wants to learn to play the piano, but she doesn't have time.
ENOUGH
Gina wishes .... to learn to play the piano.

4 I'm looking for the recipe, and then I promise to bake the same cake for your birthday as last year.
FIND
If I .... bake the same cake for your birthday as last year.

 Reading and Use of English • Part 4

Action plan

1 Read the instructions and the example.
2 Read the first sentence, think about it and concentrate on the meaning.
3 Decide what kind of word the key word is and what often follows it. You must never change the key word.
4 Use words from the first sentence if you can, or change the form of them to help you (e.g. a noun to an adjective; affirmative to negative, etc.). Do not change words unnecessarily.

Follow the exam instructions, using the advice to help you.

For questions **25–30**, complete the second sentence so that it has a similar meaning to the first sentence, using the word given. **Do not change the word given.** You must use between **two** and **five** words, including the word given. Here is an example (**0**).

Cross out words that are repeated across the two sentences:

0 ~~The boat tour~~ was full, ~~so we had to wait an hour for the next one.~~

PLACES

There .... WERE NO PLACES .... left on ~~the boat tour, so we had to wait an hour for the next one.~~

You can see that:

- *was* is transformed into *were* to match the plural noun (*places*)
- *no* is used to make a phrase with *left* – *no places left* means the same as 'full'

Advice

25 *'only when' is the same as 'not ... until'.*

26 *Think of the grammar of the verb 'apologise'.*

27 *The words you need to write mean the same as* ***be so busy that I can't****.*

28 *There is a negative element in what you have to write.*

29 *Take care with the expression of quantity.*

30 *In order to use 'have', change the adjective in the first sentence into a noun.*

---

25 'I can come out only when I've finished the last two pages of my project,' said Janie.

UNTIL

'I .... I've finished the last two pages of my project,' said Janie.

26 Martin said he was sorry that he'd upset Sarah.

APOLOGISED

Martin .... Sarah upset.

27 'I might not have time to pick up your book from the shop tonight,' Mrs Slade told her husband.

BUSY

I might .... to pick up your book from the shop tonight,' Mrs Slade told her husband.

28 Jim has decided to wait until spring to buy a new car.

DECISION

Jim has .... to buy a new car until spring.

29 I've received several letters recently from a financial company.

SENT

I've .... of letters recently by a financial company.

30 Jason was the most experienced skier in the group.

HAD

Of all the skiers in the group, none .... than Jason.

Test 1 Training Reading and Use of English Part 5

Task information

- In Part 5, you read a long text.
- After the text, there are six questions with four options A, B, C or D.
- The questions can be about main ideas or details, as well as about opinions, attitudes, or feelings. They could also be about the writer's purpose.
- Other questions are about the meaning of words or phrases in the text, or about what a reference word like *this*, *it* or *that* refers to in the text.
- The questions follow the order of the text.

Reading for detail

1a **Read the first paragraph of a story.**

Tip! Read the whole text before answering the questions. Find out what kind of text it is and what it is about.

First day at college

Nora rushed into the large college entrance hall, glad to get out of the rain. Starting college was a big enough deal, without getting completely soaked into the bargain. She looked around, just in case there were any familiar faces. Not that she expected there to be, but you just never knew. Putting on what she hoped was her most confident look as she followed the signs to the lecture hall, she tried to ignore the thoughts that had been bothering her for the last few weeks: Was this place really for her? Should she have picked somewhere less grand? Her friends had all assured her she'd have a fabulous time there, but how could they possibly know?

b **Read this question. Read the text again and underline the part which gives you the answer.**

How did Nora feel about going to college?

c **Now read the options below. Choose the best answer.**

A relieved she had managed to get in
B certain that she would do well there
C worried that she would miss her friends
D concerned about whether she would enjoy it

Tip! Always read the question carefully, so you know exactly what sort of information you are looking for.

d **Here are reasons why the other options are wrong. Match the reasons with each option.**

1 Nora hoped that she looked confident, but didn't actually feel confident.
2 Nora did not expect to see any familiar faces, and thoughts had been bothering her, but they weren't about other people.
3 Nora was pleased to get inside out of the rain, not that she had successfully applied for a college place. The question is about going to college.

2a **Read the second paragraph and the question. What does *putting paid to* mean in line 5?**

The lecture hall was huge, even bigger than Nora remembered it. She had seen it once before, during the college's annual open day for prospective students. It was also packed. She'd thought that by arriving a bit early, she'd be under less pressure and feel more relaxed. Rather too many happy, chattering students had had exactly the same idea, though, putting paid to her hopes of finding a seat comfortably near the back of the hall for the introductory lecture.

Tip! Use clues in the text to help you choose the correct answer.

b **Now read the four options below. Which one do you think is the best answer? Why are the other three options wrong?**

A raising
B predicting
C destroying
D laughing at

Action plan

1 Read the instructions, the title and the sub-title, if there is one. These will tell you important information about what kind of text it is, what it is about, and who the writer is.
2 Quickly read the text without trying to answer any of the questions. Try to get a clear understanding of what the text is about.
3 Read the first question, underlining the key words.
4 Find the relevant part of the text and draw a vertical line next to it and write down the question number. Most questions relate to a whole, single paragraph.
5 Read the relevant part of the text in detail as you answer each question.
6 Read the four options A–D. Which is closest to your understanding of what the text says?
7 If you really aren't sure, cross out any options that you think are wrong and then make a guess.

Follow the exam instructions, using the advice to help you.

You are going to read an article about a rowing race between Oxford University and Cambridge University. For questions **31–36**, choose the answer (**A, B, C** or **D**) which you think fits best according to the text.

Mark your answers **on the separate answer sheet**.

Tip! Some questions may ask you to work out the meaning of words or phrases using the context.

Tip! Some questions may focus on reference words like *one* or *this*.

Tip! If a question doesn't specify which paragraph, there will be words in the question that tell you which part of the text to look in.

The Boat Race

Olympic gold medallist Tom Ransley hasn't always known victory – losing the Boat Race was the biggest disappointment of his life.

The Boat Race is a unique event. It pulls on the tribal instincts of human nature and the desire for belonging. Everyone picks a side. The millions who watch worldwide on TV will cheer on either the Cambridge light blues or dark-blue Oxford. With an annual spot in the sporting calendar, it has wrapped itself into British culture even though the only other interest in this bizarre, backwards-moving sport is the Olympics every four years.

From an early age I shouted for the light blues; for no good reason they were always my favourites. I could never understand why the losing crew didn't simply row faster when the other boat took the lead. It all looked so terribly obvious and easy, especially when watching those wide-angled aerial shots. Like a coach in the making, my ten-year-old-self would tell the slower crew: 'You're losing! Row faster.' Little did I know that a decade later I'd be racing for Cambridge, stuck in that miserable second spot.

The hardest test I faced at Cambridge lay not in the tutorial room, the library or the exam hall, but presented itself at 5.20 am every day. With a head-splitting squeal, the alarm always tested my resolve. It presented a choice between continuing my quest to win the Boat Race, or sleep. I came agonisingly close to throwing away my Boat Race dreams on quite a few occasions. Instead, I would drag my aching body out from under the covers into the morning darkness. A typical day started with an early indoor rowing session, completed in time for a quick second breakfast and morning lectures. An equally quick lunch, often eaten in the team minibus, preceded the afternoon work on the water and then it was back to college for tutorials and dinner.

A Boat Race campaign means seven months of dedication. Juggling books and boats and avoiding injury, I somehow managed to secure myself a seat in the boat. Our sole objective was to beat a heavily favoured Oxford crew. Our crew spent the morning of the race shut away in the back of a boathouse. Two days before this, our best rower was forced to withdraw on medical grounds, as he had suffered a serious health scare. It was a brutal setback for our inexperienced crew.

Eventually, the time had come and we stepped out into the glare of the media and the cries of the crowd. We pulled up under Putney Bridge and then took the last few strokes to the start line. The umpire raised his flag. Attention. Go! The boat crashed through rough tidal waves and into a cold, unrelenting headwind. The river conditions were bleak, but less bleak than those arriving in the minds of my crew. I refused to accept the inevitable, but it was clear to the millions of people watching that Cambridge had already lost the battle. Then Oxford suddenly kicked again somewhere past halfway and at that point it really was all over. My memories of the second half of the race are hazy, but I'm sure there was a definite point at which my legs failed. Despite asking for more, there was nothing left to give. The finish line brought total exhaustion, dejection and teeth-chattering cold.

What appeals to me, as it does to many, is the simple and brutal nature of the event. Head to head. Them or us. Unlike at the Olympic Games, where I won gold in Rio 2016 and bronze in London, there are no silver medals. That is what drew me to the event. The athletes must commit fully in search of the win. This is why it matters. That is why the losing crew will hurt so much: there's no preparation for losing.

31 What point is Tom making about the race in the first paragraph?

A It is strange that it has become so popular.
B Public opinion about its importance is divided.
C More British people watch the Olympic rowing.
D It brings out the best and worst in people.

32 Tom implies that as a boy, he

A dreamt of rowing in the race himself one day.
B used to enjoy pretending to be one of the coaches.
C found the tactics used by the crews hard to work out.
D had no concept of the huge effort the crews were putting in.

33 In the third paragraph we learn that Tom

A convinced himself to look forward to the sound of his alarm clock.
B sometimes wondered whether all the pain was worth it.
C often felt he wasn't feeding his body well enough.
D thought about rowing a lot when he was studying.

34 In the fourth paragraph, what does Tom say about the Boat Race he rowed in?

A Few people gave Cambridge much chance of winning that year.
B The preparation and attitude of the Cambridge crew was perfect.
C Cambridge were confident they could overcome any setbacks.
D The Cambridge crew went into it weakened by a series of injuries.

35 What happened during the early part of the race?

A Tom's nerves got the better of him.
B Oxford conserved their efforts for later.
C The Cambridge crew got dispirited early on.
D Oxford adapted better to a sudden change in the conditions.

36 What does Tom find most appealing about the Boat Race?

A the fame it brings for the participants
B the desire not to let his teammates down
C the complex psychological challenge involved
D the excitement of being in a win or lose situation

Advice

31 *Read the words used to describe the sport at the end of the paragraph.*

32 *Think about what Tom says he could 'never understand' and also what 'looked so terribly obvious'.*

33 *This question is about the gist of the paragraph, so read the first five lines and decide what the main point is.*

34 *Look at the phrase used to describe the Oxford crew.*

35 *Read carefully about the river conditions and how these affected one of the teams.*

36 *This question tests the gist of the whole paragraph.*

Test 1 Training Reading and Use of English Part 6

Task information

- In Part 6, you read a long text with six gaps. Each gap is for a missing sentence.
- After the text, there some sentences. These sentences are in a list (A–G), but in the wrong order.
- You have to put the sentences into the correct gaps.
- There is one extra sentence which you do not need to use.
- Part 6 tests the way the text is structured, as well as the use of reference words and linking phrases.

Focus on linking and referencing

Tip! Look for linking words and pronouns which connect ideas in the text. These will help you to choose the correct sentence for each gap.

1 Complete the sentences using the words and expressions in the box.

here	his	others	nevertheless
the latter	as a result	them	this was because

1 The climbers had expected to face difficult weather conditions. .... , the storm which blew up during the night took even .... by surprise.
2 Many people come to this area to relax and have fun. .... , such as artists and writers, say that they find inspiration ....
3 Having so many demands on his time meant that John became extremely stressed. .... , the quality of .... work suffered.
4 The results of the experiment came as a surprise to the researchers. .... they had overlooked a crucial factor.
5 There were two main questions: the speed with which the waves could travel and the energy they carried. It was .... that the scientists were keen to investigate.

2 The sentences in this text have been mixed up. Put the sentences in the correct order.

The guitar

a) This may be because it is fairly straightforward to learn to play a few basic chords on it.

b) Those that can put in this time will find it a rewarding experience and, if they have the talent, be able to choose from a variety of styles.

c) Others prefer to find a good teacher.

d) These include classical, jazz, flamenco and rock, to name but a few.

e) However, despite these advantages, becoming a proficient player demands a great deal of determination and many hours of practice.

f) The guitar is a popular musical instrument.

g) Many people may have the former but lack the opportunity to do the latter.

h) Another reason for the guitar's popularity is the relative ease with which one can be carried around.

i) Some people do this by finding free lessons online.

1 *f* 2 .... 3 .... 4 .... 5 .... 6 .... 7 .... 8 .... 9 ....

Action plan

1. Read the instructions, title and subtitle if there is one so you can see what kind of text it is and what the topic is.
2. Quickly read through the main text only to get an overall idea of what the text is about.
3. Then read the seven sentences, A–G. Do any of them obviously fit particular gaps?
4. For each gap 37–42, study the ideas and words that come before and after it.
5. Look for similar or contrasting ideas in the list of sentences.
6. In both the main text and sentences A–G, underline vocabulary links, reference words such as *this* or *her*, and linking expressions like *also*, *one* and *so*.

1 **Look quickly at the text on page 33.**

1. What kind of text is it and what is it about?
2. What is each of the main paragraphs about?

2 **Follow the exam instructions, using the advice to help you.**

You are going to read an introduction to a book about polar bears. Six sentences have been removed from the text. Choose from the sentences **A–G** the one which fits each gap (**37–42**). There is one extra sentence which you do not need to use.

Mark your answers **on the separate answer sheet**.

A	However, the fact that it walks about on the sea ice like a regular land bear, and periodically comes ashore causes confusion.
B	In other words, because of their low reproductive rate, they are still vulnerable if not properly managed.
C	Consequently, polar bears are highly inquisitive.
D	This is because it is often uncertain when or where the next meal will come from.
E	I attempt to provide a broad understanding of the ecology and natural history of polar bears in accessible non-technical language.
F	It is constantly influenced by a changing environment and it interacts with other species on a daily basis.
G	At special moments when I have time to watch an undisturbed polar bear, I'm often struck by an overwhelming sense that it is simply where it belongs.

Tip! Don't forget to look out for linking words at the beginning of the sentences.

Tip! Don't waste too much time trying to work out the meaning of words you don't understand.

Advice

37 *The main idea of the paragraph before the gap is that the polar bear IS the Arctic and that its home is there.*

38 *There is a strong forward link to the idea in 'For example'.*

39 *In both sentences on either side of the gap, the writer is talking about the rest of the book.*

40 *This paragraph is about the marine ecosystem and the evolution of other animals.*

41 *You have the idea of 'energy' before the gap and hunting techniques as a predator after the gap.*

42 *There is a strong forward link here, so look at the sentence after the gap.*

My polar bear research

The polar bear, more than any other animal, symbolises the Arctic. People all around the world who will never see one know what it looks like. Like the vastness of the polar sea ice it lives on, the sheer size of an adult polar bear is impressive. Its whiteness matches the backdrop of snow and ice that we all associate with the Arctic.

37 ______ The Arctic is not a forgotten wasteland to a polar bear; it is home, and a comfortable home at that. For thousands of years, the climate, the ice, and the seals upon which it feeds have shaped the evolution of this predator. While it's easy to understand why the polar bear became such a powerful icon, it is difficult even now to comprehend its vulnerability to a changing environment.

The polar bear is a true marine mammal in the sense that it depends on the ocean for existence. **38** ______ For example, in the United States, the polar bear is considered a marine mammal for legal purposes. In Canada it is a land mammal. Ecologically, however, the polar bear is clearly an integral part of the marine ecosystem, and that's the context I will treat it in.

I began my research on polar bears forty years ago. International concern for polar bears was high, and conservation agreements were in development. Management plans were needed, and The Polar Bear Specialist Group recommended more fundamental research on the bears' ecology. I undertook a wide variety of studies of polar bears, including behaviour, genetics and denning habitat. In this book, I explain the results of that research. **39** ______

I have followed a few general themes. Firstly, the polar bear does not exist in isolation. It is both a product and part of the polar marine ecosystem. **40** ______ The polar bear has been a significant factor in the evolution of the behaviour and ecology of the arctic seal and vice versa.

Secondly, a polar bear's life revolves around energy. It obtains as much energy as efficiently as possible when there is an opportunity, and then conserves that energy as much as possible. **41** ______ Because their success as predators determines their very existence, and this is the aspect that most people have the greatest interest in, I've written the longest chapter on how they hunt and how diverse their techniques are.

A third theme is that each polar bear is an individual. A solitary predator in an extreme environment like the Arctic must live by its wits. A single solution from one bear will not answer all situations of others. Conditions for hunting or other environmental factors may change quickly. **42** ______ They often contemplate a situation before they act, and they learn quickly from new experiences. As a result, each bear is unique because of its individual combination of experiences and knowledge.

Test 1 Training Reading and Use of English Part 7

Task information

- In Part 7, there are ten questions which you match with the sections or short texts (A, B, C, etc.), according to the question at the top.
- After the questions, there are either 4–6 short texts or one long text that has been divided into 4–6 sections.
- The information you need may not be in the same order as the questions.
- Sometimes the question asks about an attitude, a feeling, or an opinion.

Tip! The words in the question are sometimes a paraphrase of the information in the text.

Tip! The information you need can only be found in one text, but there may be information in another text which distracts you.

Focus on paraphrasing

1 **Match the questions (1–5) with the sentences (a–e).**

Which person

1 says something that seemed of little importance?
2 remembers feeling disappointed?
3 had difficulty focusing?
4 learned a great deal?
5 points out that opportunities were limited?

a) I picked up all sorts of useful information.
b) Getting a job so quickly was hardly typical.
c) I considered it to be an insignificant detail.
d) It was almost impossible not to be distracted.
e) They didn't meet my expectations.

Focus on attitude, feeling and opinion

2 **Read the two extracts, then complete the sentences below with adjectives from the box.**

A Naomi

I was introduced to Diana at the university drama club. It was the annual awards evening, and I'd just got a prize! Diana was a new member, but after we'd exchanged a few words, I was so caught up in the general excitement that I ignored her completely. The next day, I felt really bad about it, and asked around to try and get her number. I messaged her but she didn't reply, and I thought, 'Well, that just serves me right!' Then one day I ran into her on campus, only to be greeted with a sunny smile. It turned out she'd lost her phone and had no hard feelings at all about my behaviour. That made me feel so much better, and we've been friends ever since.

B Lisa

When I read the letter asking me to go for national hockey trials, I couldn't believe it. I knew that I was a really good player – everyone had always told me so – but there was a great deal of competition out there, and this was a huge honour. When I told my family, my grandmother said I should get my hair cut for the occasion, which made me laugh. I went to the trials, but in the end, I didn't get on the team. I felt very bad about that for some time. Fortunately, I had another opportunity two years later, and it was second time lucky – I've never looked back.

amused	relieved	disappointed	ashamed	convinced	delighted	astonished	determined

1 Naomi was .... to communicate with someone.
2 Lisa was .... that she was skilled.
3 Naomi was .... about something she had done.
4 Lisa was .... about a result.
5 Naomi was .... to be given something.
6 Lisa was .... to receive an invitation.
7 Naomi was .... when she met someone.
8 Lisa was .... by someone's response to some news.

Test 1 Exam practice Reading and Use of English • Part 7

Action plan a)

1 Read the instructions, the title and subtitle to find out what kind of text it is and the topic.
2 Read the questions and underline key words.
3 Match the information to the questions.
4 When you have an answer, read the question again and check the evidence in the text.

Action plan b)

1 Read the instructions, the title and subtitle to find out what kind of text it is and the topic.
2 Read the first section.
3 Check which questions are answered in this section.
4 Repeat for the other sections.

Follow the exam instructions, using the advice to help you.

You are going to read an article about the first days of television. For questions **43–52**, choose from the sections (**A–E**). The sections may be chosen more than once.

Mark your answers **on the separate answer sheet**.

Tip! Different sections of the text may contain ideas that are similar, so you have to read carefully to find which say the same thing as the questions.

Tip! Don't expect to find answers in the text that use the same words as the questions. Look for words, phrases and sentences that express the same ideas.

In which section does the writer mention

a change of heart about the poor quality of programmes?	43	
a concern about how theatre and cinema might be affected by TV?	44	
a difficulty involved for the makers of one programme?	45	
the idea that a break between programmes could be good for the listener?	46	
an experimental version of TV which predated the official beginning?	47	
written evidence of someone's dislike of a programme they'd seen?	48	
a published complaint about the interest value of a programme?	49	
a practical problem for certain people who appeared on TV?	50	
a programme that featured ordinary people doing unusual things?	51	
TV being presented as something mysterious and unexplainable?	52	

Advice

43 Look for the references to people in the sections – only one person changes their opinion of TV.

44 Look for a phrase which gives the idea of 'theatre and cinema'.

45 Find references to particular programmes in the sections. One caused a difficulty for the makers.

46 Look first for the idea of 'a break between programmes'.

47 The idea of experimenting with TV is in most of the sections. Find a reference to a 'version' of TV.

48 Find references to people who dislike a programme. Which of these gives written evidence?

49 There is more than one published complaint but only one where the complaint is about a particular programme being boring.

50 There are various practical problems in the sections but only one about people on TV.

51 Find a reference to 'ordinary people' doing unusual things.

52 The idea of TV as 'mysterious and unexplainable' is present in a quotation from someone.

The first days of television

A At 3pm on 2 November 1936, BBC television officially began. Mr RC Norman, the BBC chairman, gave a speech that introduced those watching to a new word: 'viewers'. A musical star, Adele Dixon, then sang a song, Television, composed for the occasion, which gave thanks for the 'mighty maze of mystic, magic rays' that 'bring a new wonder to you'. The BBC's director-general, John Reith, attended that evening's broadcast, a single programme called *Television Comes to London*. In his diary he wrote that it was a 'ridiculous affair' and that he 'left early'.

Recently, the BBC4 channel remembered the occasion in a programme called *Television's Opening Night: How the Box Was Born*. The first broadcast was recreated using the original technology. This was quite a challenge as no recording exists, of course – all television then was live and died on the air as it was broadcast.

B John Logie Baird had first demonstrated television in 1925, but the BBC was lukewarm about his invention. The BBC yearbook for 1930 reflected the official view. 'If this power is ever brought to mechanical perfection,' it wrote of television, 'there is little reason . . . that anyone but a few should go in person to any place of entertainment again.' The BBC had trialled the new television service it was developing for two weeks in autumn 1936, in order to sell some of the new television sets at the Radiolympia show. But it was the launch on 2 November that gave us television that we would recognise today: broadcast two hours a day, at 3pm and 9pm, except Sundays.

C As time went on many more programmes were developed. L Marsland Gander, one of the first television critics, wrote in his newspaper: 'I find that next Saturday a Mr JT Baily is to demonstrate on the television screen how to repair a broken window. . . . Probably at some future time, when we have television all day long, it will be legitimate to cater for a minority of potential window repairers. Out of two hours, however, the allocation of 30 minutes to such a subject seems disproportionate.' From the start, television had more of what we'd now call lifestyle programmes than radio: cookery, and gardening, for example. Gander wasn't alone in finding the content generally mundane and banal. He did concede later that the first edition of *Picture Page*, on that opening night of 2 November, had filled him 'with an enthusiasm for a new artform that has never waned'.

D On *Picture Page* there was a series of quick-fire interviews with everyone from a bagpiper in Trafalgar Square to a London cab driver who'd driven someone to the far north of Scotland. *Picture Page* epitomised a key advantage that television had over radio: informality. Radio talk at this time was often scripted, and delivered in an extremely formal tone. On television, the announcers could not read from a script if they wanted to look at the viewer, and could not see much in the glare of the lights anyway, so they had to speak more spontaneously and learn to sound natural.

E Even so, Reith never changed his position, and said later that the arrival of television influenced his decision to leave the BBC in 1938. On his last day, the corporation presented him with a rather tactless leaving present: a television set. He barely looked at it. Were Reith alive today, what would he make of BBC television now? Mostly he would be appalled by the sheer abundance of it, the way it fills every hour of the day. This was a man, after all, who decreed that there be a few minutes' silence in between radio programmes to allow people to switch off!

Test 1 Training Writing Part 1 (essay)

Task information

- The essay task in Part 1 tests your ability to present opinions in an essay.
- The task consists of notes and information which you use to write between 140 and 190 words.
- You must write about the information and the notes given and think of a new idea of your own.
- You will need about 40 minutes for this task, including time to plan and check your work.
- Your essay must be well organised into paragraphs and include good linking expressions.
- You will need a range of structures for contrasting, comparing, disagreeing, explaining, and giving opinions with reasons or examples.
- Correct grammar and punctuation, as well as accurate spelling are important.

Useful language Expressing and justifying opinion

Tip! Keep a list of useful language for giving opinions. Try to use a variety of expressions.

1 Choose the correct phrases in *italics* for expressing and justifying opinion.

1 *Whereas / I would argue that* the internet has dramatically changed our lives. *It seems to me that / Despite* this hasn't always been for the better.

2 Young people love using technology, *rather than / whereas* older people are not so keen on it. *It could be argued that / Similarly* young people use it too much.

3 *While / On the one hand,* the internet hasn't always had a positive influence on society. *For example / To sum up,* people chat online *despite / rather than* meet face to face. *Additionally / Firstly,* it encourages cyber bullying.

4 People aren't always brought closer together by social media *despite / in my view* what companies like Twitter claim. *In my opinion / I disagree with* the opposite can happen and they become lonelier.

5 *I agree with / In my view* it's useful to have easy access to the internet because you can save time and money. *On the other hand, / On the one hand,* you can waste time and buy things you don't need. *In conclusion / For instance,* I will continue to use the internet regularly, but I will be more aware of the problems it can cause.

Exam skill Brainstorming

2 Read this essay title. What do you have to write about?

3 The third point is your own idea. Make a list of three or four things to write about. Then choose your best idea.

effect of the internet on old people ....

....

....

Tip! Practise choosing a topic and then brainstorming points and opinions to write about.

Many people think that the internet has changed our lives dramatically. What do you think?

Notes

Write about:

1 the benefits of the internet

2 personal relationships

3 .... (your own idea)

Exam skill Organising paragraphs

4 **Read the essay below and match each paragraph with its function.**

Paragraph 1 **a)** presenting writer's own idea
Paragraph 2 **b)** conclusion
Paragraph 3 **c)** explaining the benefits of the internet
Paragraph 4 **d)** introduction
Paragraph 5 **e)** giving an opinion on the internet and personal relationships

5 **Underline all the phrases for expressing and justifying opinions from Exercise 1 on page 37.**

Tip! Each paragraph should introduce a new topic.

Has the internet changed our lives?

1 Most people take the internet for granted nowadays, even though it's a fairly new innovation. I agree that it has had a huge impact on our lives.

2 On the one hand it could be argued that our working and study habits have changed dramatically. Easy access to information can save a lot of time. Additionally, booking holidays or buying and selling products online have become increasingly popular and often save people money.

3 It seems to me that social networks such as Facebook have changed personal relationships. In my view, people spend too much time looking at a screen rather than interacting with others. I would argue that it's better to go out and meet friends rather than chatting online. Personal contact is still important.

4 In my opinion, the internet does not help older people as much. If they can't use a computer or mobile phone, they have no way of benefitting from the internet despite everything that it offers.

5 In conclusion, although the internet has changed many aspects of our daily lives dramatically, it hasn't always been for the best.

Tip! Support an opinion with reasons and examples.

Tip! It is important to use relevant language (e.g. expressing opinions) and well-organised paragraphs so that your answer is easy to understand.

Understanding instructions

6 **Read this Writing Part 1 exam task and answer the questions.**

1 What is the topic of the essay?

2 What views do you have to discuss?

You recently had a discussion in class about going to another country to improve your English. Your English teacher has asked you to write an essay.

Write an essay using **all** the notes and giving reasons for your point of view.

Studying in another country is a great way of learning English.

What do you think?

Notes

Write about:

1 how you can learn English in another country

2 where to stay

3 .... (your own idea)

My Essay Plan

Paragraph 1 Introduction

Paragraph 2 Point 1

Paragraph 3 Point 2

Paragraph 4 Your own idea

Paragraph 5 Conclusion

Write your answer in **140–190 words** in an appropriate style.

7 **In your notebook, complete the essay plan opposite by brainstorming your ideas for each paragraph.**

8 **Quickly read the essay and answer these questions. Does it:**

1 have well organised paragraphs?

2 include phrases for expressing and justifying opinions?

3 give examples of how you can learn English abroad?

4 give examples of where to stay?

5 include the writer's own idea?

6 sum up points already made?

Tip! You only need a couple of ideas for each argument in paragraphs 2, 3 and 4.

Tip! List ideas for each note that you have to write about before you start writing so you can balance the essay.

Studying English abroad has become popular for students who want to improve their language skills.

Whether you attend an English course or do a summer job, it means that you can speak English 24 hours a day if you want! I think it's important to hear the language being spoken by native speakers so that you can improve your pronunciation. It might be difficult leaving your family and friends, but in my opinion, it's worth it.

Many students who study in the UK live with a host family. Older students might prefer to share a flat with native speakers. I would argue that staying with a host family would be better despite the problems you might have with the food they cook! Often the families become good friends and they can help you with your homework.

In my opinion, being in the country and experiencing the culture is also important. It seems to me that understanding the culture helps you to understand the language as well.

In conclusion, therefore, I would argue that living abroad is an excellent way of learning a language even though you might experience some minor difficulties.

Test 1 Exam practice Writing • Part 1 (essay)

Action plan

1 You always have to answer the Part 1 question.
2 Read the question carefully. Then read it again and underline any key words in the question.
3 In the notes, there are two points which you must include in your answer. You also have to add an idea of your own.
4 Brainstorm some vocabulary which is connected to the topic. You want to show the examiner that you can use a wide range of vocabulary.
5 Decide whether to present both sides of the argument, which is generally recommended. If you only present one side, you might not have enough to say and you won't be able to show the examiner you know how to present two sides of an argument.
6 Plan your answer before starting to write, and decide what information to put in each paragraph. Write between three and five paragraphs.
7 While you are writing, be aware of how much time you have left. You have 40 minutes for each part.
8 Write between 140 and 190 words.
9 Give yourself time at the end to check your work. Think about the mistakes you have made in recent pieces of writing and check that you haven't made the same mistakes again.

1 **Read the exam task below and answer these questions.**

1 Who are you writing the essay for?
2 What will be your main focus: describing your own childhood experiences, or giving opinions and reasons?
3 Which other main point will you add?

Tip! You don't have to agree with the statement, but you do have to explain your reasons for agreeing or disagreeing with it.

Tip! Try to use your own words rather than using the words in the question. For example, you could use *be out in the fresh air* instead of *spend time outdoors*.

You **must** answer this question. Write your answer in **140–190 words** in an appropriate style.

In your English class, you have been talking about children's health. Now, your English teacher has asked you to write an essay for homework.

Write your essay using **all** the notes and giving reasons for your point of view.

More needs to be done to encourage children to spend time healthily outdoors. Do you agree?

Notes

Write about:

1 benefits and disadvantages of children's outdoor activities

2 recommendations for parents and teachers

3 .... (your own idea)

2 Do the exam task.

Test 1 Training Writing Part 2 (article)

Task information

- The article task in Part 2 tests your ability to write an interesting text for a magazine, newsletter or website.
- In the actual exam, you just choose one of the three tasks in Part 2. Read all of the Part 2 questions, and choose which one you'd like to answer.
- In the exam, the Part 1 task and the Part 2 task both have the same number of marks. So you need to give yourself the same amount of time for each answer.
- You may need to write descriptions, give examples, make comments or give your opinions.
- Think about who you are writing for and whether you should use formal or informal language.
- A short title will help to engage your readers.
- You should write between 140 and 190 words.

Useful language Strong adjectives

1 **You can make your writing more interesting by using a greater variety of adjectives. Match the simple adjectives in A with the more interesting adjectives in B.**

A	**B**
angry	awful
big	fantastic
hot	fascinated
interested	freezing
good	delighted
frightened	enormous
cold	furious
small	terrified
happy	boiling
bad	tiny

2 **Complete the sentences using one of the words in box B in Exercise 1.**

1 I really didn't like the new album; I thought it was ....
2 I can't eat all that extra large pizza, it's .... !
3 We had a really .... day at the music festival; we saw some great bands!
4 Juan was .... that he passed his driving test the first time.
5 There's not enough room in this kitchen. It's really ....
6 The water in the swimming pool was .... , so Maria had to swim quickly.
7 If you don't like hot weather, don't go to Marrakech in the summer. It's absolutely ....
8 Peter was .... by the unusual paintings at the exhibition.
9 Lorna is .... of spiders.
10 James was .... that I had borrowed his bike without asking.

Exam skill Developing a personal style

3 **Quickly read the article about friendship by a First candidate and decide which description is best for each paragraph.**

a) Essential qualities in a friend ....
b) Fun qualities in a friend ....
c) The right balance ....
d) The importance of friends ....

4 **Read the article again and select the correct option for each question.**

1 How formal is the language the writer uses?
a) fairly informal **b)** very informal
2 How would you describe the style the writer uses?
a) friendly **b)** serious
3 Which of these things does the writer use to help create the style?
a) complex sentences **b)** exclamation marks and rhetorical questions

5 **Read the article carefully and underline examples of each style identified in Exercise 4.**

Important qualities in a friend

1

Having a special friend is extremely important. Friends mean a lot no matter who you are or what age you are. Have you ever wondered what makes a friend special?

2

True friendship gives us happy experiences in life and we often have friends for different circumstances. For example, if we're socialising, we look for fun friends. A sense of humour or a joke can always make you feel better. How many friends have you met doing activities at a club or socialising?

3

However, friendship is sometimes more important if we're feeling down. Then we need someone to be sympathetic and kind. In hard times, we all want a thoughtful, reliable friend to help us. A true friend should be a good listener and know how to understand your feelings. Having similar tastes in hobbies, such as music, also helps, even if we can't sing in tune!

4

Fortunately, I've stayed friends with the same people for a long time and luckily for me they have been fantastic! This balance of kindness and understanding has helped me at many stages of my life.

Tip! You will get extra points for showing your ability to use interesting adjectives in your article, e.g. *kind, reliable.*

Tip! Remember to think about who will read your article. Writing in a friendly style will help you bring the reader closer to you.

Understanding instructions

6 **Read this Writing Part 2 exam task and answer the questions.**

1 What is the topic about?
2 What two things does the writer have to do?

Tip! Brainstorming ideas for 2–3 minutes is a good idea when you are writing articles.

You have seen this announcement on an English language website.

> **Articles wanted**
> **The Home of the Future**
>
> In what ways will people's homes be different in the future?
>
> In what ways will they be the same?
>
> The writer of the best article will be published in the next few days.

Write your article in **140–190 words** in an appropriate style.

7 **Read the article and add the correct headings to gaps 1–3.**

A The same as usual
B Devices control the house
C Science fiction or reality?

8 **Read the article again and answer these questions.**

1 Is it either too short or too long for Writing Part 2?
2 Does it have a clear structure?
3 Is it written in an appropriate style?
4 Does it answer both parts of the question?
5 What other stylistic devices does it use?

1 ....

Everybody has seen science fiction films like this: the robot is cleaning the house and you are controlling the heating and lighting with the click of your fingers. Everything is automatic, super-clean and digital. Have you ever wondered about living in the house of the future? Read on.

2 ....

Will robots take over? 'Intelligent' (smart) technology, such as apps, will control your heating, draw your curtains, play music and even order your shopping online. Will we build houses using different materials? The answer is probably yes. They will be ecological buildings made to save energy, with large windows and solar panels everywhere.

3 ....

Personally, however, I don't think there will be a lot of change. Each room in your home will still have four walls and a floor. We will open the door using a key and a lock. We will still do most of the cooking and cleaning using our own hands. I believe many things will remain the same. The futuristic films I watched twenty years ago are still fiction and not reality for me.

Test 1 Exam practice Writing • Part 2 (article)

Action plan

1 Read the question carefully and underline the main points.
2 Make a plan of your answer and think of a suitable title. The title should summarise what you are going to write about and grab your reader's attention.
3 In your plan, include a few useful phrases for each paragraph.
4 Try to use a wide range of grammar and vocabulary to show the examiner what you know.
5 Think about who is going to read the article and write in an appropriate style.
6 Make sure that your answer addresses all the questions that you are asked.
7 You need to write between 140 and 190 words.
8 Check your work carefully when you have finished.

1 Read the exam task below and answer these questions.

1 What is the purpose of writing this article?
2 How many questions does the task ask you?
3 How can you make your answer memorable and interesting?

You see this announcement on an English-language website.

> Articles wanted!
>
> **Music in education**
>
> Should everyone be taught music at school?
>
> What are the advantages of learning about music?
>
> Is it always worth spending a lot of time and money trying to learn an instrument?
>
> The best articles will be published on this website.

Write your article in **140–190 words** in an appropriate style.

Tip! Think about why someone might want to read your article. People read articles for pleasure, so try to make it interesting, and include personal opinions.

Tip! Make sure you answer any questions you are asked.

2 Do the exam task.

Test 1 Training Writing Part 2 (review)

Task information

- The review task in Part 2 tests your ability to describe and express a personal opinion about something you have experienced (e.g. a TV programme, a holiday or a product) and give your opinion of it, with a recommendation to the reader.
- You read a description of the topic and then write a review of it in 140–190 words. You should allow about 40 minutes for this task, including time at the end to check your work.
- The instructions also tell you where your review will be published (e.g. on a travel website). You therefore have to write in an appropriate style.
- You should write full sentences and try to use correct grammar, punctuation and spelling, and a good range of language.

Useful language Expressing opinions

1 Put the expressions in the box under the correct headings.

One of its positive features is … I found/felt that … I felt let down by …
On the downside … I was extremely impressed by … I was disappointed by …
The big advantage of using it is … I have used it for … In my opinion, …
One thing to consider is … Unfortunately, one of the minuses is … I'm really delighted by …

General	Positive	Negative

2 Replace the phrases in *italics* in the sentences below with one of the expressions from Exercise 1 to make them more interesting. More than one answer is possible in some sentences.

1 *Something to think about* .... *is* the battery life of the mobile phone.
2 *I think* .... there are lots of similar mobile phones on the market at the moment.
3 *I like* .... the special filters included on the camera.
4 *One of the good things about this device* .... *is* that it's very light.
5 *I didn't like* .... the headphones; they were very uncomfortable.
6 *One of the bad things about the mobile phone* .... *is* its short battery life.

Exam skill Making notes

3 **Read the exam task and the notes for a review made by a First candidate. Then answer these questions.**

1 How has the writer made the notes easier to understand?
2 How did the writer indicate the most important points?
3 How many paragraphs will these notes make for the review?
4 Do the notes answer the exam question?
5 What additional information has the writer included in the notes?

You see this announcement in an online magazine.

The Latest Gadgets

Our new website is about the latest gadgets and we want your reviews! Write a review of a device you've bought or used recently. Your review should include information about the device, its features, and other relevant information. Would you recommend this device to other people your age?

We'll use the best reviews in next few days!

Title and name the device
- The cheapest new mobile phone on the market!*
- The Cosmos 11 smartphone

Description and use
- owned it for 2 months
- use it for social media*

Best features and why
- great camera, easy to use
- very light, fits in my pocket*

Worst features and why
- short battery life, always have to recharge
- screen made of plastic, easy to break*

Recommendation
- Yes, It's cheap. Doesn't have all features but reliable.*
- Good for students

Useful language:
I was disappointed by... ; reliable; affordable

Tip! Making some notes before you start writing your review is a good way to organise your ideas and think about useful language.

Tip! Organise your notes into clear paragraph headings.

4 **Make your own notes about a recent device you bought, using the format of the notes and tips in Exercise 3.**

Understanding instructions

5 Read the exam task below then answer these questions.

1 What are the key words in the exam task?
2 What situation do you have to think about?
3 What three things do the instructions say you must do?
4 What else should you add?

You see this notice in a local magazine.

> **Restaurant Critics Wanted!**
>
> Have you visited a new restaurant in your area recently? We'd love to know your opinion, please describe the food and staff and also the prices. Would you recommend this place to other people? The winning review will be published in a local magazine.

Tip! Before you plan your review, decide whether you enjoyed yourself or not.

Write your review in **140–190 words** in an appropriate style.

6 Quickly read the model review below. Did the writer enjoy eating at the restaurant?

Title

The Zebedee

The Zebedee is a new restaurant located in Lambeth, London. I recently dined there after a friend told me it served the best burgers in town.

Describes restaurant

The restaurant is very modern, with large windows and nice wooden furniture throughout. Also, the atmosphere is very relaxed, although they had a DJ playing loud music in the background when I visited. The menu had an extensive range of dishes. I was impressed that it was reasonably priced, too, with no dish more than £10.

Praises positive features

On the downside, I felt that the service and food was awful. I was given excuses ranging from being too busy, or running out of food. I had to wait for an hour for my burger. When it did arrive, the burger was overcooked and the chips were cold. I complained to the waiter, but he said nothing– it seems that the customer was always wrong!

Criticises negative features

Makes recommendation

Overall, I wouldn't really recommend The Zebedee, as the service isn't good and the quality of food is poor. It's a shame, as the atmosphere of the restaurant is fabulous, as well as its location. It's really not worth going!

7 Study the review and the notes more carefully.

1 What reasons does the writer give for not enjoying the food and service?
2 What adjectives and phrases describe the restaurant, menu and food?
3 Which contrast links can you find? Which other linking expressions can you find?
4 Which expressions similar to those in **Useful language** on page 45 does the writer use?

Test 1 Exam practice Writing • Part 2 (review)

Action plan

1 Always check that you know what you are being asked to review (e.g. a book or a film).
2 Don't worry about whether the examiner knows the film or book you are writing about. They are interested in your use of language not your knowledge.
3 If the film or book is in your language, try to include the title in English.
4 Don't try to use a review you have written before, as each review task has a different focus. The focus here is on a particular family.
5 Decide how much detail to include. A few sentences summarising the story should be enough. It's more important to focus on your reaction to the subject.
6 Write a plan in note form (i.e. not full sentences), including your ideas for each paragraph.
7 Allow a few minutes to check your work when you have finished. Look for and correct any mistakes.

1 **Read the exam task below.**
1 Is your review likely to be positive or negative?
2 How will you make your review stand out?

Tip! Use interesting vocabulary connected to the theme to make your review stand out.

Tip! Pay attention to what the announcement is asking you to review (e.g. a film or book).

You see this announcement in your college English-language magazine.

Film reviews wanted!

Have you seen a film featuring an interesting family?

Write a review of the film, explaining what was interesting about the family, and what influence they had on the story.

We will publish the best reviews in this magazine.

Write your review in **140–190 words** in an appropriate style.

2 Do the exam task.

Test 1 Training Writing Part 2 (email)

Task information

- The email task often tests your ability to write to an English-speaking friend or colleague in response to the situation described in the question.
- You are asked to respond to a situation described in the question. In your email of 140–190 words, you must include all the information asked for.
- You have about 40 minutes for this task, including time at the end to check your work.
- You have to organise your email into paragraphs and give it a suitable beginning and ending.
- You must use an appropriate style and tone, depending on who your email is for.
- A good range of language, correct punctuation and spelling will get you higher marks.

Useful language Informal and formal writing expressions

1 Mark the phrases either (I) for informal or (F) for formal.

I couldn't believe it! ....
I could not believe it. ....
I would be grateful if you could explain ... .
I want to tell you ... .
I would like to put forward ... .
I'm writing about ... .
It would be advisable to ... .
Can you tell me about ...? ....
to think about ... .
to consider ... .
Hi David! ....
Dear Mr Simpson ....
Please try to ... .
Approx. ....
approximately ....
It's a good idea ... .
It was advisable to ... .
I am writing in response to ... .

Tip! Remember to use full forms not contracted forms in formal emails, e.g. *I would* not *I'd, Do not* not *Don't*.

2 Rewrite the sentences using more formal language from Exercise 1.

1 I'm writing about the job vacancy advertised in the local newspaper.
2 Can you tell me where you plan to build the new car park?
3 It was a good idea to postpone the plans until next year.
4 You should think about the impact on the environment.
5 I want to tell you about our new initiative.
6 Please try to remember the local residents in your plans.

Understanding instructions

3 Read the writing task below and answer these questions.

1 What is the situation?
2 What does the offer include?
3 What does the writer have to do?

You see this announcement on an English-language college website.

> **Scholarships**
>
> Every year, two scholarships are offered to candidates from overseas who can show how our one-year course in English studies would help their career.
>
> Scholarships cover fees, accommodation and food but not transport or personal spending money.
>
> To apply, write an email explaining why you think you deserve a scholarship.

Write your email in **140–190 words** in an appropriate style.

Exam skill Understanding the purpose of an email

4 Read the email written by a First student and answer these questions.

1 Is the text well organised into paragraphs?
2 Where does the writer explain why he is writing?
3 Does the writer know the name of the recipient of the email?
4 Does the writer give clear reasons for why they deserve the scholarship?
5 Does the writer use the correct style and tone throughout?
6 How does the writer begin and end his email?
7 Does the writer expect a response?
8 What formal expressions from Exercise 1 on page 49 does the writer use?

Dear Sir/Madam,

I am writing in response to the advertisement on your website for scholarships at your college. I would like to apply for one of the scholarships and explain why I would be suitable.

At present, I am training to be a teacher of English and I finish my course at the end of June. However, I feel I still have a lot to learn about the language and culture of the English-speaking world and would benefit considerably from a course in an English-speaking country.

However, I cannot afford the cost of studying abroad. I have no income except for my student grant, so if I am fortunate enough to be given a scholarship, I would have to work part-time to earn some personal spending money. My parents will borrow some money for my airfare if I am successful.

I would be grateful for the opportunity to study at your college and would appreciate it if you would consider my application. Do not hesitate to contact me if you require any further information. I look forward to hearing from you in the near future.

Yours faithfully,

Pedro Iniesta

Tip! Use *Dear Sir/ Madam* and *Yours faithfully* to start and end a formal email.

Tip! If you know the person you are writing the formal email to, use their surname, e.g. *Dear Mr Jones/Miss Smith* and end it with *Yours sincerely*.

Test 1 Exam practice Writing • Part 2 (email)

Action plan

1 Read the task carefully. Make sure you understand why you need to write the email.
2 Find and underline the questions that your friend is asking you. Make sure you answer them.
3 Make notes about the answer to each question and list relevant vocabulary you could include.
4 Think about how well you know the person you are writing to; is your style going to be friendly and informal or polite and formal?
5 Open and close the email, using suitable language.
6 Make a plan before you start writing the actual answer; spend no more than 5 minutes on this.
7 Give yourself a couple of minutes at the end to check your work.

1 Read the exam task below and answer these questions.

1 Why has your friend written to you?
2 Your friend is researching parks around the world. How is the focus of your email different from this?
3 What questions do you need to answer?

This is part of an email you receive from an Australian friend.

For my college course, I'm doing a project about public parks in towns and cities around the world, and the benefits they bring to people. What problems do parks face in your country? What can be done to improve and maintain them, and who should be responsible for this work?

Write your email in **140–190 words** in an appropriate style.

2 Do the exam task.

Tip! Think about the person you are writing to, and how well you know them. This will affect the register (style of language) that you use.

Tip! Use friendly phrases at the beginning and end of the email, such as:

- *Great to hear from you!* (at the beginning)
- *Anyway, hope the project goes well.* (at the end)

Test 1 Training Listening Part 1

Task information

- In Part 1, you will hear eight short, unrelated recordings, which are either dialogues or monologues.
- The recording for each question will be about 30 seconds long.
- There is a sentence to tell you about the *context* of the recording – who will be speaking, and the topic.
- There will be eight questions or stems and three options for the answer. You will hear each recording twice.
- The questions will test whether you can understand topic, gist, detail, function, purpose, speaker's attitude, feelings or opinions and agreement between speakers.

Understanding agreement

1a Read the question below and answer these questions.

1 What's the *situation?*
2 Who will you hear speaking?
3 What are they speaking about?

Tip! Try to read quickly through the questions and options before the recording starts. Listen carefully to the context sentence in the recording for each item.

b 1 **Before you read the audioscript below, listen to the recording, and answer the question.**

You hear two friends talking about a nature walk they went on.
What do they both think about the walk?

A The amount of wildlife they managed to spot was disappointing.
B The distance they walked was further than they were prepared for.
C The unusual animals they saw were impressive.

2 Now read the underlined part of the audioscript, showing where the answer comes from. Which option does it match? Why are the other two options wrong?

Man:	Hi, April. What did you think of the guided nature walk we went on? I have to admit, I was really tired afterwards!
Woman:	Well, the guide did warn us it'd be seven or eight kilometres. Anything shorter would've been a bit of a waste of time, as we'd never have seen those rare birds down by the lake.
Man:	No, they made the walk worthwhile, I'd say. I just thought we'd spot a few other interesting creatures along the way.
Woman:	Well, the weather wasn't great, was it, so that might have affected things like the butterflies coming out. I wasn't really expecting to see those, though.
Man:	I guess not.

3 2 **Read the question below, and listen to the recording. Which is the correct answer – A, B or C? Why?**

You will hear two friends talking about a new department store in their town.
What do they disagree about?

A the appeal of the fashions there
B the convenience of the opening times
C the attitude of the staff

Tip! You may hear a word or phrase in the recording which also appears in an option. Listen carefully, as this option may not necessarily be the correct answer.

Tip! Try to use the second recording to check the answer that you've chosen. If you're still not sure, have a guess – you may be correct. Don't leave any questions unanswered.

4 3 **Listen again. Why are the other two options wrong?**

Test 1 Exam practice Listening • Part 1

Action plan

1 Use the time before each question to carefully read the first line. What's the situation? Will you hear one speaker or two?

2 If there are two speakers, does the question tell you who will give the answer? (e.g. *Why does the woman …?* or *What does the man …?*) Or, will the answer come from both speakers? (e.g. *What do they both think about …?)*

3 Read the direct question and stem (e.g. *Who is the woman?)* and underline the key words.

4 When you first hear the recording, try to think of an answer to each question in your own words. Then choose (from A, B or C) the option most like your answer.

5 Check your answer the second time you listen, making sure that you have not made a mistake – speakers may use words connected with more than one option.

6 If you're still not sure which is the correct answer, cross out any you are sure are wrong and guess.

7 When the recording has finished and you have chosen your answer, forget about that question and concentrate on the next one.

4 **Follow the exam instructions, using the advice to help you.**

You will hear people talking in eight different situations. For questions **1–8**, choose the best answer (**A**, **B** or **C**).

---

1 You hear a man talking about crime fiction.
What is his attitude to crime novels now?

A He thinks they are a useful distraction.
B He prefers to buy only one crime novel at a time.
C He finds them less memorable than other types of novel.

2 You hear two sports journalists talking about a tennis player who is retiring.
What do they agree about the tennis player?

A He will look for opportunities to work on TV.
B He is likely to start a new career as a coach.
C He has chosen to stop playing at the right time.

3 You hear an inventor talking about her work.
What does she say about inventions?

A They are the result of a lot of hard work.
B She enjoys encouraging others to create them.
C Ideas for them come to her at unexpected times.

4 You hear two friends discussing their plans for the weekend.
What is the man doing?

A persuading his friend to take up cycling
B recommending a new cycle route to his friend
C inviting his friend to accompany him on a cycle ride

Tip! Before you listen, think of other expressions for the words in the question, e.g. *What does he do? – He works in …, His job is …, He's employed as …*, etc.

Tip! Make sure you always know which question and situation you are listening to.

Advice

1 He talks about when he used to read crime fiction. But what does he say about reading crime fiction now?

2 You need to listen for the opinion that they both share.

3 A: Is inventing a lot of hard work for her? B: Does she encourage other people? C: When/How does she get ideas?

4 What language might the speaker use to persuade, recommend or invite?

5 You hear a woman talking about crossword puzzles.
How does she feel about doing them?

A relaxed while she is focused on a crossword

B excited if she can solve all the clues correctly

C satisfied that she is exercising her brain

6 You hear two colleagues talking about travelling to work.
What do they disagree on?

A that the time spent travelling is a waste of time

B that travelling to work is very expensive

C that it's better to live outside the city and travel in to work

7 You hear a researcher talking about social media.
What point does he make about it?

A It's easy to forget that social media is a recent development.

B The disadvantages of social media are often exaggerated.

C Friendships on social media cannot replace face-to-face contact.

8 You hear a woman telling a friend about her experience of using a life coach.
What has the woman decided to do differently?

A stop worrying about whether she achieves her goals

B set herself smaller goals that are easier to achieve

C reflect on which goals are most important to achieve

Advice

5 She mentions reasons why other people enjoy doing crosswords, but what does she say about herself?

*6 Listen for a phrase which means **I don't agree**.*

7 Listen to the whole piece. Is the speaker for, against or neutral about social media?

8 What does she say about how she will do things from now on?

Test 1 Training Listening Part 2

Task information

- In Part 2, you listen to one person talking about a topic, and fill in missing information in a set of notes – ten sentences in total.
- You must write down exactly the word or phrase that you hear, to fill the gap.
- You may be asked to spell a name, or write a number.
- All the questions on the page follow the order of the recording.
- You should write down only the words and phrases you hear – no more than three words for each answer. You will not be asked to make any changes to the words you hear.
- The recording will be about 3–4 minutes long.

Identifying cues

As you listen to the recording, you'll hear a 'cue' around each answer – a signal that you need to listen carefully to that part of the recording for an answer. The cues in the recording will also help you to keep your place on the page.

Tip! Try to read through the notes before listening, and think about what *type* of information is needed.

Tip! Read the whole sentence for each question. Look carefully at what comes *before* and *after* the gap, and make sure your answer makes sense.

1 **You will hear a woman called Sally talking about a gallery she visited with a friend recently. Read the first question. What kind of word will fill the gap?**

Sally was hoping to see a painting showing a .... at the gallery exhibition.

2 5 **Before you read the audioscript below, listen to the recording and try to answer the question.**

3 **Read the audioscript below. Which is the cue for the answer? Which are the distractors?**

> When my friend and I arrived at the gallery, the exhibition was quite crowded, so I wasn't sure that we'd see much. I knew my friend wanted to see a painting by her favourite artist, which had a rainbow in the sky. We managed to spot that, although the one of a horse I was really keen to find was nowhere to be seen, sadly, as it had been taken away for repair. However, we did spend time looking at another picture by the same artist, of a castle, and that was beautiful.

4 6 **Listen again to the recording.**

5 7 **Listen to the next section of the recording and complete the sentence.**

Sally uses the word .... to give her opinion of the artist's talk they went to.

6 8 **Listen to the recording again. What is the cue? Which words are distractors?**

Test 1 Exam practice Listening • Part 2

Action plan

1 Read the instructions to get an idea of the situation.
2 Quickly go through the incomplete sentences, including the words after the gaps. This will help you get an idea of what the recording is about.
3 For each gap, decide what kind of information you need to listen for (e.g. a noun, adjective or verb. Many of the answers are often nouns, so think about whether you are listening for an object, place, person, title.)
4 The first time you listen, write your answer in pencil, in case you want to change it on the second listening.
5 When the recording has finished, check the sentences all make sense – and check your spelling, too.

9 **Follow the exam instructions, using the advice to help you.**

You will hear a talk by a woman called Kelly who ran a long-distance hiking route from the top to the bottom of New Zealand. For questions **9–18**, complete the sentences with a word or short phrase.

Running the 'Long Pathway' – a 3,000km route in New Zealand

Kelly trained for running the Long Pathway near where her **(9)** .... lives.

Kelly took her **(10)** .... with her to New Zealand to provide practical support.

Kelly uses the word **(11)** '........................' to describe the beaches she ran along.

The hardest day of the run was when Kelly lost her **(12)** ....

Kelly says she enjoyed running in the **(13)** .... most of all.

For part of the route, Kelly did a trip in a **(14)** .... for 128 kms.

Kelly was amazed by the **(15)** .... she saw.

Kelly used a ferry to cross from the North to the South Island because of the **(16)** .... on the day she was there.

Despite training well, Kelly had issues with her **(17)** .... near the end of the race.

Kelly says she felt **(18)** .... when she finally got to the finish line.

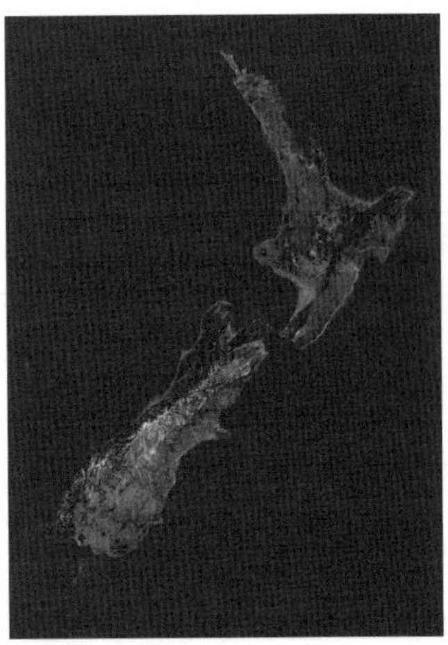

Advice

9 Which family member lives near the perfect place to go running?
10 Listen for who actually went to New Zealand with Kelly.
11 How were the beaches different from those where Kelly lives?
12 Kelly says various things went wrong, but what did she actually lose?
13 Listen for a phrase that matches to 'enjoyed' most.
14 What type of word is likely to complete the phrase 'a trip by'?
15 Which word in the recording matches to 'amazed'?
16 What were the weather conditions on the day Kelly made the crossing?
17 The question asks about issues 'near the end of the race'.
18 Don't be distracted by how Kelly had expected to feel.

Test 1 Training Listening Part 3

Task information

- In Part 3, you hear five short monologues.
- You have to choose from a list of eight options which one best matches what you hear. There are three options that you won't need to use.
- Each monologue will be about 30 seconds long.
- The options on the page, A–H, don't follow the order of the information in the recording.
- Part 3 tests your understanding of gist, detail, attitude, opinion, feeling and purpose.

Identifying keys and distractors

1 10 **Read the exam task below. Listen to Speaker 1 and answer these questions.**

1. Why is E the key? What does the speaker say?
2. Which options are the *distractors*? Distractors may sound similar to what you hear, but they aren't *exactly* a match.

You will hear five different people talking about the magazine they buy. For questions **19–23,** choose from the list (**A–H**) the reason each speaker gives for buying the magazine.

A The puzzles are great fun.

B The stories are by well-known writers.

C It has adverts for what I want to buy.

D It offers great free gifts.

E There are discounts on events.

F It has photos of famous bands.

G The letters page has useful advice.

H It tells me what's on in my area.

Speaker 1	E	**19**
Speaker 2		**20**

2 **Now read the audioscript. Look at where the key and the distractors (B, D and F) are located in the audioscript. Why are they wrong?**

Speaker 1

I've always read lots of fashion magazines, but I think *Starlight* is probably the best one. Most fashion mags usually have something on the front that they're giving away, although *Starlight* tends to go for giving you money off the big fashion shows and things like that, which I couldn't possibly afford otherwise, and that's the appeal for me. It does always feature things like the latest pictures of pop groups, too, which I have to admit I usually skip over to find something to read. The writing's not bad, although even though famous authors contribute to the magazine, I think I prefer getting absorbed in a long novel, really.

D
E
F
B

Tip! What sort of information do you have to listen out for in distractors? The information might be similar to the correct answer, but will be incorrect in some way.

3 11 **Listen to Speaker 2 and read the options in Exercise 1 again. Which is the key? Which other options sound similar to what you heard? Why are they wrong?**

Test 1 Exam practice Listening • Part 3

Action plan

1 Quickly read the instructions and options A–H. What is the link between the five speakers?
2 Study options A–H and underline the key words in each.
3 Before you listen, think of words or phrases that the speakers might use to talk about different aspects of the topic.
4 The first time you hear the recording, listen for the general idea of what each speaker says.
5 Choose the answer to each question that you think is correct.
6 The second time you listen, check that each of your choices exactly matches what the speaker says.

12 **Follow the exam instructions, using the advice to help you.**

You will hear five short extracts in which people are talking about camping trips. For questions **19–23**, choose from the list (**A–H**) what opinion each speaker gives about the camping trip they went on. Use each letter only once. There are three extra letters which you do not need to use.

Tip! Be careful if a speaker says something connected with two or more options: there is only one correct answer.

A It was more comfortable than I had thought.
B It made me want to go camping again.
C It brought the family closer together.
D It was easy for me to choose a good camp-site.
E It cost less than my usual holidays.
F It made me feel healthier.
G It brought back happy memories.
H It was a great way for me to relax.

Speaker 1		19
Speaker 2		20
Speaker 3		21
Speaker 4		22
Speaker 5		23

Advice

A *Listen for something that one speaker was expecting to be uncomfortable.*

B *Three speakers mention going camping again, but only one of them actually wants to go again.*

C *Four speakers talk about family camping trips, but only one of them felt closer to their family.*

D *Take care. Two speakers talk about other people choosing the campsite.*

E *Who compares the cost of this camping trip with other holidays?*

F *Take care with the difference between 'feeling relaxed' and 'feeling fit'.*

G *Three speakers went camping in the past, but only one talks about happy memories of it.*

H *'for me' means that the speaker has to say they felt relaxed*

Test 1 Training Listening Part 4

Task information

- In Part 4, you will hear an interview or an exchange between two or more speakers. There are seven multiple-choice questions, and each one has three options.
- You will be tested on your understanding of gist and detail and also on the speaker's attitudes, feelings and opinions.
- The questions follow the order of the recording as you are listening.
- The rubric will give you information about who the speakers are, and what they will be talking about.
- The recording will be 3–4 minutes long.

Understanding feelings, attitude and opinion

1 13 **Read the multiple-choice question below and listen to the recording.**

You will hear a woman called Alice talking about her job as a florist, selling flowers. What does Alice feel about the way she runs her business now?

A She misses having contact with the customers.
B She's relieved to have moved it all online.
C She's proud of the unique service she offers.

Tip! Before the recording begins, you have 1 minute to read through the rubric and the questions. This will help you understand what information to listen for.

2 **Now read the audioscript below. Why is B correct? Why are A and C wrong?**

Int: So, Alice, you've made some changes to your business. How do you feel about the business now? (cue)

Alice: Well, just to give you some of the background, I started by selling flowers from my own shop, and that attracted a lot of passing customers – often people who'd pop in to buy flowers when they'd forgotten someone's birthday, and they'd often stop to chat. (A) But running the premises just became too expensive, so I was really glad when I started operating solely on the internet, which has just been so much better (B) – I've saved a lot of time and money. So people look on my website and choose what they'd like or, as many florists will do, (C) I can make up a bouquet if they have something special in mind.

3 14 **Read the question for the next part of the interview and listen to the recording. Which is the correct answer – A, B or C? Why?**

In Alice's opinion, her job

A requires greater sensitivity than people realise.
B is far more creative than is generally recognised.
C can sometimes be more stressful than she'd like.

Tip! As you're listening, try to answer the question in your own words, and then look at the options to see which one matches your answer the most closely.

4 15 **Listen to the recording again. Why are the other two options wrong?**

Test 1 Exam practice Listening • Part 4

Action plan

1 Quickly read the instructions. What is the situation? What's the topic? Who will you hear?
2 Before you listen, read the first line of each question. What kind of information, e.g. somebody's opinion, do you need for each?
3 Underline the key words in each item.
4 Listen for expressions with similar or opposite meanings to the key words you underlined.
5 Think of an answer in your own words. Then choose the option most like your answer.
6 Check all your answers on the second listening.

16 **Follow the exam instructions, using the advice to help you.**

Tip! After you hear the instructions, there's a one-minute pause before the recording begins. Use this time to look through the questions, underlining the key words.

You will hear an interview with a man called Jamie Cole, who is talking about his experience of writing his first recipe book. For questions **24–30**, choose the best answer (**A**, **B** or **C**).

---

24 When Jamie was a recipe tester, he decided to write a recipe book because
- **A** he was persuaded by a colleague that his book would do very well.
- **B** he thought his own recipes were better than the ones he was testing.
- **C** he knew he had a good understanding of what makes a successful recipe.

25 How did Jamie succeed in getting a book deal with a publisher?
- **A** He found an agent who helped him.
- **B** He had a useful contact in the business.
- **C** He wrote to every publisher of food books.

26 What aspect of writing the book did Jamie find most challenging?
- **A** having to spend so much time shopping for ingredients
- **B** practising the same recipe many times in order to perfect it
- **C** researching background information to include about his recipes

Advice

24 *Listen for what Jamie says he was confident about.*

25 *Jamie says he didn't get a book deal in the usual way.*

26 *Which thing was the most difficult for Jamie?*

27 *Jamie explains what questions he's been asked, and what he might be asked one day.*

28 *Which option is Jamie's opinion?*

29 *Think about possible phrases for giving advice, e.g. 'It's a good idea to …' / 'I'd suggest …?'*

30 *Look at the phrase 'immediate priority' in the question. Which option describes what he plans to do next?*

27 Jamie says he has been asked by the public
- **A** whether the pictures in his book are real.
- **B** whether he had help with writing the recipes.
- **C** whether his recipe book has earnt him lots of money.

28 Why does Jamie think his recipe book is popular?
- **A** He uses unusual flavour combinations in his recipes.
- **B** His recipes are aimed at people with little time to cook.
- **C** He has included recipes for cooks of different abilities.

29 What advice does Jamie give to people thinking of writing their first recipe book?
- **A** focus on a particular style or type of cooking
- **B** develop food preparation skills by taking courses
- **C** get a job where you work in a kitchen every day

30 What is Jamie's immediate priority for his career?
- **A** planning a series of TV programmes about food
- **B** travelling widely to gather ideas for future books
- **C** starting a blog as a way to communicate with readers

Test 1 Training Speaking Part 1

Task information

- Speaking Part 1 lasts about 2 minutes.
- There are two examiners. One of the examiners tells you their names, then asks you for your name. You then give the examiner your mark sheet.
- One of the examiners asks you questions about yourself, and you answer. The other examiner listens only.
- The examiner asks each candidate questions in turn. You don't talk to the other candidate in this part.
- Part 1 tests your ability to talk about everyday topics such as your work or studies, your family, your free time and your future plans.
- To find out how your speaking will be assessed, go to the Cambridge Assessment English website.

Useful language Useful expressions

1 Write the words and expressions in the box next to the correct function.

~~also~~	and	as well	because
Could you repeat that, please?	for example	for instance	
I think	I would say that	like	Sorry, can you say that again?
such as	the reason for this is	too	

To add extra information: also ....

To give a reason: ....

To give an example: ....

To give your opinion: ....

To ask for repetition: ....

Tip! One aim of Part 1 is to help you to relax by getting you to talk about familiar topics. Try to relax and talk naturally about yourself and your life.

Tip! Use full sentences to answer the questions. Add reasons, examples and extra information to support your answer, and express your own opinion. If you don't understand a question, you can ask the examiner to repeat it.

2 Read the four questions *in italics* that the examiner asks. Then complete parts of Ana's answers with words and expressions from Exercise 1.

Where are you from?

1 I'm from Madrid. It's the capital of Spain, and it's .... the largest city.

What do you like about living in your home town?

2 It's a really exciting city .... there are lots of things to do. .... example, there are lots of cafés where I can meet my friends.

3 There are plenty of events .... as concerts and festivals, ...

What sort of things do you do in your free time?

4 I .... say that I'm a very sociable person, so my friends are important to me.

In what ways do you think you will use English in the future?

5 I .... that English will be very important for me in my work.

6 The .... for this is that I'd like to work for an international company, and I'd like to travel in Europe and the United States.

3 17 **Now listen and check. Which question does Ana ask the examiner to repeat?**

Remember! There are no 'right' and 'wrong' answers to the questions in Part 1. Just try to be yourself!

Test 1 Exam practice Speaking • Part 1

Action plan

1 Try to look friendly and confident when you meet the examiners.
2 Listen to the examiner's questions carefully.
3 Speak clearly so that both examiners and your partner can hear you easily.
4 Give full answers to the questions with reasons and examples, rather than just saying *yes* or *no*.
5 Don't prepare answers in advance as your speech will not sound natural.
6 If you don't understand a question, ask the examiner to repeat it. You won't lose marks if you do this.

Part 1 2 minutes (3 minutes for groups of three)

1 **Work in pairs. One of you take the role of the examiner and ask the questions, while the other answers the questions. Then swap roles.**

Interlocutor First, we'd like to know something about you.

- What do you like about the town you live in? ….. (Why?)
- How do you usually spend your evenings?
- What do you like to do at lunchtime? ….. (Why?)
- Do you enjoy studying English? ….. (Why are you studying it?)

Tip! Chat to your exam partner in English before you go into the exam room. It will help you feel more relaxed once the exam starts.

2 **Now swap roles.**

Interlocutor First, we'd like to know something about you.

- What do you like about where you study/work? ….. (Why?)
- How do you usually spend your Saturdays? ….. (Why?)
- What do you like to do when you get home after work or college?
- Do you enjoy using a computer? ….. (What do you use it for mainly?)

Tip! Practise answering questions about yourself so that you feel comfortable and relaxed, and can make a good first impression in Part 1.

Test 1 Training Speaking Part 2

Task information

- In Speaking Part 2, each candidate is given a one-minute 'long turn'. No one will interrupt you.
- The examiner gives you both two photographs to compare, and answer a question above the photographs.
- Part 2 tests your ability to organise your speaking, and to compare, describe and give your opinions.
- The examiner then asks you a question about your partner's photographs. You have about 30 seconds to answer.

Exam skill Understanding the task

1 **Study photographs A and B on page C1 and read the question above the photographs. Then circle the points below you should do when you compare these photographs.**

1 Describe the people.
2 Say what topic links the photographs.
3 Say briefly what the people are doing.
4 Say how many people there are.
5 Suggest who the people might be.
6 Say what is different about the forms of exercise.
7 Talk about what might happen next.
8 Suggest how the people might be feeling.
9 Say why people might choose each form of exercise.
10 Say which form of exercise you would prefer, and why.

2 18 **Listen to Paul comparing the two photographs. Check your answers to Exercise 1.**

Useful language Comparing and expressing preferences

3 19 **Complete the sentences with the words in the box. Listen to Paul again and check.**

as	both	difference	more	other	whereas

1 .... photos show people doing exercise.
2 The people in the gym don't seem to know each other … . On the .... hand, the people playing basketball are probably friends.
3 The class looks quite serious, ... the basketball game looks very relaxed.
4 The people in the gym don't look .... happy as the people playing basketball.
5 I think the people playing basketball are probably enjoying themselves ....
6 Another .... is that the basketball is outside.

4 **Choose the correct words to complete the sentences expressing personal preferences.**

1 I'd *prefer / rather / choose* do exercise with friends, in a fun way.
2 I don't *want / enjoy / rather* going to the gym.
3 I'd *prefer / rather / enjoy* to do a team sport than exercise alone.
4 I'd rather *wouldn't / don't / not* exercise in a gym.

Exam skill Answering the question

5 **20 Listen to Ela answering a question about Paul's photos. Tick the things she does.**

1 describes and compares the photos ☐
2 mentions something that Paul said ☐
3 expresses her own opinion and preferences ☐
4 gives an example or reason to support her opinion ☐
5 disagrees with Paul's opinions ☐

Tip! Listen carefully when the other candidate compares their photos. If you wish, you can refer to some of their ideas when you answer your question about their photos.

Exam skill Organising your answer

6 **Study photographs A and B on page C2 and read the question above the photographs. Then organise the ideas (a–h) under the headings (1–4).**

1 What topic links the two photos? ....
2 What is similar about the achievements? ....
3 What is different about the achievements? ....
4 How are the people in the two photographs feeling? ....

a I think the mountain climbers probably feel exhausted.
b Both achievements involve a lot of physical effort.
c Both photos show people who have achieved something important, and are celebrating.
d The football players have competed against other people, whereas the mountain climbers have only competed with themselves.
e I think the football players must be really proud of themselves.
f To achieve both these things, you have to train very seriously for a long time.
g The mountain climbers can only celebrate their achievement with each other, whereas the football players can see all their fans cheering for them.
h The football players can relax and celebrate now. On the other hand, the mountain climbers still have to get back down the mountain safely.

7 **21 Compare the two photographs and answer the question. Remember to start by saying what topic links the two photographs. Listen to Natalie and compare your ideas.**

Exam skill Understanding the follow-up question

8 **Read the follow-up question that the examiner asks the second candidate. What should he do?**

George, which achievement do you admire the most?

a say which photograph he prefers and give reasons ☐
b explain which achievement impresses him more and give reasons ☐
c explain why some people choose to do difficult or dangerous things ☐

9 **22 Listen to Natalie again, then listen to the follow-up question and answer it. Remember, you can refer to ideas that she mentions if you like.**

10 **23 Listen to George answering the question and compare your ideas.**

Test 1 Exam practice Speaking • Part 2

Action plan

1 Listen carefully to the instructions, look at the pictures and read the question.
2 Talk about things that are similar and different in the two pictures. Don't describe everything.
3 If you can't find the right word for something, paraphrase it (i.e. use other words to explain).
4 Speak at a natural speed.
5 Try to keep talking for the full minute.
6 When your partner is talking about his/her pictures, listen but don't interrupt.

Part 2 4 minutes (6 minutes for groups of three)

1 **Work in pairs, A and B. One of you takes the role of the examiner and gives the instructions, while the other follows the instructions. Then swap roles.**

Interlocutor In this part of the test, I'm going to give each of you two photographs. I'd like you to talk about your photographs on your own for about a minute, and also to answer a question about your partner's photographs.
(Candidate A), it's your turn first. Here are your photographs on page C3. They show **people at home.** I'd like you to compare the photographs, and say **what you think the people are enjoying about being at home.**
All right?

Candidate A

1 minute ....

Interlocutor Thank you.

Tip! Try to organise what you say by using connecting words and phrases, e.g. *so, because, whereas,* etc. This will help you to get higher marks.

2 **Now A can read the examiner's question to B.**

Interlocutor *(Candidate B),* which of these things do you prefer to do at home?

Candidate B

approximately ....
30 seconds

Interlocutor Thank you.

Tip! The more you practise talking for a minute, the easier it will be in the exam.

3 **Now swap roles.**

Interlocutor Now, *(Candidate B),* here are your photographs on page C4. They show **people who are busy.** I'd like you to compare the photographs, and say **why you think these people are busy.**
All right?

Candidate B

1 minute ....

Interlocutor Thank you.

4 **Now B can read the examiner's question to A.**

Interlocutor When are you busiest – in the week or at the weekends?

Candidate A

approximately ....
30 seconds

Interlocutor Thank you.

Task information

- Speaking Part 3 lasts about 4 minutes.
- In this part of the test, you must work with a partner.
- The examiner gives you a piece of paper with written prompts that show different ideas or possibilities, and explains what you have to do.
- First, you must talk together and discuss all the prompts, giving your opinions about each one.
- The examiner then asks you to try to reach agreement about something.
- Part 3 tests your ability to talk about different possibilities, make suggestions, express opinions and give reasons, agree or disagree, and try to reach agreement.

Understanding the task

1 **Read the exam instructions below. Answer these questions.**

1 What is the topic of the discussion?
2 How many of the ideas should you discuss?
3 Should you try to reach agreement immediately?

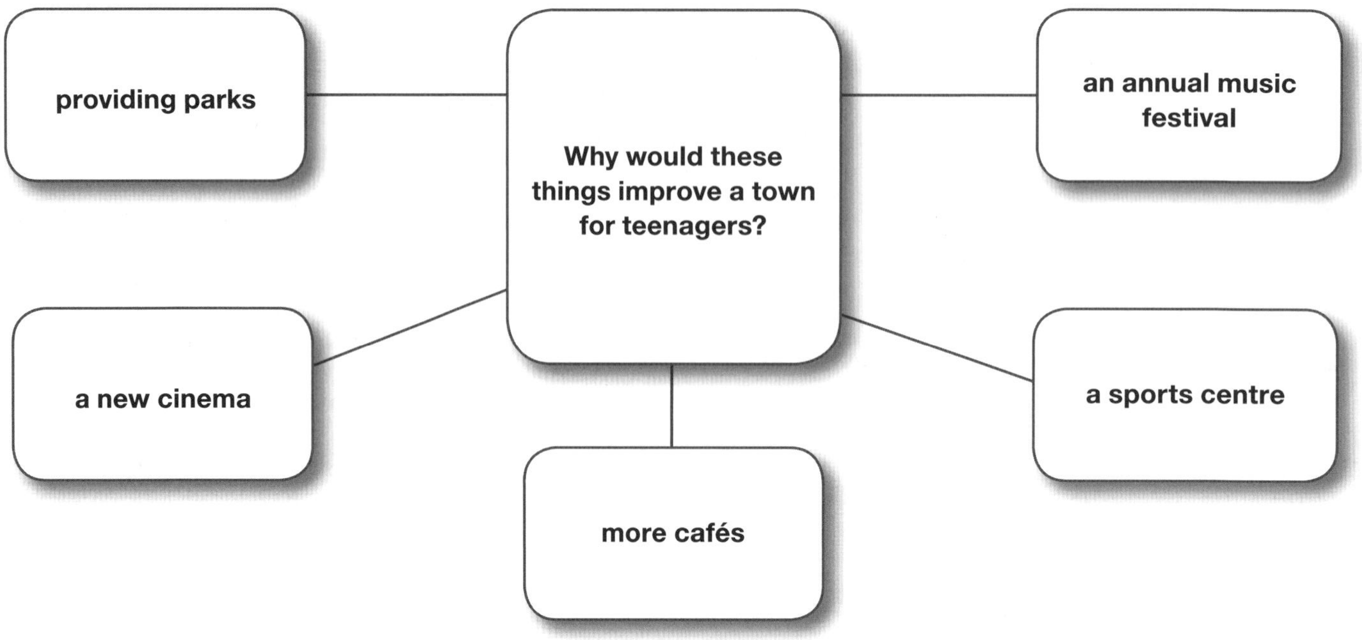

Tip! It is important that both you and your partner speak. Take turns in the discussion so you both spend about the same amount of time speaking.

Useful language Making and responding to suggestions

2 Match the groups of expressions 1–4 with the categories a–d.

a asking for someone's opinion
b agreeing with someone
c disagreeing politely with someone
d making a suggestion

1 ....
I can see what you mean, but ...
I'm not sure about that.
I think ... might be a better idea.
Yes, that's true, but ...

2 ....
Do you agree?
What do you think about ...?
Would you agree with that?
Do you think that's true?

3 ....
It might be a good idea to ...
Perhaps we/they should ...
... sounds like a good idea.
We / They could ...

4 ....
I think so, too.
That's true.
Yes, you're right.
I completely agree with you.

Tip! Using these expressions helps to make your ideas clearer, helps your partner to understand your opinions and helps the discussion to continue smoothly.

3 24 Complete the sentences with words from Exercise 2. Then listen to Sofia and Chang doing the task and check your answers.

1 Shall we start with providing parks? This .... like a good idea.
2 I can .... what you mean, but parks are no good when the weather's bad.
3 I think more cafés might be a better ....
4 Yes, you're .... I hadn't thought about that.
5 What do you .... about the idea of a new cinema?
6 Yes, that's .... , but it's quite expensive to go to the cinema.
7 With sports centres, you can go every day and do something different. Would you .... with that?
8 Yes, I .... agree with you.

4 25 Listen to Sofia and Chang doing the final part of Part 3. What do they agree?

Remember!
It's important to listen to your partner during the discussion and respond to their ideas, as well as expressing your own opinions.

Test 1 Exam practice Speaking • Part 3

Action plan

1 It's important that you and your partner both have a chance to speak in the time given. Share the conversation equally.
2 Encourage your partner to respond to your ideas by saying things like *Do you agree?* or *What do you think?*
3 Show that you are listening when your partner is speaking, e.g. by nodding or smiling.
4 Remember that there are no right or wrong answers – just give your opinion about the topic.
5 Don't worry if you haven't discussed all five points in the time available. However, you should continue the discussion until the examiner stops you.
6 Make sure you express your opinions clearly and give reasons for what you say.
7 Don't feel that you have to agree with each other during the decision making stage. It's fine to disagree.

Part 3 4 minutes (5 minutes for groups of three)

Interlocutor Now, I'd like you to talk about something together for about two minutes.
Here are some things that young people have to think about when deciding whether to leave home after they finish school, and a question for you to discuss. First, you have some time to look at the task.

[Show candidates the diagram on page C5. Allow 15 seconds.]

Now, talk to each other about **whether it's a good idea for young people to leave home after they finish school**.

Candidates

2 minutes ....
(3 minutes for groups of three)

Interlocutor Thank you. Now you have about a minute to decide **what the most important thing is for young people to think about when deciding whether to leave home or not**.

Candidates

1 minute ....
(for pairs or groups of three)

Interlocutor Thank you.

Tip! Listen carefully to your partner. Respond by agreeing or disagreeing, and give reasons. Showing that you can interact in a conversation will get you higher marks.

Test 1 Training Speaking Part 4

Task information

- You answer general questions based on the same topic as Part 3.
- Part 4 tests your ability to talk about issues in more depth.
- You need to express your opinions, and give reasons or examples to support your opinions.
- The examiner may also ask you to reply to your partner's opinions.
- You don't have to talk directly to your partner, but you may want to bring them into the discussion when you answer a question.
- After you finish Part 4, the examiner will thank you and say that the test has ended.

Understanding the task

1 Read the sentences about Part 4. Mark them T (true) or F (false).

1 You should give your own opinion when you answer. ....
2 You should add an example or a reason to support your opinion. ....
3 You must encourage your partner to join the discussion. ....
4 You should only answer when the examiner speaks to you. ....

2 26 Listen to Hans and Maria answering some Part 4 questions.
Which speaker, Hans (H), Maria (M) or both (B) ...

1 asks for their partner's opinion? ....
2 gives a reason or example to support their opinion? ....
3 extends the discussion by responding to their partner's opinion? ....
4 asks the examiner to repeat a question? ....

Tip! Listen carefully when your partner is answering their questions. The examiner might ask you for your opinion.

Useful language Opinions

3 27 Choose the correct words in *italics* in expressions 1–8 below. Listen to some opinions about sport and check.

Giving your opinion

1 I'd *say / think* that ...
2 I *argue / think* that ...
3 In my *opinion / thought*, ...
4 My own *view / idea* is that ...

Asking for someone's opinion

5 What's your *thought / opinion* of ...?
6 What do you *think / agree* about ...?
7 What are your *views / opinion* about ...?
8 How do you *feel / say* about ...?

4 28 Match the expressions in 1–5 with a–e. Listen and check.

1 Yes, but on the
2 But don't you
3 Yes, but wouldn't
4 Yes, but you could also
5 Another way of

a) you agree that ...?
b) other hand, ...
c) argue that ...
d) looking at it would be ...
e) think that ...?

5 29 Listen to the opinions from Exercise 2. Practise extending the discussion using expressions from Exercise 4.

Test 1 Exam practice Speaking • Part 4

Action plan

1 Listen carefully to the examiner's questions. You can ask the examiner to repeat something if you don't understand.
2 Give yourself thinking time by saying things like *That's an interesting question …* or *Let me think, …* .
3 As in all parts of the test, give full answers to the questions by including reasons and examples.
4 Be ready for more challenging questions than the ones in Part 1. The questions will usually require you to give your opinion about a topic.
5 If you haven't got an opinion about the topic, say something like: *I've never thought about that, but I would say that …* . You can make up an answer as it is your language that is being tested, not your ideas.
6 As in Part 3, try to develop the ideas and opinions of your partner, and show that you are responding to what he / she says.

Part 4 4 minutes (6 minutes for groups of three)

Take it in turns to answer these questions. Use the questions in the box to move the conversation along or get your partner to join in.

- What are the advantages of going to university in a different town from your hometown?
- Should there be a minimum school leaving age? ….. (Why? / Why not?)
- Do you think young people have enough free time? ….. (Why? / Why not?)
- Should parents give their children advice after the age of 18? ….. (Why? / Why not?)
- Is it better to live in an apartment or a house? ….. (Why? / Why not?)
- Is there a 'right' age to get married? ….. (Why? / Why not?)

Select any of the following prompts, as appropriate:

- What do you think?
- Do you agree?
- And you?

Tip! You can develop your partner's answers to questions in Part 4 and give your own opinion or idea – but try not to interrupt your partner!

Tip! Look at the examiner when you are answering his or her questions, but at the other candidate when you are speaking together.

Test 2 Training Reading and Use of English Part 1

Useful language Words with similar meanings

1 Complete the sentences with the correct forms of the words in the boxes.

> **Tip!** The words in the options to fill each gap will usually be very close in meaning.

occur	appear	happen	arise

1 The issue of what to do with the land .... during one of the council planning meetings.
2 This chemical .... naturally in some plants.
3 So what exactly .... at the end of the film? I didn't really understand the story!
4 She's a good actor, and will be .... in a new TV series on Channel 4 soon.

risk	threat	uncertainty	danger

5 It's important not to put other people's financial security at ....
6 He's in .... of losing his job if he continues to arrive late every morning.
7 No-one knows exactly what the future will hold – we all have to live with that ....
8 The message contained .... that the company's computer systems would be attacked by hackers.

control	direct	conduct	guide

9 It was wonderful to have such a knowledgeable person to .... us around the city!
10 Scientists say that once the reaction has started, it's very difficult to .... it.
11 My friend .... us to the station, but he couldn't come with us himself.
12 The experiment was .... by an international team of researchers.

opinion	idea	attitude	view

13 It was George's .... to have a barbecue on the beach.
14 I'm delighted that you have such a positive .... towards your work!
15 My boss takes the .... that new staff members should be given as much training as possible.
16 .... are divided on the need for a new motorway.

Useful language Phrases and collocations

2 Complete the sentences with the correct form of the verbs in the box.

> **Tip!** Read the sentences carefully to make sure you use any phrases and collocations in the correct tense.

raise	put	bear	leave	cross	draw	play	deliver

1 The supervisor .... our attention to the new safety regulations.
2 Thanks for your advice, I'll .... it in mind.
3 The film director .... a speech and then answered questions from the press.
4 Liam said the idea of starting his own business had never .... his mind.
5 Nobody .... the issue at the meeting, so it wasn't discussed.
6 I'm planning to .... a trick on him – I'm sure he'll think it's funny, too.
7 .... her alone until she's finished replying to all her emails.
8 This waste plastic could be .... to good use making water pipes.

Useful language Linking words and expressions

3 For sentences 1–8, decide which linking words and expressions (A, B, C or D) best fits each gap.

> **Tip!** Think about what the linking words have to do – add ideas, contrast them or show reason.

The first telephone exchanges

When telephones first started to become available to the public, many businesses used them, **(1)** .... few private individuals did. **(2)** .... the fact that phones were so expensive, most people used public telephone boxes **(3)** .... having their own phone at home. People's calls were routed via a telephone exchange that was manually operated. The operators had to plug the correct wires into the correct sockets **(4)** .... connect the two speakers. The operators had to listen to the speakers at the beginning of a call **(5)** .... put it through, and often carried on listening to the whole conversation. **(6)** .... this, telephone operators often knew all about what was going on in local people's lives. In some exchanges, there was a minimum height requirement for telephone operators, **(7)** .... the fact that they had to be tall enough to reach the sockets located higher up. In the countryside, the exchanges were often located in local post offices, (8) .... these were eventually replaced by larger exchanges that could serve a wide area.

	A	B	C	D
1	**A** in spite of	**B** instead of	**C** despite	**D** whereas
2	**A** Because	**B** Owing to	**C** As	**D** Thanks to
3	**A** unless	**B** instead of	**C** until	**D** by contrast
4	**A** in spite of	**B** in addition to	**C** in view of	**D** in order to
5	**A** so as to	**B** due to	**C** instead of	**D** as long as
6	**A** In spite of	**B** As long as	**C** As a result of	**D** In addition to
7	**A** due to	**B** apart from	**C** as well as	**D** except for
8	**A** whereas	**B** although	**C** despite	**D** unless

Test 2 Exam practice Reading and Use of English • Part 1

Follow the exam instructions, using the advice to help you.

Tip! If you're not sure of an answer, cross out any you know are wrong, and choose from the remaining ones.

For questions **1–8**, read the text below and decide which answers (**A**, **B**, **C** or **D**) best fits each gap. There is an example at the beginning (**0**).

Mark your answers **on the separate answer sheet**.

Example:

0 **A** sits **B** rests **C** lies **D** falls

0	A	B	C	D
	▭	▭	▬	▭

Ice-cream farm

Deep in the heart of beautiful Irish countryside **(0)** .... Willow Farm café. Its proprietor is Martha Lindsay, wife of farmer Derek who has a herd of 100 cows. It is an extremely popular **(1)** .... for tourists with young families because of the wonderful ice cream it sells. There are 20 regular flavours, but the number one bestseller is Willows Own, a unique vanilla-based recipe whose contents are a **(2)** .... guarded secret! Everyone who tries it **(3)** .... it for its rich, creamy, natural taste – one that mass-produced ice cream cannot **(4)** .... The café also sells teas and cakes to **(5)** .... for the tastes of older customers.

The ice cream is made using only natural ingredients from the farm, including milk, eggs, and even the strawberries or apples which give each product its **(6)** .... flavour.

The café is hard to **(7)** .... to, but Martha reckons this is all part of the attraction for visitors. Certainly it is well worth the **(8)** .... , as the views of the surrounding countryside are stunning.

	A	B	C	D
1	visit	objective	intention	destination
2	narrowly	precisely	closely	thoroughly
3	praises	compliments	thanks	congratulates
4	balance	match	compare	measure
5	supply	offer	deliver	cater
6	divided	disconnected	distinct	dissimilar
7	arrive	come	reach	get
8	effort	task	feat	act

Advice

*1 One of these means here **place to visit**.*

2 Only one of these words completes this fixed phrase and common expression.

3 Look at the word after the gap – only one of these fits with this word.

*4 The meaning you need here is similar to **reach** or **achieve**.*

5 Which verb can be followed by 'for'?

*6 The meaning here is similar to **individual** or **particular**.*

7 Only one of these verbs can be followed by 'to', with this meaning.

8 This is part of a fixed phrase and common expression.

Test 2 Training Reading and Use of English Part 2

Useful language Articles, quantifiers and determiners

1 **Correct the sentences by adding an article, quantifier or determiner where necessary. Some of the sentences are correct.**

1. Could you send me some more information about place where you're living?
2. That was strange thing to say!
3. There aren't biscuits left.
4. I'd love to have dinner with you on Wednesday!
5. There's interesting course I'd like to do in the evenings.
6. My two sisters all like coffee ice cream.
7. Where's best place to have coffee in this area?
8. Lot of people at the meeting said they rarely used public transport.
9. That's so easy, it must be the least difficult exercise I've ever done!
10. Lucy's doing a college project on history of film.

Tip! Remember that most of the words tested in Part 2 are grammatical words like articles and modal verbs.

Useful language Auxiliary verbs

2 **Complete the sentences with the correct auxiliary verb. Use only one word. Sometimes more than one tense is possible.**

1. When .... we going to be told where the new car park will be built?
2. The sculpture looked even more beautiful than I .... imagined before I went to see it!
3. I think I must .... dropped one of my gloves while I was walking to work.
4. It .... said to be the earliest example of a comb ever discovered.
5. They have .... given all the information they need to do the puzzle.
6. Where .... the rare bird last seen?

Tip! You always have to complete each gap. It will never be correct to leave it empty.

Useful language Spelling

3 **Correct the spelling mistake in each sentence.**

1. I wasn't tall enogh to reach the top shelf.
2. This photograph is better then that one.
3. You can choose wichever one you like.
4. We had to walk trough the woods to get to the beach.
5. Whoose bag is this?
6. I don't know weather to stay or to go!

Tip! Incorrect spelling will lose you marks.

Useful language Time expressions

4 **Complete the sentences with time expressions from the box. There is one sentence with two possible answers.**

until	yet	as soon as	by the time	since
in time	in the meantime	already	once	

1 If you run, you might just get to the station .... to catch the train.
2 .... the music started, they got up and danced.
3 We can't start eating .... all the guests have arrived.
4 Has Barbara arrived ....? I can't see her anywhere.
5 Frank spent the morning working in his office. .... , James went fishing.
6 Have you .... finished that book I lent you?
7 .... we got to the cinema, the film had already started.
8 I'm exhausted! I've been up .... five o'clock in the morning.

5 **Read the text below and choose the correct time expressions in *italics*.**

My brother is an artist. **(1)** *Already / By the time / Until* he was seven, he could **(2)** *still / already / in time* paint and draw very well. His teacher wanted to enter one of his paintings into an art competition, but our parents refused. They could see that when he was older, he might be able to earn a living as a professional artist, but **(3)** *in time / in the meantime / by the time*, they wanted him to have an ordinary childhood. So it wasn't **(4)** *yet / as soon as / until* he was sixteen that his paintings appeared in our local art gallery. Things have never been the same **(5)** *in the meantime / since / yet.*

(6) *As soon as / By the time / Already* the public saw his work, he became a local celebrity. And **(7)** *in time / once / in the meantime* the critics had reviewed the exhibition and praised my brother's paintings, his career really took off. He hasn't had a major exhibition in the National Art Gallery **(8)** *already / yet / in the meantime*, but I'm sure he will some day.

Test 2 Exam practice Reading and Use of English • Part 2

1 **Read the article quickly without filling in any gaps. What would be a good summary of the text?**

A the pros and cons of being ambidextrous

B being ambidextrous in the world of sport

C it's more complicated than it sounds

2 **Follow the exam instructions, using the advice to help you.**

For questions **9–16**, read the text below and think of the word which best fits each gap. Use only **one** word in each gap. There is an example at the beginning (**0**).

Write your answers **IN CAPITAL LETTERS on the separate answer sheet.**

Example: | 0 | | W | O | U | L | D |

Tip! Try reading the previous words or the previous sentence to help you choose the gapped word.

The ability to use both hands

If asked, most people **(0)** .... say that most individuals are right-handed, some are left-handed and a few are 'ambidextrous' – they can use both hands equally well. In fact, the truth **(9)** .... the matter is somewhat more complicated. For one thing, the true scientific definition of 'ambidextrous' is **(10)** .... able to write equally well with either hand, and only 1% of people fall into **(11)** .... category.

Certainly, some people are very strongly right or left dominant when it **(12)** .... to using their hands and legs. But many people are **(13)** .... entirely individual mix: for example, someone might be a right-hander for playing tennis but a left-footer in football.

Of course, top sportspeople sometimes try to train themselves **(14)** .... be equally capable with both sides of the body. The **(15)** .... can be said of people in other professions. A carpenter or mechanic who can learn to use tools with his weaker hand will find things much easier and is far **(16)** .... likely to suffer from repetitive strain injuries.

Advice

9 You need a preposition here to complete a very common fixed phrase.

10 You could put 'the ability to' here, which you can see is a noun phrase. So you need a grammatical word which can be a kind of noun.

11 The word you need refers back to the previous bit of information. Which grammatical word fulfils that function?

12 You need a verb here to complete a very common fixed phrase.

13 Read forward to the word 'mix' and think grammatically! You know that 'mix' must be a noun here because of the adjective 'individual' immediately before it.

14 'themselves' is a reference to somebody, a person. So what is the grammar of the verb 'train'?

15 Read the previous sentence to follow the argument here.

16 Consider the argument around the gap so that you don't fall into the obvious trap!

Tip! Remember that the gapped words are often part of bigger phrases.

Useful language More word building

1 **Read the definitions and match them with the base words. Then, using a suffix from the box and any other changes necessary, write the correct form of the word.**

-er -ible -ish -ism -ist -or -ship -y

> **Tip!** Learn spelling rules, e.g. how to form the plural of nouns ending in a consonant followed by *y* (*-y* > *-ies*).

Definition	Base word	Word
1 courageous behaviour	CRITIC	
2 which can be seen	FOOL	
3 the way in which two things are connected	SUPPLY	
4 a person who runs something	MOTOR	
5 saying that something is bad	VISION	
6 not wise	OPERATE	
7 a company which delivers goods to someone	BRAVE	
8 a person who drives a car	RELATE	

2 **Complete the sentences with a word using the base word in CAPITALS.**

1 That was a .... thing to say! Please try to be more sensible. **FOOL**
2 The tour .... organised everything for us, even our meals. **OPERATE**
3 Scientists are trying to discover the .... between the two events. **RELATE**
4 She was given a medal for her .... **BRAVE**
5 Most people agree that there are too many .... on the roads in this city. **MOTOR**
6 The spots on the painting were almost .... to the naked eye – that's why we didn't notice it until now. **VISION**
7 There are only a few .... of parts for this type of camera now. **SUPPLY**
8 Novelists often have to deal with .... from readers of their work. **CRITIC**

> **Tip!** Think about whether nouns need to be singular or plural.

> **Tip!** You may need to add a prefix to the word. Some words need both a prefix and a suffix.

Useful language Word building (irregular word formation)

3 **Complete the table with the correct forms of the words where possible.**

adjective	noun	verb	adverb
free			
hot			
strong			
wide			
long			
anxious			
deep			

4 **Complete the sentences with a word using the base word given in CAPITALS.**

1 The factory has to do a lot of tests to check the .... of the furniture it produces. **STRONG**
2 Jackie watched her daughter go sailing with some .... **ANXIOUS**
3 This doorway is far too narrow – I think it should be .... **WIDE**
4 All the information you need is .... available on the internet. **FREE**
5 Have you any idea of the .... of the river here? **DEEP**
6 This soup needs .... up before you eat it. **HOT**
7 These trousers are a bit short, but I can .... them. **LONG**

Test 2 Exam practice Reading and Use of English • Part 3

1 **Quickly read the text below, without completing any of the gaps, and say which of the following best summarises it:**
- A Birdwatching's similarity to extreme surfing
- B Birdwatching in a state in the US
- C The simple, relaxing pleasures of birdwatching

2 **Read the example (0) and answer these questions.**
1. What kind of word is 'fascinate'?
2. What kind of word is needed and what suffix is added to form it?
3. Are any other changes made?

Tip! Don't forget to change *all* the words in capitals.

3 **Follow the exam instructions, using the advice to help you.**

For questions **17–24**, read the text below. Use the word given in capitals at the end of some of the lines to form a word that fits in the gap **in the same line**. There is an example at the beginning (**0**).

Write your answers **IN CAPITAL LETTERS on the separate answer sheet.**

Example: | 0 | F A S C I N A T I O N |

The attraction of birdwatching

When asked to explain their **(0)** .... with their hobby, some birdwatchers might	**FASCINATE**
mention the simple **(17)** .... of getting out and walking in woods and noting	**PLEASE**
what birds you come across. But the authors of a highly **(18)** .... new book,	**ENTERTAIN**
The Attraction of Bird Watching, describe a particularly thrilling occasion when they were	
(19) .... to see an extremely rare visitor to the shores of Maine in the USA. They	**DESPAIR**
compare the **(20)** .... of preparing and researching for this expedition to that of	**EXCITE**
extreme surfers, who eagerly chase the big wave, wherever it might occur. There is the same	
sense of anticipation, the **(21)** .... checking of internet sightings and	**CARE**
(22) .... guides, and above all the sense of having to be ready for	**REFER**
(23) .... that might appear only very briefly, if indeed it appears at all. The authors	**SOME**
attempt to give an **(24)** .... for this feeling, and speculate that it is perhaps a	**EXPLAIN**
throwback to what primitive hunters would have felt.	

Advice

17 *This is testing a well-known collocation.*

18 *Choose from the following: 'entertainer', 'entertainment', 'entertaining'.*

19 *Take care with a spelling change.*

20 *The word you need is a noun.*

21 *There are several possible adjectives from 'care' – you need to choose one with the right meaning!*

22 *The word you need will form a compound noun.*

23 *There is a grammatical element to this word formation.*

24 *Be careful with the spelling when you form a new word.*

Test 2 Training Reading and Use of English Part 4

Useful language Past modals, third conditional and regrets

Tip! Reported speech, conditional sentences and modal forms are often tested in this part, as well as fixed phrases.

1 Choose the correct verb forms in *italics*.

My first ever job interview didn't go very well. I wish I **(1)** *had done / did* a lot of things differently. First of all, I **(2)** *should checked / should have checked* exactly where I was supposed to go. If I **(3)** *would have / had*, I wouldn't have gone to the wrong metro station. If I **(4)** *didn't / hadn't* done that, I **(5)** *might have / might have had* a chance of arriving on time. In fact, I was over twenty minutes late. They **(6)** *must have thought / must thought* I wasn't very keen to get the job. I learnt my lesson, though, because I knew that if **(7)** *I'd been / I was* better prepared, I **(8)** *could get / could have got* the job. And I did get one in the end, with another company, and I love my work.

Useful language Active and passive forms

Tip! If you have to change a verb from active to passive, or from passive to active, make sure you keep the tense the same.

2 Complete the second sentence so that it has a similar meaning to the first sentence.

1 Anna has been shown how to operate the printer.
Someone .... how to operate the printer.
2 The rare bird had never been seen outside the jungle before.
No-one .... the rare bird outside the jungle before.
3 Your food is being prepared by our chef as we speak.
Our chef .... your food as we speak.
4 This picture couldn't have been painted by Jana!
Jana .... this picture!
5 Somebody gave them some free cinema tickets last week.
They .... some free cinema tickets last week.
6 Someone must have told him how to get to party.
He .... how to get to the party.
7 Did anybody actually see her leaving the house?
Was she .... the house?
8 Where do they keep the staff uniforms at this hotel?
Where are .... at this hotel?

Tip! Learn the grammar of phrasal verbs as well as their meaning, e.g. you can say *call it off*, but not *call off it*.

Useful language Phrasal verbs

3 Match the phrasal verbs with their meanings.

1 call off	**a)** start to suffer from an illness, especially one that is not serious
2 give in	**b)** accept that a difficult situation exists
3 come up with	**c)** like someone and become friendly immediately
4 point out	**d)** decide that a planned event, especially a sports event, will not happen, or to end an activity because it is no longer useful or possible
5 face up to	**e)** finish, use, or sell all of something so that there is none left
6 come down with	**f)** tell someone about some information, often because you believe they do not know it or have forgotten it
7 run out of	**g)** suggest or think of an idea or plan
8 hit it off	**h)** accept that you have been defeated and agree to stop competing or fighting

4 **Complete the sentences with the correct form of the phrasal verbs from Exercise 3.**

1 I wouldn't have realised my new phone had so many features if they hadn't been .... to me by my friends.
2 I don't feel very well – I think I might be .... flu.
3 They had to .... the football match because of the bad weather.
4 Sally needs to .... the fact that she'll never be a champion swimmer.
5 When I met Gary, we .... straight away, and we've been friends ever since.
6 OK, I .... , you win – but let's play another chess game soon.
7 Freya went to the supermarket because she'd .... milk.
8 Tess .... a possible solution to the problem while she was out for a walk.

Useful language Review of Tests 1 and 2 Training Part 4

5 **Choose the correct words in *italics*.**

1 After training hard for an hour, the players stopped *having / to have* a rest for a few minutes.
2 I wish I *knew / had known* exactly what the weather's going to be like tomorrow.
3 I can't remember *taking / to have taken* this photo!
4 I'm sure your phone can't *be / have been* stolen. Let's have another look for it.
5 Paul felt tired, but his friends persuaded him *to go / going* out.
6 We may have to face up *with / to* the fact that we'll lose this football match.
7 Let's go by car, otherwise, we risk *getting / to get* soaked if it rains as much as it did yesterday.
8 Jenny denied *having / to have* known anything about the surprise party.

Test 2 Exam practice Reading and Use of English • Part 4

1 **Read the exam instructions and the example below. The words that are the same in both sentences have been crossed out.**

0 ~~It took James~~ ages to repair ~~the clock~~.

LONG

~~It took James~~ .... ~~the clock~~ working again.

You have to change the underlined words.

The gap can be filled by the words *a long time to get*, so you write:

1 mark for 'a long time', 1 mark for 'to get'.

Example: | **0** | A LONG TIME TO GET |

Tip! Do not include any 'repeated' words from the first sentence in your answers.

2 **Now follow the exam instructions, using the advice to help you.**

For questions **25–30**, complete the second sentence so that it has a similar meaning to the first sentence, using the word given. **Do not change the word given**. You must use between **two** and **five** words, including the word given. Here is an example (**0**).

Write **only** the missing words I**N CAPITAL LETTERS on the separate answer sheet.**

---

25 Lizzie wasn't able to train for two weeks when she injured her ankle.

PREVENTED

An ankle injury .... two weeks.

26 The pasta dish was so salty that Jim could only eat a little of it.

LEAVE

The pasta dish was so salty that Jim had .... of it.

27 'This summer I've done less swimming than I normally do,' said Barry.

MUCH

'I .... swimming this summer as I normally do,' said Barry.

28 When she heard that her sister had had a baby, Maura took the first train to go and see her.

BECOME

When she heard that her sister .... Maura took the first train to go and see her.

29 'If you think you know the answer, please don't shout it out,' said the teacher to his class.

KEEP

'If you think you know the answer, please .... yourself,' said the teacher to his class.

30 'If you decide you do not want this policy, you have ten days to inform us,' said the manager.

MIND

'If you .... this policy, you have ten days to inform us,' said the manager.

Advice

25 The meaning is that because of an injury Lizzie couldn't train for two weeks.

26 What is the connection between 'salty' and 'leave'?

27 Transform this using a negative form.

28 Use a maximum of five words.

29 You need a fixed phrase here.

30 You need a collocation with 'mind' that means ***decide that you do not want.***

Test 2 Training Reading and Use of English Part 5

Reading for detail

1a Read this paragraph in an article about extreme sports. Then read the question and the options below. Choose the option which is the best answer.

> **Tip!** Read each question/incomplete sentence. Try to answer the question or complete the sentence yourself before reading the options.

The value of research into risk taking and the people who take part in extreme sports has been questioned by some. Given the limited funds available, is it really worth spending time and money investigating this particular aspect of human nature? I think this is a fair question, and it also seems to me that extreme sports tend to attract those with less concern than most not only for their own safety, but also for that of others. When things go wrong, rescuers are frequently put at risk because someone else was deliberately putting themselves in danger. Thrill-seeking and a wish to escape from everyday routine hardly excuses an outcome such as this. Even relatively well-established sports, such as snowboarding and paragliding, involve a level of risk-taking that many would consider unacceptable.

What is the writer doing in this paragraph?

A justifying research into extreme sports
B explaining the attraction of extreme sports
C criticising people who take part in extreme sports
D recommending participation in certain extreme sports

b Read through the paragraph again and <u>underline</u> the parts of the text which give you the answer.

c Which parts of the text do the incorrect options relate to?

2a Now read this question about the same paragraph and choose the correct answer.

> **Tip!** The questions can be the first part of a sentence. The options are then four different ways of completing the sentence.

In line 10, 'this' refers to

A rescuers being put at risk.
B people deliberately putting themselves in danger.
C looking for thrills.
D wishing to escape from everyday routine.

b Explain how you found the correct answer.

Test 2 Exam practice Reading and Use of English • Part 5

1 **Read the instructions, title, sub-title and the text. Then read the following statements and write T (true) or F (false).**

1 The writer interviews Porter about his life and work. ....
2 Porter has been famous as a singer all his adult life. ....
3 The writer keeps giving opinions and making comments. ....
4 The writer is generally quite critical of Porter's music. ....

Tip! Read each part of the text with its question. Look either at the question first and then read the part of text, or the other way round.

Tip! The three other options for each question may sound correct, but they are wrong.

2 **Follow the exam instructions, using the advice to help you.**

You are going to read an article about a jazz musician. For questions **31–36**, choose the answer (**A**, **B**, **C** or **D**) which you think fits best according to the text.

Mark your answers **on the separate answer sheet.**

Jazz musician

Reporter John Bungey meets the US singer Gregory Porter, one of the hottest names in jazz.

Gregory Porter may be tired – he arrived from Zurich just 40 minutes ago – but at least he knows where he is. This is not always the case. There is a smile as he sinks into a comfortable hotel chair. 'Yeah, it happens all the time. I wake up slowly, I'm kind of brain dead and I'm not sure where I am. . . . and then you can lose days – fly over some date line, and what happened to Thursday?' If any singer has a right to be disorientated it is Porter, thanks to a midlife surge that propelled him from obscurity into becoming jazz's music's number one vocal draw. Last year he spent 300 days on the road playing 250 dates. Every one sold out.

Porter sings jazz, gospel and soul in a rich baritone voice, often in a style that many thought had died out with black-and-white TV. He's a road dog whose career depends on profitable live shows, not on the slim pickings of digital music streaming services. Hence a performing tour that sees him in Europe, with the odd American detour, all spring and summer. 'To be the most streamed artist in jazz, what does that mean? A cheque for about $120.' Good job, then, that he loves the roar of the crowd. 'There are certain nights when the voice is perfect and there's nothing you can't do. Your hearing is crystal-clear. You never know when that's going to happen and that's the magic of it.'

Porter, at 1.9 metres, has the build of the professional American football player he hoped he would be before injury intervened. He's wearing trainers and jogging bottoms plus a smart tweed jacket and waistcoat – sort of half off-duty, half on. And then there's the famous cap with its enveloping chin strap. No marketing department could dream him up.

At the age of 45, delayed success is all the sweeter. After college he tried odd jobs in a dog-food factory and mixing aromatherapy oils. He was a barista and in his mid-20s began to think that cookery might be his professional calling. In his free time he acted occasionally, but singing was a constant. 'I had a great voice when I was 22, but I was looking for someone to make me – a producer and an arranger – and they never came. And I suffered.'

He says he has often reflected on the forces that shape a life. 'What fascinates me is: how do you find your soil? Where is the best place to grow, to be what you can be?' Perhaps some people never do find their place. 'Yeah,' he says. 'Maybe that's the angry person behind the window when you've got to buy your ticket. Some people have settled in their discontent. I was pretty near there ... I just needed to make a statement, however small, even if nobody heard it.'

That small statement – a demo, not a finished record – earned a hearing in Russia, where he played in concert halls to great acclaim. While there, he met his Russian wife, Victoria.

Porter writes more of his material than most singers in his field and says that spending so much of life being transported around between concerts does not get in the way; in fact sitting in the back of a car watching the scenery trundle by can inspire. 'Something about my eyes darting back and forth as things pass. Something about motion always triggers me and my brain goes into a place where I start thinking about my past, my dreams, my future. The poetry comes to me; the melody comes to me; they come together.'

---

31 When he meets the writer, Porter is
- **A** relieved to find he has the right time and place.
- **B** more alert than he can sometimes be.
- **C** unaware of how late he is.
- **D** apologetic for being tired.

32 The phrase 'slim pickings' (line 16) tells us that Porter
- **A** is now in a position to choose the work he wants.
- **B** is listened to by relatively few younger people.
- **C** likes the simplicity of the idea of streaming.
- **D** earns little from streaming services.

33 In his description of Porter's appearance, the writer suggests that Porter
- **A** doesn't care much about how he looks off-stage.
- **B** doesn't yet have a well-planned individual image.
- **C** doesn't fit with the marketing image created for him.
- **D** doesn't use his muscular physique enough when performing.

34 When Porter says he 'suffered' in his twenties, he is referring to the fact that
- **A** none of the jobs he tried suited him.
- **B** certain people he trusted didn't support him.
- **C** the opportunity he longed for didn't happen.
- **D** he was often too busy to keep up his singing.

35 The 'angry person behind the window' (line 45) represents someone who
- **A** has no capacity for deep thoughts about life.
- **B** thinks of themselves before other people.
- **C** should make more of an effort in their job.
- **D** has accepted they're never going to achieve their dreams.

36 Porter says that travelling in the back of a car
- **A** is something he's had to get used to.
- **B** enables him to think creatively.
- **C** is less than ideal for writing down new songs.
- **D** has become his way of switching off and relaxing.

Advice

31 *Porter talks about being alert in lines 4–7.*

32 *To get this you'll need to read on, because Porter comments again on this later in the paragraph.*

33 *Look at the end of the paragraph – especially the reference to 'off-duty'.*

34 *Find the reference to Porter suffering, and work out what he's talking about when he says this.*

35 *Read on either side of this quote to get the answer.*

36 *Look at everything Porter is quoted as saying in this paragraph, and the answer summarises this.*

Test 2 Training Reading and Use of English Part 6

Focus on structure

1 **Read the article then complete each gap using one of the sentences (A–E). There are three sentences which you do not need to use.**

Tip! In this part in the exam, there is one sentence option which you do not need to use.

Tip! Clues to help you choose the correct answer can come from the sentence after the gap as well as the sentence before the gap.

Sleep and memory

A great deal of research has been done on memory. There are apparently many reasons why we remember certain things but forget others. **1** ______ One of the conclusions they have come to is that much of this happens while we are asleep.

The quality and duration of our sleep appears to affect whether or not our brains can successfully convert experiences and knowledge we have acquired whilst awake into long-term memories. To do this, our brains rely on regular periods of sleep every day. **2** ______ That is one of the reasons why sleep has become such an important area of research.

In the future, sleep experts may finally understand all the connections between sleep and memory. **3** ______

A This means that interruptions to these patterns matter.

B As a result, interest in sleep research has increased significantly.

C Until they do, much of what happens after we have closed our eyes at night will remain a mystery.

D Scientists are also interested in how we process what we have seen or has happened to us.

E So our memories are formed in ways that are still not fully explained.

2 **Underline the pronouns and other words in the article and options which helped you find the correct answers. Explain how these words helped you.**

Reading and Use of English • Part 6

1 **Read the instructions, the title and sub-title. Then quickly read the main text and answer the following questions:**

1 Is the writer Sarah present in the text?
2 Who is being quoted throughout the text and who is she?
3 What is the Queen of Kalahari?
4 What are the Gardens of Kalahari?

2 **Follow the exam instructions, using the advice to help you.**

Tip! If you take some time to get a clear understanding of the text first, it is much easier to complete the gaps.

Tip! Some of the gaps will have clear language links such as pronouns, which refer directly to something before or after.

You are going to read an article about a famous diamond bought by a jewellery company. Six sentences have been removed from the article. Choose from the sentences **A–G** the one which fits each gap (**37–42**). There is one extra sentence which you do not need to use.

Mark your answers **on the separate answer sheet.**

The Queen of Kalahari

Sarah Royce-Greensill tells the story of a famous diamond.

Among the many photographs on the walls of the Swiss headquarters of the jewellery company Chopard, one stands out: an image of a 342-carat rough diamond. The stone was discovered in Botswana's Karowe Mine two years ago. Of all the many colossal roughs discovered at Karowe, Chopard's co-president Caroline Scheufele believes hers is the purest. 'I was really lucky to put my hand on this one. It's not the biggest but the others don't have the same purity,' she says.

Scheufele first saw the stone in Botswana in September 2015. 'Our partner at the mine called me and said, "We've found something you should not let pass,"' she recalls, handling an exact replica of the rough, made from crystal. **37** ______ Indeed, it's flat along one side which, she says, hints that it was once twice as large, and a similarly sized sibling (the King of Kalahari) may still be found.

'It was an emotional moment when I opened the package,' she says: a moment that is recreated in a dramatic 50-minute documentary film charting the discovery of the stone. **38** ______ There were various possibilities. 'We could have cut two big 80-carat stones from it and maybe made a pair of drop earrings,' Scheufele muses. 'Somebody else would have done that, but Chopard is all about creativity. I didn't just want one piece, I wanted a whole set.'

After naming her newly acquired stone the Queen of Kalahari, she started figuring out the best possible combination of stones that would work commercially. **39** ______ After a nerve-racking few months with expert polishers in Belgium, Scheufele had all the ingredients for 'the most prestigious set of jewellery ever to emerge from Chopard's High Jewellery workshop' – a six-piece set entitled the Gardens of Kalahari.

40 ______ Two rings, a necklace, a bracelet, a pair of earrings and a secret watch all shine a brilliant pure white. Among the 23 stones cut from the Queen of Kalahari, five are above 20 carats. Each represents a different flower. While the dry Kalahari desert may never see such species in bloom, the botanical theme reflects Scheufele's passion for gardening and the fact that 'nature gave us this stone'.

The collection's versatility is remarkable. 'I've always wanted to do a whole set that you can play with, detach, wear in different ways for different occasions,' Scheufele says. 'If I'm not mistaken there are 17 different possibilities.' **41** ______

I can barely begin to comprehend the painstaking work involved in shaping that beautiful rough into these exquisite jewels. In total, it took over 3,200 hours to create the Gardens of Kalahari. **42** ______ This varied from melting the gold, through sketching the pieces, to setting and polishing each diamond. It is a remarkable achievement.

A She used computer modelling to assist her, which indicated it was possible to cut 23 diamonds of various shapes and sizes, all of them in the highest grade of clarity.

B When worn in this way, it makes a definite statement.

C Almost every pair of hands in Chopard's workshop touched the product at some point.

D There was no doubt about whether she'd buy the stone – the only question was, what to do with it once it was in her possession.

E For example, the necklace can be worn as a simple choker, built up with further rows of petal-shaped diamonds, or adorned with a detachable flower, and one, two or three pendants.

F About the size of a tennis ball, it fills the palm of the hand with a mixture of jagged edges and cool, smooth planes.

G Although I had seen sketches of each individual piece, nothing quite prepared me for the impact of the jewels, presented in a velvet-lined case.

Advice

37 *The text before the gap refers to 'something', i.e. the diamond that has been found.*

38 *The stronger link is forwards to the short sentence after the gap.*

39 *The stronger link is backwards. Look for a sentence which gives details of how she'd figure out the best commercial combination for the jewels.*

40 *The sentence after the gap seems to be the writer describing what she sees.*

41 *Before the gap, Scheufele is talking about the collection's versatility, so you need a sentence which develops this idea.*

42 *Before the gap you have a reference to 'painstaking work' that is continued in one of the gapped sentences.*

Reading and Use of English Part 7

Focus on recognising attitude

1 **Match the reporting verbs (1–8) with extracts from texts (a–h) which show how the writer feels.**

Tip! The reporting verbs in Exercise 1 are often used in Part 7 questions. You need to learn what these verbs mean.

Which person

1 accepts?
2 explains?
3 admits?
4 appreciates?
5 insists?
6 regrets?
7 approves?
8 describes?

a) Some managers are very strict whereas others can be friendly and approachable.
b) I'll always be grateful for all the help I received.
c) I should never have believed this claim.
d) I am quite sure that this was a moment of great importance in the history of physics.
e) Although I'd initially doubted this, it was, in fact, the case.
f) First, they divided the volunteers into two groups, and then they gave them different puzzles to solve.
g) I understand I'll have to work hard to succeed.
h) They made the right choice.

2a **Answer questions 1–4 using information from extracts A and B below. One of the questions does not have an answer in either of these extracts.**

Tip! You may find the information you need for an answer in more than one part of the text.

In which section does the writer

1 challenge a claim?
2 argue against a change of plan?
3 agree with a decision?
4 recommend a course of action?

b **Underline the parts of the extracts where you found the answers.**

A When announcing new measures, local councils frequently say these have been approved following extensive consultation amongst the local residents. However, in the case of policies designed to reduce the impact of traffic in cities, this is frequently not the case. It would be in the interests of all concerned if the views of residents were adequately researched, preferably by an agency approved by those on all sides of the debate. Those who wonder whether this is necessary, given the costs involved, should consider the response to previous initiatives, and how effective the outcome was when local opinion was not fully taken into consideration.

B A few years ago, the local government of my city reached the conclusion that a good way to reduce congestion would be to institute days on which only drivers whose car registration number began with an even number would be allowed on the road. The following day, it would be the turn of those driving cars displaying odd numbers on their number plates. This idea was excellent, and aimed to encourage car sharing and increased use of public transport. Unfortunately, because of local opposition, this initiative had to be abandoned. In my view, the council should not have backed down. If they had kept the policy in place for longer than a couple of weeks, residents, including drivers, would have had the chance to experience the benefits, and would, I believe, have ended up in favour of the scheme.

1 **Read the instructions, the title and subtitle, and quickly read the text. Answer the following questions:**

1 Are the writer and the runner the same person or different people?
2 How does the writer feel about the dog at the beginning and at the end of the text?

Tip! If you have a general understanding of the text first, this may give you some help in answering the questions.

2 **Follow the exam instructions, using the advice to help you.**

You are going to read an article about the effects of tourism on local people. For questions **43–52**, choose from the people (**A–E**). The people may be chosen more than once.

Mark your answers **on the separate answer sheet**.

In which section does the writer

decide not to take responsibility for the dog although it is following him?	43	
fear that the dog may hurt him?	44	
comment on other people's observations of the dog's actions?	45	
appear to be less generous towards the dog than some other racers?	46	
say that personal circumstances gave him an improved chance of coming first?	47	
say he was inspired in his running by the dog's presence?	48	
express his concern that the dog might be accidentally harmed by the other runners?	49	
first become aware that the dog had made a decision about which person to stick with?	50	
risk losing his place in the race for the benefit of the dog?	51	
imply that the racers have to be very well prepared?	52	

Advice

43 The writer decides not to take responsibility for the dog in more than one section, but the detail about following him is only in one.

44 There are two references in the text to being hurt, but only one refers to the writer.

45 Look for a reference to other people commenting on what the dog does.

46 This is about the writer's changing attitude, which you have identified on your quick read of the text.

47 From your quick first read of the text, you will hopefully remember which section mentions the runner's personal circumstances.

48 Find the reference to the writer being inspired by his running.

49 The writer expresses concern about the dog in more than one section, but only one mentions the possibility of the dog being harmed.

50 From your quick read of the text, you have identified the writer's changing attitude, so this should help you.

51 The writer only talks about his place in the race in one section.

52 Think about the running situation – what would an ultra-distance runner need if he was running all day?

Gobi the dog athlete

Dion Leonard is followed by a dog across the desert on an ultra-marathon.

A I had just finished the first stage of a seven-day ultra-marathon in China when I saw 'Gobi' for the first time. It was a cold night and I'd walked out of the yurt I was staying in to get some hot water when I noticed her next to the campfire, a scruffy little dog getting food from people. This surprised me somewhat. These races are about self-sufficiency – you carry your food for the week and the situation would normally have to be pretty desperate for someone to give any away. I thought: 'There's no way I'm feeding it.'

B This race was important to me. I'm 42 and after three years of competitive ultra-distance running I wanted to win. Normally my wife runs alongside me and we're quite sociable, but when it's just me I concentrate more on the race. I'd taken up running several years earlier, partly because my wife, Lucja, seemed to get so much out of it. This was a 200-kilometre race across the Gobi Desert – one of the most challenging I had attempted. It was mentally and physically demanding.

C The day after spotting the dog I would later name 'Gobi', I stood at the start line. I was nervous because we were racing over the extremely hilly Tian Shan mountain range. I looked down and there was this little dog with these big beautiful brown eyes looking up at me. There were a hundred runners and I thought it had better get out of the way or it'd get squashed. The race started and I forgot about the dog. Soon after, I was running along, aware of the little shadow at my feet. We ran into the mountains and I didn't see her for some time, but I jumped a small river crossing and heard a dog barking. I thought: 'Ah, the dog's not going any further. Someone else can help it.'

D I reached the mountain top, and the first checkpoint. People stared and started cheering the dog. I thought: 'That's a long way for a little dog.' When I reached the finish line for the first day stage, in fifth place, people said: 'The dog has followed you all the way.' I hadn't called it, or whistled at it. I didn't even know it was a she. That evening I went to my tent. She came too and lay down next to me. Then I got thinking about what must have been going through her mind. She'd crossed that river, she'd climbed that mountain, such a massive job for a little dog. Gobi ran close to a marathon that day. I dished out my food to her.

E The next day there was a massive river to cross: rushing water, chest-high. I heard her whimpering on the bank. There was no way she could have swum across. There were two runners ahead of me. I stopped thinking about the need to prove myself and turned back to get her. I realised that if I didn't stop to help Gobi, no one would. I put her in my arms, warily, in case she bit me. She relaxed completely, and closed her eyes. She knew she was safe. I thought: 'Ah well, I'll come in third.' But, flushed with happy togetherness, towards the finish we raced past the others. It was the best day ever. From that point on, Gobi was my constant companion. On the final day, I came in second but I wouldn't have cared had I come first – it was magnificent. My wife saw pictures online and said: 'It's the first time I've ever seen you smile at the end of a race!'

Tip! All sections of the text are used in the answers.

Test 2 Training Writing Part 1

Useful language Introductions, contrasting arguments and conclusions

1 **Put the expressions in the box under the correct headings.**

Lastly, ... ~~I would argue that~~ ... The question of ... To sum up, there are arguments ...
However, ... Although ... in contrast to ... I have come to the conclusion that ...
Nevertheless, ... whereas ... in spite of In conclusion, (I believe that) ... First of all, ...

Introductions	Contrasting linkers	Conclusions
I would argue that		

2 **Underline the best alternative from the expressions in *italics*.**

1 The rate of unemployment has increased *in contrast to / although* the rate of inflation.
2 She didn't know much about the book. *Nevertheless / Whereas* she attempted to describe the plot.
3 *The question of / In conclusion* the effect of cars on the environment has been discussed for many years.
4 *In spite of / In conclusion*, I believe that our cities should become totally car-fee.
5 There is still a lot of serious disease in the world *in spite of / although* the advances in medical science.

Exam skill Using topic sentences

3 **Read the sample essay on the next page and underline the topic sentences. Explain why each sentence is used.**

Paragraph 1: introducing the topic
Paragraph 2: ....
Paragraph 3: ....
Paragraph 4: ....
Paragraph 5: ....

Tip! A topic sentence generally appears near the beginning of each paragraph and summarises what that paragraph is about.

Tip! A good way to help your reader understand your essay is to use topic sentences in each paragraph.

Understanding instructions

4 **Read the sample essay again and answer these questions.**

1 What is the writer's opinion and where is it stated?
2 In which paragraphs does the writer discuss each of notes 1 and 2?
3 Which other main point does the writer discuss, and where?
4 What examples are provided to support the writer's main points?
5 What expressions from Exercise 1 are used in the essay?

In your English class, you have recently had a discussion about science and young people. Now, your English teacher has asked you to write an essay.

Write an essay using all the notes and give reasons for your point of view.

Science is very important in the 21st century. How do you think it could be made more appealing to young people?

Notes

Write about:

1 television programmes

2 interactive museums

3 .... (your own idea)

Write your essay in **140–190 words** in an appropriate style.

First of all, young people love gadgets and technology, whereas they see science as uninteresting. I would argue that the number of young people pursuing science and technology studies and careers has dropped.

One way to make science more attractive is to have television programmes presented by celebrities, with subjects which are relevant to young people. We live in a celebrity culture and children identify with well-known people.

Another idea would be to set up interactive science museums in every town, where parents could take their children. It is much better to teach children the principles of science through hands-on experiments than to teach them in a classroom.

Of course, it would help if scientists were better paid and young people were made aware of the range of jobs available. A lot of people are put off a scientific career because they think it means working in a badly-paid job in a boring laboratory.

In conclusion, it is vital that more young people are attracted to science, since society's future depends on scientific progress. If this happens, then I'm sure more young people would choose a career in science.

Tip! In an essay, it's important to have a strong introduction and conclusion. This gives structure to your writing.

Tip! Make sure you provide clear examples or points to support your argument.

Test 2 Exam practice Writing • Part 1 (essay)

1 **Read the exam task below and answer these questions.**

1 Are you going to agree or disagree with the statement?

2 What reasons can you provide for this opinion?

You **must** answer this question. Write your answer in **140–190 words** in an appropriate style **on the separate answer sheet**.

In your English class, you have been talking about the consequences of growth in online shopping. Now, your English teacher has asked you to write an essay for homework.

Write your essay using all the notes and giving reasons for your point of view.

**If online shopping continues to grow in popularity, shops in our town centres will close because fewer people will use them.
Do you agree?**

Notes

Write about:

1 the kind of shops that are most at risk

2 any evidence that town centres are already facing problems

3 .... (your own idea)

2 **Do the exam task.**

Tip! Look at the list of vocabulary you have written down and tick the words as you include them in your writing.

Tip! If you wish, give examples from a town or city that you know. Otherwise, you can invent a place as the examiners are checking your language not whether the information you give is correct.

Test 2 Training Writing Part 2 (report)

Task information

- The report task expects you to give some factual information and make recommendations or suggestions.
- The instructions include a description of a situation. You have to write a report of between 140 and 190 words.
- Allow about 40 minutes for this task, including time at the end to check your work.
- The report may be for a teacher or school director, or classmates, etc. You therefore have to write in an appropriate style.
- Organise your text into report format and use headings if needed.
- Write full sentences and try to use correct grammar and punctuation with a good range of language with accurate spelling.

Useful language Expressions for reports

1 Match the headings in the box with the groups of expressions 1–4.

Introduction	Description and findings	Recommendations and suggestions	Conclusions

1 ....
In conclusion, …
I strongly recommend …
All things considered …

2 ....
It has been found that …
It would seem / appear that …
It is said to be …
According to …,

3 ....
The aim / purpose of this report is to …
This reports looks at …
This report is intended to show that …

4 ....
I believe we should …
I would suggest …
I would recommend …
Taking all the factors mentioned into account, …

2 Replace the informal expressions in *italics* in these sentences with more formal expressions from Exercise 1. More than one answer is possible in some sentences.

1 *I want to write this report* to give an overview of the city's sporting facilities.
2 *People are saying that* most of the sports centres and football pitches have closed in recent times.
3 *Why don't* the council fund the building of new sports facilities and make them free to use?
4 *To finish off*, the council should take more responsibility for the health of the public.
5 The council may lose the next election, *so* a recent poll *says*.

Understanding instructions

3 Study the exam instructions and underline the key words.

> After a class discussion, your English teacher has asked you to write a report on where people can play sports in your local area. You have to include the views of visitors as well as local people and make a recommendation on how the facilities could be improved.

Write your report in **140–190 words** in an appropriate style.

4 **Now answer the following questions about the exam instructions.**

1 What is the situation?
2 Who must you write a report for?
3 Should the style be formal, informal or neutral?
4 What three things do the instructions say you *must* do?

Tip! It's a good idea to use the passive forms in a report, as it provides a more impersonal, formal style, e.g. *It was reported that …*

Exam skill Checking your writing

5 **Read the report below and add the correct paragraph headings to gaps 1–4.**

A Recommendations
B Problem areas
C Available facilities
D Introduction

Tip! Allow a few minutes at the end to check your writing for spelling, grammar and punctuation errors. Read your text, concentrating on one type of error at a time.

6 **Read the report again. The writer has made some errors commonly found in First writing tasks. Find and correct the following:**

1 Wrong style: Where has informal language been used instead of formal language?
2 Spelling errors: Find four examples of incorrect spelling and correct them.
3 Grammar errors: Find two mistakes of verb forms.
4 Punctuation errors: Find three punctuation errors.
5 Length: The essay is about 30 words too long. Which sentences would you remove?

(1) ....

I wanted to write a report to give an overview of the town's sporting facilities As part of the survey, both tourists and local residents was asked for their views. It was very interesting to do the survey.

(2) ....

There are a number of good quality gyms in the area, which are modern and have a good range of equipement. There are also two swiming pools which are open every day of the year, apart from public holidays. We, are also fortunate to have several football pitches, which are very popular at lunchtime with school children and office workers in the evening.

(3) ....

It was reported that in recent years people were saying that most gyms have increased their membership fees by 20%. It would appear that the swiming pools are often dirty and crowded, especially in the summer months. I don't like using them. According to three school principals, the football pitches are in poor condition and the floodlights are rubbish.

(4) ....

In conclusion, the two main areas of concern among the people interviewed were the rising prices and the poor condition of some of the fasilities. Why don't the counsil repair the facilities and subsidise the gym membership fees? This will allow more people in the area to enjoying themselves and get fit as well?

Test 2 Exam practice Writing • Part 2 (report)

Action plan

1 Read the instructions carefully, and make sure you understand exactly what you are being asked to do, and who it is for.
2 Think of a suitable subject to write about.
3 When planning what to write, consider using headings. They can help you and your reader understand how the report is organised.
4 Think about what the reader already knows (or doesn't know) about the topic and decide if there are any basic details you need to include.
5 Start by making clear what the purpose of the report is.
6 Make sure that you write at least 140 words. If you write less, you probably won't be able to address the question in enough detail.
7 Don't make the report too technical or too detailed.

1 **Read the exam task below and answer these questions.**

1 What three things do you have to cover?
2 How formal should your report be?

You see this announcement on an English-language website.

> We are conducting research into new buildings and construction projects around the world. We want to hear people's opinions about a new building or construction project in your area. What are its strengths and weaknesses? What impact will it have on the area?

Write your report in **140–190 words**.

2 **Do the exam task.**

Tip! When you are asked for opinions, you don't need to include technical information.

Tip! When asked for strengths and weaknesses, make sure you include at least one strength as well as a weakness.

Test 2 Training Writing Part 2 (letter)

Task information

- The letter task in Part 2 tests your ability to write, for example, a formal job application or a letter to a magazine editor. You must write in an appropriate style.
- The instructions include a description of a situation. In response to this situation, you have to write a letter of between 140 and 190 words.
- You should allow about 40 minutes for this task, including time at the end to check your work.
- You have to organise your letter into paragraphs, with a suitable beginning and ending.
- You should write full sentences with correct grammar and punctuation, and use a good range of language with accurate spelling.

Useful language Informal expressions

1 Match the headings in the box with groups of expressions 1–5.

Requests	Thanking someone	Making suggestions and recommendations
Giving news	Apologies	

1 ....

This is just to let you know that I got the job
I thought you might be interested to hear about my brother. (*more formal*)
By the way, have you heard about the concert?

2 ....

I'm writing to ask for your help.
Could you do me a favour?
I hope you don't mind me asking, but could you send me payment? (*more formal*)

3 ....

How about buying her a new dress?
I would recommend that you think about this carefully. (*more formal*)
Don't forget to visit the Tate Modern.

4 ....

I'm really sorry that I missed your call.
So sorry about not writing sooner.
I am writing to apologise for missing your party but I was ill. (*more formal*)

5 ....

I am writing to thank you for your hospitality. (*more formal*)
Thanks so much for everything!
Thanks for being there when I needed you.

Understanding instructions

2 **Study the exam task below and answer these questions.**

1 Who has written to you?
2 What is the situation?
3 What questions does the writer ask you?

You have received this letter from your English-speaking friend, Joan.

I hear you organised a surprise birthday party for your brother. I'd love to hear about it.
What kind of party did you organise? Who did you invite? How did it go? Do tell me.
Love,
Joan

Write your letter in **140–190 words** in an appropriate style.

Exam skill Organising letters

3 **Read the letter written by a First candidate and add these guidelines in the correct gaps 1–7.**

A Open with an informal greeting.
B When you close, make an excuse to finish.
C Use an informal linking word/phrase.
D Make sure you finish with an informal phrase.
E Start a new paragraph as the topic has changed slightly.
F Start your reply by referring to the sender's letter.
G Give reason for replying.

Hi Joan, [**1** ....]
How's it going? It's good to hear from you again. [**2** ....] I hope you're still enjoying your course and I'm sorry about not writing sooner.
So you want to hear about the party I planned for my brother's birthday. [**3** ....]
Well, it was fantastic! I told my brother we were taking him out for a quiet meal at a local restaurant with just the family, but, in fact, I'd hired a DJ and invited all his work friends!
I picked my brother up from work and told him I had to pop home first. [**4** ....] I'd arranged for everyone to be at the house waiting for him. You should have seen his face when he walked into the room and everyone started cheering! He couldn't believe it and his face turned bright red! Then the party got going and it didn't finish until two in the morning. The music and the DJ were great! We were tired, but we had a great time.
Anyway, [**5** ....] I've got to run, as I want to catch the post. [**6** ....] Hope to hear all your news soon.
Lots of love, [**7** ....]
Bernadette

Tip! When you write to a friend you can use informal language and punctuation, including exclamation marks, e.g. *How's it going? … his face turned bright red!*

Tip! It's a good idea to use Informal language, including phrasal verbs, informal vocabulary and contractions, e.g. *pick my brother up, I've got to run, I'd changed my mind.*

4 **Read the letter again and answer these questions.**

1 Is the letter well organised into paragraphs?
2 Does the writer answer all of Joan's questions? In which paragraphs?
3 What reason for writing does she give?
4 How does the writer encourage Joan to write back?
5 What examples of informal language does the writer use?

Test 2 Exam practice Writing • Part 2 (letter)

Action plan

1 Read the instructions carefully, underlining any key points.
2 Think about who you are writing to. Use a friendly style if you are writing to friends.
3 Start and finish the letter in a suitable way.
4 Consider when and where the letter will be read and think of a good opening sentence. In this case, you could say something like *'I hope you've arrived safely and found everything you need.'*
5 Use separate paragraphs for the opening and closing sections. Include one or two longer paragraphs in the middle part.
6 Check your letter to make sure the tone is the same throughout, that is, informal or formal.

1 Read the exam task below and answer these questions.

1 Who exactly are the friends?
2 Where are you are going to be, and why?
3 What jobs do they need to do in your home?

> Some English-speaking friends are coming to stay in your home while you are away. Write a letter to them, welcoming them and explaining what you would like them to do to look after your home while you're away.

Write your letter in **140–190 words**.

2 Do the exam task.

Tip! You can write informally, but always be polite in letters and emails, especially if you are asking people to do something for you.

Tip! This is a letter, not an email. Think about how you start and finish a letter.

Test 2 Training Writing Part 2 (article)

Useful language Expressions for articles

1 Put these expressions under the correct headings.

Have you thought about ...? Go online and find out about ... Another advantage of ...
Are you one of those people who ...? I was absolutely terrified when I ...
More importantly, it was something ... Give it a try! Unsurprisingly, I ended up ... On top of that, ...
It was the most amazing experience I have ever had. You also have to ... Take my advice and ...
Just imagine ... How would you feel if ...?

Involving the reader	Adding interest	Developing your points	Making suggestions

2 Replace the words in *italics* with one of the expressions from Exercise 1. Remember that verb forms may change in the sentences.

1 *It wasn't a surprise when I finally* arrived two hours late.
2 I *was scared when I* did my first bungee jump.
3 *Additionally*, I had left my passport at the hotel.
4 *You should* stay at one of the recommended hotels.
5 *Have you ever considered* going on a round-the-world trip?

Understanding instructions

3 Read the exam task and answer these questions.

1 What situation do you have to think about?
2 Who are you writing for?
3 What two things do the instructions say you must do?
4 Do you have to include a title for the article?

You see this announcement in a travel magazine.

> **Articles wanted**
>
> **A really special holiday**
>
> Have you ever had a really special holiday? Where did you go? What did you do there?
>
> Write us an account of your holiday.
>
> The best article will be published in the next issue.

Write your article in **140–190 words** in an appropriate style **on the separate answer sheet**.

Exam skill Creating an appropriate style

4 **It's important to develop a clear style for your article. Read the sample article below and add examples of the different stylistic features 1–5.**

1 Using imperatives and rhetorical questions:

....

2 Making a connection with the reader:

....

3 Using examples to bring your article to life:

....

4 Summarise your article to encourage the reader to continue reading:

....

5 Introducing the article in an interesting way:

....

5 **Read the article again and answer the questions.**

1 Is the text well organised into paragraphs? What key information does each paragraph contain?
2 Does the article answer all the questions in the exam task?
3 Does the writer use the correct style and tone throughout?
4 Does the article use any of the expressions from Useful language, Exercise 1 on page 101?

Fabulous Japan – Live the dream!

Have you ever thought about the perfect holiday? Just imagine my surprise when my parents booked a holiday in Japan as my birthday present. I went on a ten-day tour and it was the most amazing experience I have ever had.

I had no idea what to expect because I didn't know much about Japan. Why worry about that though? I quickly got used to the food, humidity and even tried out some of my Japanese, although it's not very good!

Japan was very clean, everyone was really friendly and the hotels were superb. I took the bullet train from Tokyo to Kyoto and I loved it. In Kyoto I slept on a matted floor and then bought a beautiful Kimono for my mother. I also did a fun sushi making class. Unsurprisingly, I ended up making some horrible sushi, but the chef was very kind to me!

My holiday in Japan and its influence on my life has totally changed me as a person. If you're looking to spend an amazing time while completely changing your outlook, Japan is the answer. Give it a try!

Tip! Add a short title to catch the reader's attention. Make sure it is relevant. You can use the one in the question or invent one of your own.

Tip! Use a personal or more neutral style but not formal (you can use contractions).

Test 2 Exam practice Writing • Part 2 (article)

1 **Read the exam task below and answer these questions.**

1 What different things does the question ask you to do?
2 What skill could you write about?
3 Which vocabulary (related to your skill) could you include?

You see this announcement in a lifestyle magazine.

> *Next month, we're going to publish a special issue of the magazine, all about learning new skills. Tell us about a skill that you have learned, the challenges you faced while learning, and the benefits the skill can bring. What advice would you give to others starting to learn the same skill?*

Write your article in **140–190 words**.

2 **Do the exam task.**

Tip! Articles always need to be interesting to read. Using a variety of vocabulary and structures will help.

Tip! Try and think of a way to get your reader's attention right at the beginning. For example, *I never realised that learning to cook could save my life.*

Tip! You need to include all the points in the question. Make sure you don't use up all your words before the final point.

Test 2 Training   Listening   Part 1

Identifying function and purpose

1 **Before you read the audioscript below, read the exam question. Who is talking, and what is he talking about?**

2 30 **Listen to the recording. What's the correct answer?**

You will hear a city guide taking a group around a city.
What is he doing?

A advising them of the most worthwhile sights to see
B inviting them to give feedback on his opinion
C persuading them to visit one of his favourite places

Tip! Learn as many function verbs as you can before the exam, such as *criticising*, *confirming* and *justifying*. Make a list.

3 **Read the audioscript below. Underline the section which gives the answer.**

Guide: Now everyone, we're currently standing in what's probably the most beautiful square in the whole city – in my view, of course! Anyway, there are certainly plenty of other nice places for you to explore and compare it with. So maybe you can decide at the end of your stay whether you agree with me, and let me know! Anyway, I'm going to give each of you a map, so you'll be able to follow exactly where we are as we walk round the main sights together. And then you can have some time on your own to have a look around at the places that appeal to you.

4 31 **Listen to the recording again, and mark where the other two options are located. Why are they wrong?**

5 32 **Read the options A–C, and listen to the next recording. What do you think the *question* is?**

You will hear a woman phoning a friend.

A to make a suggestion
B to correct some information
C to express her disappointment

6 **Read the options again. Which one matches what the woman is doing as she is speaking?**

Tip! You may get a question asking you *why* a speaker is doing something. Listen carefully and think what their purpose is.

Tip! You may get questions that ask you what the speaker is doing (function) and why they are doing it (purpose).

Test 2 Exam practice Listening • Part 1

1 **Read the first two lines of questions 1–8 below. For each one, answer these questions where possible.**
1 What is the situation?
2 Will you hear one female, one male, or two speakers?

2 **What is the focus of the question in the second line?**

3 33 **Follow the exam instructions, using the advice to help you.**

Tip! Read the question and try to imagine the situation. Who's talking to whom? Where? Why? When? How do they feel?

Tip! Remember that you can change your mind about an answer while you listen for the first or the second time.

You will hear people talking in eight different situations. For questions **1–8**, choose the best answer (**A**, **B** or **C**).

---

1 You hear two neighbours talking about a new statue in their town.
What does the woman say about it?
A She suspects many people won't like it.
B She doesn't understand what it represents.
C She is convinced it should be removed.

2 You hear a music teacher talking about his job.
He regrets that
A music is rarely considered to be an essential subject.
B there are so few advanced level music students.
C he cannot teach the music that he personally likes.

3 You hear two journalists talking about driverless cars.
What do they both think about them?
A Most drivers would be keen to try them out.
B More tests have to be done on their reliability.
C There will need to be many changes to driving laws.

4 You hear a doctor talking on the radio about colds.
She says many of her patients are unaware that
A antibiotics are ineffective at treating colds.
B healthy eating may help the symptoms of colds.
C there are things they can do to avoid colds.

Advice

1 The question is asking what she thought after she saw the statue.

2 A: What do other people say about teaching music? B: Does he teach high-level students? C: Does he teach music he likes?

*3 Listen for a phrase that means **I agree**.*

4 She mentions these three things about colds, but which one is something she says people don't know.

5 You hear a brother and sister talking about a musical they have seen.
Why does the woman like the musical?

A It explores themes that are important to her.
B She feels sympathetic to its central character.
C The songs are entertaining and easy to remember.

6 You hear a woman talking about horse riding.
How has the woman benefited from going riding again?

A She now has a new group of friends.
B Riding has helped to improve her balance.
C It has enabled her to deal effectively with stress.

7 You hear a customer complaining in a department store.
What does the shop assistant agree to do?

A exchange the item for a different size
B offer a refund for the unsatisfactory item
C give him a credit to spend in the store

8 You hear a food critic talking about a chef called Peter Tinney.
What is she doing?

A describing Peter's creative approach to cooking
B justifying why Peter deserves the award he has won
C defending Peter's decision to close his restaurants

Advice

5 *Listen carefully to what she says about the theme of the musical, the central character and the songs.*

6 *Listen for a phrase that means* ***I've benefited from.***

7 *Be careful. One of the options is something the customer wants but can't have.*

8 *Words in these options that are also heard on the audio won't necessarily lead you to the correct answer.*

Predicting keys

1 **You will hear a woman called Heather giving a talk about honey. Read the question below. What kind of word could fit in the gap?**

Many people use honey to improve their .... , according to Heather.

2 34 **Listen to the recording. Complete the sentence in Exercise 1.**

3 **Now read the audioscript. Circle the answer, and underline the words that are distractors. Why are they wrong?**

Hello everyone! Today I'm here to tell you all about a type of food that you probably eat a lot but don't really know much about – honey! Now, did you know that honey has been used all over the world for centuries?

And people have used it for very different purposes. For example, some scientists believe that it can boost people's ability to fight diseases, such as ones that affect the heart.

It's also common practice for people all over the world to try and make their skin better by drinking milk and honey. And some athletes also use it to give them extra energy and help their performance.

4 **Read the sentence below, and think about what the missing word or phrase might be. What aspect of honey might be affected by different factors? The *colour* of the honey, for example?**

Heather reports that many different factors can affect the .... of the honey we buy.

5 35 **Now listen to the recording and complete the sentence.**

Tip! You have 45 seconds to look through the task.

Tip! As you read through the task before the recording starts, think about what *kind* of information is missing in the sentences.

Tip! Make sure the word you choose fits the sentence grammatically.

Test 2 Exam practice Listening • Part 2

1 **Read the exam instructions below.**

1. What kind of recording (e.g. *a talk*) is it?
2. What's the topic?
3. Who will you hear?
4. For each gap, what kind of information (e.g. *a verb, a day of the week*) do you need to listen for?

Tip! Only write one answer, even if you can think of two or more good ones.

Tip! There is always plenty of time between each answer for you to write down the missing words.

2 36 **Follow the exam instructions, using the advice to help you.**

You will hear a cameraman called Chris Jones giving a talk about filming a wildlife documentary in Gabon, Africa. For questions **9–18**, complete the sentences with a word or short phrase.

Filming African wildlife in Loango National Park, Gabon

Chris wanted to visit Gabon after seeing an unusual **(9)** .... featuring some of its animals.

When researching his trip, Chris says that a **(10)** .... was most useful to him.

Chris's boss advised him that he needed a **(11)** .... visa for his trip.

A **(12)** .... offered to be Chris's local guide in Gabon.

Chris appreciated the ride by **(13)** .... on his way to Loango National Park.

Chris's guide explained that forest elephants visit the beach to get **(14)** ....

Chris was convinced that the buffalo looked like they were **(15)** .... in the sea.

Chris didn't manage to film any **(16)** .... during his trip.

Chris uses the word **(17)** .... to describe the people he stayed with.

Chris says the National Park has had difficulties in increasing **(18)** ....

Advice

*9 Listen for something in the audio that suggests **unusual**.*

10 He used various things, but only one of them is described as the most useful.

11 Which modal verb does Chris use to report advice?

12 Someone took Chris to his hotel, but who offered to be his guide?

13 Listen for a word that matches with 'appreciated'.

14 The elephants get some things in the forest but only one thing on the beach.

*15 Listen for a phrase that means **looked like**.*

16 There were signs that certain animals had visited in the night.

17 There is a difference between how Chris expected them to be and how they actually were.

18 Listen for which numbers have gone up and which have gone down.

Test 2 Training Listening Part 3

Ruling out distractors

1 You are going to listen to two speakers from a Part 3 exam task. Read the following complete task:

Tip! In each recording, you may hear the speaker refer to two or three of the options, but only *one* will be the correct answer.

You will hear five different people talking about their experience of starting a new job. For questions **19–23**, choose from the list (**A–H**) the advice that each speaker gives about starting a new job. Use each letter only once. There are three extra letters which you do not need to use.

A Ask for help when you need it.
B Get to know your colleagues.
C Make sure you don't arrive late.
D Check what you're expected to wear.
E Don't try to understand everything immediately.
F Have a positive attitude.
G Learn all you can about your employers.
H Try to get plenty of sleep.

Tip! Make sure you read the rubric carefully to check what you are listening *for.*

2 Now read what Speaker 1 says about starting a new job and do the following tasks.
1 Underline the advice he gives.
2 What is the advice about? Match it with one of the options in the list above.

3 37 **Listen to the recording and read the audioscript.**

Speaker 1

Starting a new job can be stressful. I remember feeling nervous the night before, and not being able to sleep that well. But by the time the first day was over, I was really wondering what I'd been so worried about! Anyway, I soon made friends with my new work colleagues, and luckily I'd done some research on the company beforehand, so I knew who the boss was and who her team were. Sounds really obvious, but that's pretty important I'd say, so that you know exactly who it is you might be talking to. Anyway, I'm pleased to say, I'd chosen the right kind of clothing to put on that morning, so I didn't stand out because of the way I was dressed!

4 Read the audioscript again. Which other options does the speaker refer to? Why are they wrong?

Tip! Make sure you listen to the *whole* of each speaker's turn before you choose your answer. There may be something at the end that you need to hear, so you may choose the wrong answer if you decide too soon.

5 38 **Now listen carefully to Speaker 2 and answer these questions.**
1 What *advice* does she give?
2 What phrase does she use?
3 Which other options are referred to in the recording? Why are they wrong?

6 39 **Listen to the recording again to check your answers.**

Test 2 Exam practice Listening • Part 3

1 **Read the exam instructions and sentences A–H.**

1. What is the topic?
2. What information do you need to listen for?

2 40 **Follow the exam instructions, using the advice to help you.**

Tip! Remember that three of sentences A–H aren't needed.

Tip! Don't worry about understanding every word. It isn't necessary.

You will hear five short extracts in which people are talking about their experiences of doing part-time courses. For questions **19–23**, choose from the list (**A–H**) how each speaker says they benefited from doing a part-time course. Use each letter only once. There are three extra letters which you do not need to use.

A It helped me get promoted at work.
B It made me reconsider my priorities in life.
C It gave me a way to fill my time.
D It introduced me to like-minded people.
E It enabled me to relax after work.
F It allowed me to use my creativity.
G It provided the chance to gain a new qualification.
H It encouraged me to consider taking further courses.

Speaker 1		**19**
Speaker 2		**20**
Speaker 3		**21**
Speaker 4		**22**
Speaker 5		**23**

Advice

A *Several speakers mention past promotion or the possibility of promotion, but only one actually got promotion after doing a course.*

B *Look at the phrase 'reconsider my priorities in life'. Who changed what was important to them as a result of doing a course?*

C *How might someone feel if they needed to fill their time?*

D *Three speakers mention other people, but think about what the phrase 'like-minded' means.*

E *Think about phrases you would expect to hear if somebody said the course helped them to feel relaxed.*

F *What words would you expect to hear if someone is talking about* ***creativity****?*

G *Did any of the part-time courses described offer a qualification at the end?*

H *Who uses a phrase that means the same as* ***take further courses****?*

Identifying feelings

> Tip! After the instructions, you have a minute to read through the questions. Use this time to highlight key words.

1 41 **You will hear an interview with a young man called Dennis, who is talking about playing musical instruments.**
Read the first question. It's asking how he felt as a child.
Listen carefully to the recording. Which is the correct answer? Why?

When Dennis was a child, he
A realised almost immediately that he didn't enjoy the piano.
B continued his piano playing to avoid upsetting his family.
C wished he could play an instrument as skilfully as his parents.

2 **Now read the audioscript and underline the part of the text that gives the answer.**

Int: So you started playing the piano at an early age, didn't you? How did you feel about learning to play?

Dennis: Well, you're right – I started learning to play the piano when I was about four, I think. I come from a very musical family, where everyone played some instrument or other – my father's a professional violinist, my mother's a music teacher, and my older brother was a brilliant guitar player from an early age. As time went on, though, I came to see that the piano just wasn't my thing, and that I'd much rather be outside playing football with my mates – something that I guess never occurred to my family. But for the sake of peace, I just kept quiet and carried on practising.

> Tip! Remember that, when you're listening for the correct answer, what you hear in the audioscript won't be exactly the same as what you read in the option.

3 42 **Read the question below. It is asking about his feelings at a concert. Listen to the next part of the recording. Which option is correct?**

How did Dennis feel at the concert he went to?
A sorry he hadn't continued with his music
B jealous of his brother for his success
C relieved that he no longer had to perform in public

> Tip! You may be asked questions about how the speaker felt about something, so learn as many adjectives and verbs to do with feelings as you can, e.g. *disappointed, impressed, concerned, relieved, confused, jealous, determined*. Make a list.

4 43 **Listen to the recording again, and check your answer. Why are the other two options wrong?**

> Tip! The questions follow the order of the listening. If you haven't managed to answer one question, move onto the next. The recording is repeated, so you may find the answer then.

Test 2 Exam practice Listening • Part 4

1 **Read the exam instructions.**
1 What kind of recording (e.g. *speech*) is it?
2 What's the topic?
3 Who will you hear?

2 44 **Follow the exam instructions, using the advice to help you.**

Tip! Don't choose an answer just because you hear the same word or phrase. Listen for the same *idea*.

Tip! For each question, wait until the speaker finishes talking about it before you decide on your answer.

You will hear an interview with a retired sportswoman called Gemma Porter, who now runs her own business. For questions **24–30**, choose the best answer (**A**, **B** or **C**).

---

24 Why did Gemma retire from sport?
A She had won all the major championships.
B She wanted to spend less time travelling for work.
C She was starting to get injured more often.

25 How did Gemma feel immediately after her retirement?
A She was dissatisfied at not training every day.
B Her financial situation was a concern to her.
C She missed her former competitors.

26 What did Gemma feel was a disadvantage for her when applying for jobs?
A She lacked formal qualifications.
B She wasn't used to fixed working hours.
C She had never worked in an office.

27 Why did Gemma start a business helping retired sportspeople to find new careers?
A She still had many friends in the world of sport.
B No other recruitment companies offered this service.
C Her experience meant she could offer the best advice.

28 What motivated Gemma in the early days of her business?
A the determination to prove other people wrong
B the belief that she was doing something worthwhile
C the desire to gain a reputation as a business woman

29 Gemma says some sportspeople can have problems joining a company because
A they can be impatient with colleagues.
B they dislike receiving negative feedback.
C they object to having to follow company rules.

30 Gemma thinks companies will hire more retired sportspeople in the future because
A sportspeople are better at accepting change than other employees.
B both companies and sportspeople are focused on achieving goals.
C companies will only survive if they have staff who are competitive.

Advice

24 *What was Gemma 'fed up with'?*

25 *'immediately after' is a key phrase in the question.*

26 *What happened to Gemma when she was 16?*

27 *A: What does she say about friends? B: Was Gemma's company the only one to offer this service? C: What did Gemma's experience give her?*

28 *Listen for a phrase that matches with 'motivated'.*

29 *Two options are things Gemma says about other workers, but only one option relates to sportspeople.*

30 *Listen for something that businesses and companies have in common.*

Test 2 Training Speaking Part 1

Understanding the task

1 **Read the sentences about Part 1. Write T (true) or F (false).**

1 The questions are all on familiar topics. ....
2 You should discuss the questions with your partner. ....
3 You should express your own opinion when you answer. ....
4 You should add reasons, examples and extra information to support your answers. ....
5 You cannot ask the examiner to repeat the questions. ....

Exam skill Useful language (revising tenses)

2 **Read the questions. Do they ask about the present, past or future?**

1 How often do you watch TV? ....
2 Which country would you most like to visit? Why? ....
3 What kinds of food did you like or dislike when you were younger? ....
4 Which famous person would you like to meet? Why? ....
5 What do you usually do at the weekend? ....
6 Tell us about your last holiday or trip. ....

3 **Choose the most suitable verb form (A, B or C) to complete each answer to the questions in Exercise 2.**

1 I .... TV very often during the week.
A didn't watch **B** don't watch **C** am going to watch

2 I .... to the United States.
A have been **B** went **C** would love to go

3 I .... bananas!
A hate **B** hated **C** would hate

4 I .... Lionel Messi because he's the best footballer in the world.
A would love to meet **B** once met **C** meet

5 I .... together with my friends.
A usually got **B** hope I can get **C** often get

6 I .... to London with two friends.
A am going **B** went **C** would love to go

Tip! Look carefully at the verb tense in each question. Think about whether it asks you about your present habits or opinions, something you did in the past or something you would like to do one day.

Test 2 Exam practice Speaking • Part 1

Part 1 2 minutes (3 minutes for groups of three)

1 **Work in pairs. One of you take the role of the examiner and ask the questions, while the other answers the questions. Then swap roles.**

Interlocutor	First, we'd like to know something about you. • Do you have a favourite colour for clothes? ..... (Why?) • What do you wear when you relax? ..... (Why?) • Do you enjoy spending time on your own? ..... (Why? / Why not?) • Tell us about a day you've really enjoyed recently.

Tip! Try to respond naturally rather than giving learnt responses. Learnt responses can sound 'false' and may not match the question properly.

2 **Now swap roles.**

Interlocutor	First, we'd like to know something about you. • Do you have favourite clothes you like to wear? ..... (When do you wear them?) • What do you wear when you go to parties? ..... (Why?) • What do you enjoy doing with other people? • Tell us about a place you really enjoyed visiting. ..... (What did you do there?)

Tip! If you can't think of the exact word you need, use a few other words to explain what you mean.

Test 2 Training Speaking Part 2

Useful language Speculating

1 45 **Look at the photographs on page C6. Match these sentence halves. Listen and check.**

1 The people in the first photo look
2 I think they probably
3 Maybe they're going to
4 The man in the second photo looks like
5 He seems
6 I guess he might be
7 I'm sure the tourists
8 The professional photographer might

a) quite serious.
b) will feel happy when they look at their photo.
c) want to remember their trip.
d) feel proud if it's a good photo.
e) like tourists.
f) a professional photographer.
g) send the photo to their friends and family.
h) taking this photo for a newspaper or a magazine.

Exam skill Giving relevant answers

2 **Look at the two photographs on page C7 and read the question. Tick which ideas are suitable for your answer.**

1 There are four people in the first photo. ☐
2 The people in the first photo look like professional musicians. ☐
3 The teenagers in the second photo look very relaxed. ☐
4 The people in first photo are all concentrating on playing. ☐
5 There are some tents in the background of the second photo. ☐
6 I think the teenagers are playing music just for fun. ☐

Remember!
You can describe the photos, but only to help you make comparisons or answer the question.

Useful language Describing unknown words

3 **Look at the photographs again. Where are the people? Complete the descriptions of the places with the words in the box.**

kind	like	something	special

1 It looks like a .... place for giving concerts.
2 It's .... a theatre but for music shows.
3 They're in a theatre, or .... like that.
4 Maybe they're at a .... of summer camp.

Exam skill Points to remember

4 **Compare the two photos and answer the questions. Tick the boxes.**

1 Did you explain the topic linking the two photos? ☐
2 Did you talk about similarities and differences? ☐
3 Did you answer the question? ☐
4 Did you express your opinion? ☐

5 46 **Listen to Andreas and compare your ideas.**

Tip! Your guesses about the photos don't have to be right, but it's important to speculate about what might be happening.

Tip! Don't panic if you don't know the word for something in one of the photos. Just explain what you are talking about.

Test 2 Exam practice Speaking • Part 2

Part 2 4 minutes (6 minutes for groups of three)

1 **Work in pairs, A and B. One of you takes the role of the examiner and gives the instructions, while the other follows the instructions. Then swap roles.**

Interlocutor In this part of the test, I'm going to give each of you two photographs. I'd like you to talk about your photographs on your own for about a minute, and also to answer a question about your partner's photographs.
(Candidate A), it's your turn first. Here are your photographs on page C8. They show **people using laptops**.
I'd like you to compare the photographs, and say **why you think the people are using the laptops**.
All right?

Candidate A

1 minute ....

Interlocutor Thank you.

2 **Now, A can read the examiner's question to B.**

Interlocutor Do you often use a laptop? (Why? / Why not?)

Candidate B

approximately 30 seconds ....

Interlocutor Thank you.

3 **Now, swap roles.**

Interlocutor Now, *(Candidate B),* here are your photographs on page C9. They show **people eating together.**
I'd like you to compare the photographs, and **say what you think the people are enjoying about eating together**.
All right?

Candidate B

1 minute ....

Interlocutor Thank you.

4 **Now, B can read the examiner's question to A.**

Interlocutor Do you enjoy eating meals with other people?

Candidate A

1 minute ....

Interlocutor Thank you.

Tip! Speak calmly and clearly. If you don't speak clearly, you could get lower marks for pronunciation.

Test 2 Training Speaking Part 3

Understanding the task

1 Complete the text about Part 3 using words in the box.

all of these	different possibilities	one minute
reach agreement	three minutes	with a partner

In Part 3, you work **(1)** .... The examiner gives you some prompts which show **(2)** .... , and you have to discuss **(3)** .... with your partner. You have about **(4)** .... to do this. The examiner then asks you to work with your partner to **(5)** .... about something. You have about **(6)** .... to do this.

Useful language Suggestions and reaching agreement

2 Read the suggestions about places to stay. Choose the correct words in *italics* to complete the reasons.

1 I don't think that camping is a good idea. *It's because / That's because* it can be very cold at night in the mountains.
2 Staying with friends seems like a good idea. *The one thing / For one thing,* it would be much cheaper than a hotel.
3 I would suggest that they stay in a hotel. *After all / For all,* it's a holiday, so they want to be comfortable.
4 I don't think they will be able to find a cheap hostel. *This reason / The reason for this* is that there aren't many hostels in the countryside.

3 47 Complete the expressions the students use to reach agreement. Listen and check.

choice	choose	either	go	happy

1 Well, I'd suggest .... a hotel or staying with friends.
2 Are you .... with that?
3 My .... would be the hotel.
4 So shall we .... a hotel?
5 Yes, let's .... for that.

Tip! You and your partner may sometimes have very different ideas. You don't have to reach agreement with your partner, but you have to *try* to reach agreement.

Test 2 Exam practice Speaking • Part 3

Part 3 4 minutes (5 minutes for groups of three)

Interlocutor Now, I'd like you to talk about something together for about two minutes.
Here are some things that people might think about when deciding whether it is a good idea to become an expert in a subject, and a question for you to discuss. First, you have some time to look at the task.
[Show candidates the diagram on page C10. Allow 15 seconds.]

Now, talk to each other about **whether it's better to become an expert in one subject or to know a lot about many things**.

Candidates

2 minutes ....
(3 minutes for groups of three)

Interlocutor Thank you. Now, you have about a minute to decide **which two things are the most important when considering this question**.

Candidates

1 minute ....
(for pairs or groups of three)

Interlocutor Thank you.

Tip! Try to discuss all the points. They will help you talk about different aspects of the question and help show the extent of your language.

Test 2 Training Speaking Part 4

Understanding the task

1 **Choose the correct words in *italics* to complete the sentences about Part 4.**

1 In Part 4, the examiner asks you questions about *your life / your opinions.*
2 When you answer, you should give your opinion and add *examples and reasons / other people's opinions* to support it.
3 You *can / must* ask your partner for their opinion, to encourage a discussion.
4 When they give their opinion, you *should / shouldn't* respond to what they say.
5 Your partner *might / will definitely* ask you to join in when they answer their questions.

Useful language Giving and asking for opinions

2 **Correct the mistakes in the sentences giving opinions and asking for opinions. Two sentences are correct.**

1 I say that shopping in town is more fun than shopping online.
2 I'd think that shopping online can be quicker than going to the shops sometimes.
3 For my opinion, you need to try clothes on before you buy them.
4 My own view is that everyone will buy things online in the future.
5 What's your opinion for designer clothes?
6 What do you think about buying expensive brands?
7 What are your views in the quality of clothes in most clothes shops?
8 How are you feeling about the fact that most clothes are made in developing countries?

3 48 **Match the sentence halves for responding to what your partner says. Then listen and check.**

1 That's an
2 I hadn't
3 Yes, I see
4 Yes, I think I
5 Yes, I can

a) thought of that.
b) see your point of view about that.
c) what you mean.
d) interesting point.
e) agree with you about that.

Tip! Listen carefully to what your partner says so that you can respond and give your own opinion.

Test 2 Exam practice Speaking • Part 4

Part 4 4 minutes (6 minutes for groups of three)

Take it in turns to answer these questions. Use the questions in the box to move the conversation along or get your partner to join in.

- Is there a subject that you'd like to be an expert in?
  ..... (Why? / Why not?)
- What personal qualities are needed to become an expert in something?
- Is there someone you particularly admire who's an expert in something?
- What are the advantages of doing an online course?
- What do you think about the reliability of online information when you are researching a subject?
  ..... (Why? / Why not?)
- Why do you think people do general knowledge quizzes?

Select any of the following prompts, as appropriate:

- What do you think?
- Do you agree?
- And you?

Tip! Remember that there are no right answers to the questions and you won't be judged on your opinions, only on the language you use to express your ideas and views.

Test 3 Reading and Use of English • Part 1

For questions **1–8**, read the text below and decide which answer (**A**, **B**, **C** or **D**) best fits each gap. There is an example at the beginning (**0**).

Mark your answers **on the separate answer sheet**.

Example:

0 **A** risen **B** increased **C** lifted **D** enlarged

0	A	B	C	D
	▭	▬	▭	▭

Urban heat islands

Scientists now fear that global warming may be **(0)** .... by what they call the 'urban heat island effect'. This refers to considerable rises in temperature in big cities, when **(1)** .... to surrounding rural areas, that affect local climate patterns in **(2)** .... of rainfall and wind. Basically when plants and trees are cut down and concrete is put in their **(3)** ...., the natural state is already altered. Then the way the concrete itself absorbs, **(4)** .... and releases heat further alters the natural balance. Then waste heat from traffic and buildings, together with ozone pollution, **(5)** .... still further to the problem.

Scientists claim it is important to **(6)** .... action to counter this effect in cities – by planting as much vegetation as possible. In addition, they are **(7)** .... city developers to use a more expensive concrete for pavements that absorbs rainwater, thus cooling them down. They also advise that rooftops and pavements should be made of light-coloured materials, as dark objects **(8)** .... energy into heat whereas white objects reflect light.

1 **A** balanced **B** connected **C** measured **D** compared

2 **A** regard **B** terms **C** concern **D** relation

3 **A** position **B** room **C** place **D** situation

4 **A** stores **B** maintains **C** stays **D** possesses

5 **A** supplies **B** contributes **C** gives **D** provides

6 **A** take **B** make **C** be **D** do

7 **A** pointing **B** urging **C** proposing **D** suggesting

8 **A** translate **B** exchange **C** adapt **D** convert

Test 3 Reading and Use of English • Part 2

For questions **9–16**, read the text below and think of the word which best fits each gap. Use only **one** word in each gap. There is an example at the beginning (**0**).

Write your answers **IN CAPITAL LETTERS on the separate answer sheet.**

Example: | **0** | O | F |
|---|---|---|

Preparing for my first running race

For the first 24 years **(0)** .... my life, I strongly disliked running. At school, I'd been completely put **(9)** .... running after being made to do cross country running in shorts in the middle of winter. But when I started my first job I found **(10)** .... socialising with a different set of people, who persuaded me to come and **(11)** .... a go at training in a gym.

(12) .... thing led to another, and I began to **(13)** .... my fitness seriously. I agreed to try a ten-kilometre race my friends had entered. I had three months in **(14)** .... to train. My very first training runs were **(15)** .... much of a success, so I combined gentle running and walking by myself, until my legs got more used to the activity.

My cautious approach seemed to be working. By the time I joined my friends for some practice runs, I was pleasantly surprised to find I could keep **(16)** .... with them.

Test 3 Reading and Use of English • Part 3

For questions **17–24**, read the text below. Use the word given in capitals at the end of some of the lines to form a word that fits in the gap **in the same line**. There is an example at the beginning (**0**).

Write your answers **IN CAPITAL LETTERS on the separate answer sheet.**

Example: 0 | F | O | U | N | D | E | R |

Florence Nightingale

Florence Nightingale is considered to be the **(0)** .... of modern **FOUND**
nursing. Before her **(17)** .... in the mid 19th century, nurses were **INVOLVE**
relatively **(18)** .... and lacked basic skills and knowledge, but **TRAIN**
Florence was an influential figure who **(19)** .... the profession. **REVOLUTION**
Born into a rich English family which did not consider nursing to be a
(20) .... profession for her, she surprised her parents when she **SUIT**
announced her **(21)** .... to become a nurse. But she rose rapidly **INTEND**
within the profession and was soon in charge of nursing at a London hospital.
She was **(22)** .... to go and lead a team to nurse British soldiers **CHOICE**
wounded in the Crimean War.
She arrived to find a serious **(23)** .... of nurses, badly informed **SHORT**
about basic hygiene and nutrition, and she worked tirelessly to improve this
situation. The soldiers adored her for her caring attitude. On her return the
grateful British public thanked her for what she had done in many
(24) .... letters, articles and poems. **EMOTION**

Test 3 Reading and Use of English • Part 4

For questions **25–30**, complete the second sentence so that it has a similar meaning to the first sentence, using the word given. **Do not change the word given.** You must use between **two** and **five** words, including the word given. Here is an example (**0**).

Example:

0 The boat tour was full, so we had to wait an hour for the next one.

PLACES

There .... left on the boat tour, so we had to wait an hour for the next one.

The gap can be filled by the words *were no places*, so you write:

Example:

0	WERE NO PLACES

Write **only** the missing words **IN CAPITAL LETTERS on the separate answer sheet**.

---

25 My last visit to Brazil was for my sister's marriage twelve years ago.

GOT

I haven't been to Brazil .... twelve years ago.

26 'Are you feeling well enough now for a little walk, Joe?' asked his mother.

RECOVERED

Joe's mother asked him .... enough for a little walk.

27 Mr Garside had only ever let two neighbours go inside his house.

ALLOWED

Only two neighbours had .... go inside Mr Garside's house.

28 'I'll only go on the boat trip if Dad comes,' said Tania.

LONG

'I'll go on the boat trip .... there,' said Tania.

29 The tour leader told everyone about the danger of getting too close to the edge of the waterfall.

WARNED

The tour leader .... too close to the edge of the waterfall.

30 Brian's gardening is the most important thing to him in the world.

MORE

Nothing .... than his gardening.

Reading and Use of English • Part 5

You are going to read an article about travel. For questions **31–36**, choose the answer (**A**, **B**, **C** or **D**) which you think fits best according to the text.

Mark your answers **on the separate answer sheet**.

The experience of travelling

I have just returned from a long weekend break in Lisbon, to enjoy the southern European weather. From a base in the old town which forms the heart of the city, I tested my calves on long uphill walks to districts that qualify the Portuguese capital as Europe's 'in' city, according to the people who write travel reviews on the internet. I ate poorly in tourist traps and exquisitely at the hands of genius chefs. I took in the central monuments and the hidden wonders in the industrial part of the Lisbon shoreline. I covered a good few kilometres, I can tell you, as you would in most large cultural towns.

Lisbon is a great city that is really open to tourists, and I like it enough to return soon. I felt refreshed and pleased not to have to think about work. But did I learn much or emerge an improved person? No. On my travels, I rarely do, and I am not sure that anyone does. The more of the world I see, the less confident I am that there is anything innately educational about travel. It is worth doing because it is fun. Travel is for the senses, not the character. Fun is a good enough reason to do anything, as long as we do not kid ourselves that something more profound is at work.

The most frequent travellers I know are not wiser or smarter than anyone else. At worst, travel can make people a bit too sure of themselves. They tend to rely all the time on personal anecdote: whatever they saw of a place represents the truth. They tend to under-rate the character formation that takes place at home: the quarrels, the disappointments, the mistakes learned from. And our culture tends to encourage them in their misbeliefs.

Imagine you are an employer staring at two job applications that are identical in all respects save one. Candidate A spent a gap year between school and university seeing the world – funded, incidentally, by Mum and Dad. Candidate B spent the same year stacking shelves in a local supermarket. One of the hopefuls showed self-reliance, commitment, co-operation and a certain grown-upness. The other is Candidate A. Yet ours is still a world that rewards the gap-year wanderer with the big well-paid job, a world where 'well-travelled' is still a synonym for 'clever'.

In a sense, travel is kind of hangover from a time when few people went abroad, and when little knowledge about the wider world was available to those who did *not* go abroad. The effect was that people who had done a couple of international trips could feel they'd done a great thing: they felt more cultural and intellectual. That era of travel ended in the mid-1990s when the internet was born. We can now not just read in detail about anywhere on earth, but instantly see videos of it with high-definition clarity. Our potential to be surprised or educated by a visit to a place has diminished. I would go as far as to say that anyone who is consistently 'discovering' things on their travels is uncurious when at home, and not perceptive when abroad.

In the modern world, the only way to learn much more about a place than you could remotely, is to live there for a sustained period, paying taxes and using local services. Mere travel is no great source of insight, which leaves just one reason to do it: fun. That's more than enough. I enjoy travel, including the bits many people hate. I enjoy the boring atmosphere of airports, the anonymity of hotel rooms where there are no distractions, the useful isolation of long-haul flights. If I could afford it, I would go on regular London-to-Sydney trips just to finish long and interesting books in one sitting. But precisely because I take so much pleasure from travel, I can see through any attempt to cover it in virtue.

31 The writer says that internet reviewers seem to rate Lisbon highly on the basis of

A the unusual layout of the city.

B the wonderful cuisine available there.

C how pleasant (easy) it is get around on foot.

D the areas of interest away from the city centre.

32 What point is the writer making in the second paragraph?

A We can't expect travel to be continually enjoyable.

B We shouldn't pretend that travelling is a deep experience.

C We can't expect a place to feel the same when we revisit it.

D We shouldn't see holidays as a chance to escape from ordinary life.

33 The writer believes that people who travel a lot

A fail to learn from mistakes they have made.

B choose to ignore the unpleasant aspects of travelling.

C think their own views and impressions must always be right.

D think everyone will be interested in their travel stories.

34 The writer implies that students who travel around the world on gap years

A should stay at university if they want to be considered clever.

B are wrong to assume that employers will be impressed.

C would be better off earning some money at home.

D usually end up in lower paid jobs.

35 What is the writer objecting to in the fifth paragraph?

A the idea of travelling to broaden your cultural knowledge

B the fact that some people dismiss travel as a waste of time

C the way digital technology has affected the travel industry

D the superiority that some travellers display when abroad

36 In the final paragraph, what part of travel does the writer enjoy personally?

A the feeling of living somewhere different for a long time

B the thought that it makes him a nicer person

C the opportunity to be alone and undisturbed

D the sense of being as far from home as possible

Test 3 Reading and Use of English • Part 6

You are going to read an article about a natural phenomenon in the night sky. Six sentences have been removed from the article. Choose from the sentences **A–G** the one which fits each gap (**37–42**). There is one extra sentence which you do not need to use.

Mark your answers **on the separate answer sheet.**

The aurora borealis

A new book explores the many myths and legends attached to the magical displays in the skies we know as the aurora borealis. Adrian Bridge reports.

To the ancient Greeks, the magical dancing lights that occasionally appeared in the night sky were known as Aurora, the goddess of the dawn. When the lights filled the skies with their dramatic displays of colour, it was said that Aurora was riding her chariot across the heavens to announce the arrival of Helios the sun, and another new day. The twisting, dancing forms the displays took were the result of the efforts of Boreas, one of the four winds.

There are, of course, many myths that over the millennia have been passed down to explain the extraordinary spectacle of the aurora borealis – more commonly termed the Northern Lights. **37** ______ And in a recently published book, *Life Beneath the Northern Lights*, a research team led by Lizzy Pattison is well aware of this.

In the book, Pattison and her team have sought to throw light on some of the more colourful stories that have grown up around the phenomenon. **38** ______ This strategy is cleverly handled so that the reader's imagination is engaged.

Much of the book focuses on the legends and lifestyles of the Sami people, indigenous to Norway, Sweden, Finland and Russia. Some Sami still have the traditional belief that the lights emanate from their ancestors and must be treated with immense respect. **39** ______ In one account, a sacred bear rescues someone taken in that way.

Elsewhere in the northern hemisphere, there have been many other interpretations. The Chinese saw in the lights fire-breathing dragons; the Fox Indians of North America believed that they were the ghosts of enemies who brought ill fortune. More cheerily, the Scots believed they were merry dancers. **40** ______ The Canadian Indians saw the lights as spirits engaged in a ball game!

Of course we know better now and have scientific explanations for the Northern Lights – displays occur when solar particles enter the Earth's atmosphere and emit burning gases that produce different coloured lights. We know that the aurora borealis occurs in an oval doughnut-shaped area located above the magnetic pole and that the best sightings are within the 'doughnut' and away from artificial light and moonlight.

The opening chapter of the book is devoted to a comprehensive review of the scientific explanations for the aurora borealis, with a further chapter offering practical advice on how best to capture the lights on film. **41** ______

'Knowing the background to the myths and stories that have grown up around the lights can only improve the experience of seeing them,' said Jonny Cooper, the founder of *Off the Map Travel*, a soft adventure specialist. He helped with the book by flying the research team to northern Sweden. **42** ______ 'You can stand under the night skies and watch in awe, just as our forefathers did,' Cooper says. 'The experience can … be so powerful that unless we knew better we would find ourselves asking if there were not some other force at work.'

A Traditionally, they remained inside during a display; even today, if caught outside, few dare to whistle in case the lights carry them away.

B More scientific explanations are available now, of course, but the legends are what fascinate people.

C In other words, even with a scientific understanding of the phenomenon, the tales lose none of their magic.

D That way they could explore the phenomenon first-hand.

E We are transported back to the times when those who witnessed the spectacle could only attribute it to the supernatural.

F This theme, with variations, is relatively common in the mythology.

G Undoubtedly these are both invaluable, but there is something in the naivety and the drama of those early explanations that can still fire the imagination.

Test 3 Reading and Use of English • Part 7

You are going to read an article about a composer of background music called Michael Reed. For questions **43–52**, choose from the sections (**A–D**). The sections may be chosen more than once.

Mark your answers **on the separate answer sheet**.

In which section does the writer mention

Michael being unsure which programme his music will be used for?	43	
evidence of the wide range of Michael's professional expertise?	44	
Michael appreciating the opportunity to try out different things?	45	
the need to be strict about scheduling the composing of music?	46	
Michael getting fed up at one point in his musical career?	47	
some music which gives the listener a false impression?	48	
Michael enjoying a new feeling of being in total control of his work?	49	
the difficulty of working for an unpredictable financial reward?	50	
Michael briefly forgetting that he was the composer of certain music?	51	
the factors which affect how long Michael needs to compose some music?	52	

Striking the right note

David Waller goes to meet Michael Reed, a composer of background music.

A Your ears slowly fill with sound, first with some foreboding cello, then an eerie female vocal and the occasional bang of a drum. The sounds gain in intensity before suddenly breaking into the epic sweep of a full orchestra. Eyes closed, it sounds like the soundtrack for a nightmarish futuristic film landscape, but this is a simple house in Devon, England. Michael Reed welcomes me and shows me to his self-built studio in the basement. There the composer of music for film, commercials and television has a giant sound desk, monitor speakers, piles of dusty synthesisers, and a full drum kit. Reed has produced hundreds of pieces of music in this room, layering a mix of computer samples and live instrumentation. A piece, he says, 'could take anything from 15 minutes to five days, depending on everything from the complexity of instrumentation to how tired you are. It's really difficult to say, 'Right, on this day I'm going to write this bit of music.' But when it comes down to it, you have to.'

B The majority of Reed's output is library music, pieces written to a brief but with no specific purpose, to be picked up later by shows and film trailers that need a soundtrack. It's usually not until he receives his four-monthly statement of earnings that he sees where his work has ended up. In the last period, that meant a soap opera, a cookery show and a documentary about dogs. 'I once went on holiday to Lake Geneva,' he says. 'I turned on the TV and saw an advert for Visit Turkey and my music was in the background. Another time I was in my old house and heard some music I recognised coming through the wall. I liked it. Then I realised I'd written it!'

C It's an odd way to encounter your own work and certainly it's not the music career he had envisaged. At university, Reed studied musical composition and afterwards had his heart set on becoming a drummer. He ended up playing in sessions at the prestigious Abbey Road recording studios. But the reality of life as a professional drummer was rather tedious, with endless car journeys all over Britain, transporting his drums around. But then some music industry friends introduced Reed to composition work. His first successful pitch for a television commercial earned him $3,000 and provided a valuable lesson: it was better paid and being in charge of the whole process was far more fulfilling. He goes back through his millions of files and digs out samples of his work, from classical pieces recorded with a full live orchestra through pop, drum and bass to specific work he has produced for films.

D Yet from a business point of view, working in the music industry is like sailing on a rocky sea. Reed risks producing work that he never gets paid for. While his four-monthly earnings statement will have hundreds of individual entries, the total for each individual track could be anything from thousands of pounds to pennies. 'I've been doing it 15 years now and there doesn't always seem to be a correlation between what you're most proud of and what makes you the most money.' Still, Reed is happy about the unexpected direction his music has taken him in. 'You have to remember that you can do something cool with each piece and experiment with new sounds. Then you suddenly find yourself really enjoying what you're writing. . . . I'm really lucky.'

Test 3 Writing • Part 1

You **must** answer this question. Write your answer in **140–190 words** in an appropriate style **on the separate answer sheet**.

---

1 In your English class, you have been talking about libraries. Now, your English teacher has asked you to write an essay for homework.

Write your essay using **all** the notes and giving reasons for your point of view.

Libraries are no longer needed, as people can learn all they need to online.
Do you agree?

Notes

Write about:

1. college libraries and public libraries
2. different services libraries can offer
3. .... (your own idea)

Test 3 Writing • Part 2

Write an answer to **one** of the questions **2–4** in this part. Write your answer in **140–190 words** in an appropriate style **on the separate answer sheet**. Put the question number in the box at the top of the answer sheet.

---

2 You see this announcement on an English-language website about food.

> Articles wanted!
>
> What can be done to encourage people to eat healthier snacks between meals, rather than something tasty but unhealthy? The best articles will be published on our website.

Write your **article**.

3 This is part of an email you receive from a friend in Canada.

> *I'm doing a project about how films can help people to learn about history. Could you tell me about a film which helped you understand a particular time or event in history? What made the film an effective way to learn?*

Write your **review**.

4 This is part of an email you receive from a friend who is a school teacher in another country.

> *I'm planning a trip with my pupils to your country. Can you recommend one region where we will be able to learn about various aspects of your country, such as its wildlife, history and architecture? What would be the best way to make the trip really educational? Hopefully we can meet up too!*
>
> *All the best,*
>
> *Frankie*

Write your **email**.

Test 3 Listening • Part 1

49 You will hear people talking in eight different situations. For questions **1–8**, choose the best answer (**A**, **B** or **C**).

---

1 You hear a man talking about flying long distances.
What does he say about it?
A He still finds some trips challenging.
B He now keeps business trips short.
C He always travels in business class.

2 You hear a woman telling her friend about a jewellery-making course she did.
What does she say about it?
A It has given her the confidence to make jewellery to sell.
B Meeting the other participants added to her enjoyment.
C She liked the peaceful atmosphere of the sessions.

3 You hear a woman talking about moving home.
What will the woman do differently the next time she moves home?
A hire a professional company to help her move
B get rid of unwanted possessions before she moves
C research her new neighbourhood in advance of moving

4 You hear two film critics discussing a film starring an actor called Tania Fry.
They agree that
A Tania manages to find humour in the script.
B the film doesn't allow Tania to show her acting ability.
C there should be more films for actors of Tania's generation.

5 You hear a football referee talking about his job.
How does he deal with the pressure of his job?
A by taking regular exercise to keep himself fit
B by sharing his experiences with other referees
C by reminding himself that players argue with all referees

6 You hear two friends discussing a photography exhibition they have just been to.
How does the woman feel now?
A enthusiastic about improving her own photography skills
B motivated to find out more about the photographer
C inspired to visit the places shown in the photos

7 You hear a travel and tourism student talking about a project she is doing about pop-culture tourism.
What does she say about fans who travel to pop-culture destinations?
A They are often disappointed by their experience.
B They are unpopular with residents in these locations.
C They are dissatisfied that so few destinations are available.

8 You hear two friends discussing a local market.
Why does the man recommend the market to the woman?
A There aren't too many shoppers there.
B The prices are generally competitive.
C It helps to support local producers.

Test 3 Listening • Part 2

50 You will hear a man called Pete talking about a cycling holiday in the UK that his company organises. For questions **9–18**, complete the sentences with a word or short phrase.

Cycling holiday in the UK

Pete calls the 15-day cycle trip **(9)** '...' level.

A wider range of dates is available to those who choose the **(10)** '...' option.

In terms of weather, cyclists experience less **(11)** .... in the middle of the trip.

Pete's company has won an award for its **(12)** .... for the last three years.

Starting this year, the company is providing a greater choice of **(13)** .... for cyclists.

If you book this holiday, it is not necessary to buy **(14)** ....

Pete uses the word **(15)** .... to describe the majority of the hills on this trip.

Through major cities, cyclists will need to use local **(16)** ....

Cyclists need to be in good condition as there are no **(17)** .... on this trip.

All cyclists receive a **(18)** .... at the end of the trip.

Test 3 Listening • Part 3

51 You will hear five short extracts in which people are talking about learning to drive a car. For questions **19–23**, choose from the list (**A–H**) what advice each speaker gives. Use the letters only once. There are three extra letters which you do not need to use.

A Ask others to recommend an instructor.

B Learn to drive in a small car.

C Save money by booking a series of lessons.

D Watch other people's driving techniques.

E Accept that you may need a lot of lessons.

F Don't start learning if you're very nervous.

G Avoid taking lessons when there is heavy traffic.

H Be aware that learning continues even after the driving test.

Speaker 1		**19**
Speaker 2		**20**
Speaker 3		**21**
Speaker 4		**22**
Speaker 5		**23**

Test 3 Listening • Part 4

52 You will hear an interview with a woman called Helena Best, who has been a contestant on three TV quiz shows. For questions **24–30**, choose the best answer (**A**, **B** or **C**).

---

24 What does Helena say about being a contestant on the show *Full Marks*?

A She was frustrated at not remembering the correct answers.

B She was annoyed by some of the people in the audience.

C She was distracted by the studio lights and cameras.

25 When Helena appeared on *Great Minds*,

A she felt inferior to the other contestants.

B she was relieved that she had prepared well.

C she thought her questions were harder than other people's.

26 What helped Helena to feel relaxed on *Brainbox*?

A competing in a team

B being given a suitable topic

C knowing the show was not live

27 What aspect of being a contestant did Helena particularly enjoy?

A chatting to the show's host during the breaks

B being given expensive clothes to wear for filming

C being treated like a celebrity by the staff at the studio

28 What point does Helena make about applications to be on a quiz show?

A State if you've been a contestant on other shows.

B Be honest about your education and previous work.

C Make yourself sound interesting on your application.

29 Helena mentions that, because of the contract contestants are given, it's important not to

A publish any of the questions online.

B give interviews to newspaper journalists.

C tell anyone in advance whether you've won.

30 Helena advises anyone who is going to take part in a quiz show to

A believe strongly in their own ability to win.

B enjoy the experience of being seen on television.

C watch as many episodes of the show as possible.

Test 3 Speaking • Parts 1 and 2

Part 1 2 minutes (3 minutes for groups of three)

Interlocutor First, we'd like to know something about you.

- Do you enjoy cooking? ..... (Why? / Why not?)
- What's your favourite snack food? ..... (Why?)
- What do you use the internet for most? ..... (Why?)
- Tell us about a website you often use.
- Do you prefer to spend free time indoors or outdoors? ..... (Why?)

Part 2 4 minutes (6 minutes for groups of three)

Interlocutor In this part of the test, I'm going to give each of you two photographs. I'd like you to talk about your photographs on your own for about a minute, and also to answer a question about your partner's photographs.

(*Candidate A*), it's your turn first. Here are your photographs on page C11. They show **people taking exercise in different situations**.

I'd like you to compare the photographs, and say **why you think these people are taking exercise in these ways**.

All right?

Candidate A

1 minute ....

Interlocutor Thank you.

(*Candidate B*), **how important is it to you to take exercise**?

Candidate B

approximately 30 seconds ....

Interlocutor Now, (*Candidate B*), here are your photographs on page C12. They show **people listening to music in different places**.

I'd like you to compare the photographs, and say **what these people are enjoying about listening to music in the different places**.

All right?

Candidate B

1 minute ....

Interlocutor Thank you.

(*Candidate A*), **do you prefer going to live concerts or listening to recorded music**?

Candidate A

approximately 30 seconds ....

Interlocutor Thank you.

Test 3 Speaking • Parts 3 and 4

Part 3 4 minutes (5 minutes for groups of three)

Interlocutor Now, I'd like you to talk about something together for about two minutes. (*3 minutes for groups of three*)

Here are some things that can influence a good day out and a question for you to discuss.

First, you have some time to look at the task.

[Show candidates the diagram on page C13. Allow 15 seconds.]

Now, talk to each other about **how important money is for having a good day out**.

Candidates

2 minutes ....

(3 minutes for groups of three)

Interlocutor Thank you. Now you have about a minute to decide **which two activities money will help you with most**.

Candidates

1 minute ....

(for pairs or groups of three)

Interlocutor Thank you.

Part 4 4 minutes (6 minutes for groups of three)

Interlocutor *Use the following questions, in order, as appropriate:*

- What is a good place for a day out where you live?
  ..... (Why?)
- Is shopping a satisfying way to spend free time?
  ..... (Why? / Why not?)
- How important is money when choosing a job?
  ..... (Why?)
- Should some jobs offer a higher salary than they do now?
  ..... (Why? / Why not?)
- What would you do if you became extremely rich?
  ..... (Why?)
- What are the disadvantages of being rich?

Select any of the following prompts, as appropriate.

- What do you think?
- Do you agree?
- And you?

Thank you. That is the end of the test.

Test 4 Reading and Use of English • Part 1

For questions **1–8**, read the text below and decide which answer (**A**, **B**, **C** or **D**) best fits each gap. There is an example at the beginning (**0**).

Mark your answers **on the separate answer sheet**.

Example:

0 **A** hunt **B** look **C** search **D** quest

0	A	B	C	D
	▭	▭	▬	▭

Wasps and picnics

How can you stop a pleasant summer picnic from being ruined by wasps in **(0)** .... of a sugary treat? Well, scientists have **(1)** .... some interesting information on the subject. The **(2)** .... is evidently to spot any single wasps which arrive on the **(3)** .... unaccompanied. Such wasps are likely to be 'scout' wasps which are out looking for suitable food, with the intention of reporting back to the nest and getting other wasps to help come and collect the food. Scientists advise people to simply trap such a scout wasp under a glass for the **(4)** .... of the picnic, before freeing it again. The advice makes good **(5)** .... but supposes that several spare glasses have been packed for this **(6)** .... !

The scientists also **(7)** .... what many picnickers have discovered from experience: if wasps are circling around your picnic, the worst thing you can do is start waving your arm to get them away. They will interpret this as an aggressive **(8)** .... and may sting you to defend themselves.

1	**A** got through to	**B** come up with	**C** made up for	**D** gone over to
2	**A** craft	**B** trick	**C** result	**D** art
3	**A** scene	**B** location	**C** place	**D** situation
4	**A** time	**B** duration	**C** term	**D** interval
5	**A** worth	**B** point	**C** sense	**D** reason
6	**A** view	**B** purpose	**C** idea	**D** aim
7	**A** agree	**B** witness	**C** settle	**D** confirm
8	**A** threat	**B** effort	**C** fear	**D** risk

Test 4 Reading and Use of English • Part 2

For questions **9–16**, read the text below and think of the word which best fits each gap. Use only **one** word in each gap. There is an example at the beginning (**0**).

Write your answers **IN CAPITAL LETTERS on the separate answer sheet.**

Example: **0** | T | O |

Waiting at the diner

After fifteen minutes waiting for her order **(0)** .... come, Sylvie began to regret her decision to stop at the diner. She'd been led to a seat at the back with a view of a small lake. At least that would pass the time pleasantly, she thought, watching the ducks and texting a message to Alan. She told him it was something of an exaggeration to call **(9)** .... a lake – more like a pond, really, and then deleted the message for being far **(10)** .... trivial and chatty.

She'd come in at half past four, hoping to have a quick coffee and a cake and **(11)** .... on her way again, but already the diner was starting to fill **(12)** .... with travelling families looking **(13)** .... they were settling for an early meal. The waitress looked stressed and kept her head down, so despite several attempts, Sylvie was **(14)** .... to make eye contact with her. **(15)** .... this rate, Sylvie risked being late for her appointment with Alan, **(16)** .... already been on the road since the early morning.

Test 4 Reading and Use of English • Part 3

For questions **17–24**, read the text below. Use the word given in capitals at the end of some of the lines to form a word that fits in the gap **in the same line**. There is an example at the beginning (**0**).

Write your answers **IN CAPITAL LETTERS on the separate answer sheet.**

Example: | 0 | A F F E C T S |

Birth order

A good deal of research has been carried out by scientists on how birth order
(0) .... children from large families. **AFFECT**

It would appear that first-born children are the most likely to imitate their parents
throughout life, because they had the **(17)** .... attention of the **DIVIDE**
parents until the birth of the next child. But first-borns can also be quite
(18) .... people because they lost this complete attention when later **ANXIETY**
siblings were born. **(19)** .... reason is that their mother and father **OTHER**
were first-time parents, often nervous and **(20)** .... about what they **SURE**
should be doing and **(21)** .... by what might happen. **FRIGHT**

Conversely, if a third child is born, the parents are much more
(22) .... and confident in bringing up infants, so there is a **RELAX**
(23) .... for the child to grow up being fun-loving and **TEND**
(24) .... in group situations such as parties. Both second and third- **SOCIETY**
born children are likely to have had to compete to get their parents' attention,
and scientists think this makes them more independent.

Test 4 Reading and Use of English • Part 4

For questions **25–30**, complete the second sentence so that it has a similar meaning to the first sentence, using the word given. **Do not change the word given.** You must use between **two** and **five** words, including the word given. Here is an example (**0**).

Example:

0 It took James ages to repair the clock.

LONG

It took James .... the clock working again.

The gap can be filled by the words *a long time to get*, so you write:

Example:

0	A LONG TIME TO GET

Write **only** the missing words **IN CAPITAL LETTERS on the separate answer sheet**.

---

25 Tom's mum said he should have some food before going to football practice.

SOMETHING

Tom's mum told him to .... eat before going to football practice.

26 The waterfall walk took much longer than Lee had expected.

SUCH

Lee hadn't expected the waterfall walk .... long time.

27 'Do you mind if my junior colleague observes this consultation?' Dr Matthews asked her patient.

OBJECTED

Dr Matthews asked her patient .... a junior colleague observing the consultation.

28 'Having to wait in the traffic all the time used to be annoying, but now I've got used to it,' said Julian.

ANNOY

'It .... more when I have to wait in the traffic,' said Julian.

29 'Thank you everybody – you've made my birthday a really happy occasion.'

THANKED

Lynn .... birthday a really happy occasion.

30 Graham practised every day because he desperately wanted to beat his old rival in the tennis match.

DESPERATE

Graham practised every day because he .... the tennis match against his old rival.

Test 4 Reading and Use of English • Part 5

You are going to read an article about a professional cycling team. For questions **31–36**, choose the answer (**A**, **B**, **C** or **D**) which you think fits best according to the text.

Mark your answers **on the separate answer sheet.**

Preparing for the big one

Jeremy Wilson joins Team Sky's cycle training camp in Tenerife as they prepare for the Tour de France.

Day ten of Team Sky's two-week training camp in mountainous Tenerife has just been completed, and I join the exhausted riders in the dining room of their hotel. The diet is strictly protein, fruit and vegetables for the riders, with carbohydrates eaten only when absolutely necessary. Chris Froome, a previous Tour winner – is 1.86 metres but weighs only 68 kilos. Team etiquette has it that staff do not eat forbidden foods in front of the riders. An exception to the diet was made when day eight of the camp coincided with Geraint Thomas's and Ian Stannard's birthdays. Both were presented with a mini chocolate bar.

The next morning there's a brief talk from Tim Kerrison, head of athlete performance. The riders listen intently. Kerrison – formerly an Australian rowing coach was a sports scientist for the swimming teams before being headhunted by Dave Brailsford, Sky's team principal. Hiring someone he regarded as the best in the world, regardless of his cycling inexperience, was a typical Brailsford decision. So was the remit in Kerrison's first year, 2010. He simply followed in a camper van and watched, listened and learnt. 'He then sat down and … rattled off a load of things we probably didn't pick up on or took for granted,' Brailsford later tells me. An example was the introduction of fast interval sessions during the winter months when cyclists had traditionally just built up a slow endurance base of high mileage.

Brailsford speaks to Kerrison every day but, with 28 Team Sky riders following their own training programmes around the world, he keeps his schedules flexible and has felt no need to be in Tenerife. 'If the boss turns up it can add that bit of pressure,' Brailsford says. Mind you, that may not always be a bad thing. 'Sometimes you need that. Sometimes you need to get the job done, recover and relax.'

I am deep in conversation with Kerrison in his support car, when there is a sudden bang in front of us. Luke Rowe has had a puncture on the descent. Within 20 seconds, team mechanic Gary Blem has jumped out of the car and changed the wheel for Rowe to catch up with his teammates. The riders have been touching speeds of 80kph, fast enough to occasionally lose Kerrison's car but not to inhibit Stannard from suddenly sitting bolt upright, taking both hands off the bars and putting on some arm and leg warmers. An acceptance of danger, the Dutch rider Wout Poels later tells me, is a prerequisite. 'When you are going 80kph downhill, if you think too much, it is over,' Poels says.

Over a lunch break, there's another discussion about how the riders will approach the remaining 20km mountain stretch. This is when they practise the team tactics they're going to utilise in the Tour de France. Some of the lesser stars in the group act as support riders to the two best climbers, sheltering them from the wind to ensure they have the best possible chance of getting first to the finish line. The sacrifices made by the teammates will put the two top riders in a privileged but also pressurised position over the 23 days of the Tour. Rider Chris Froome says: 'These guys have literally spent months away from their families. It is a burden but also a motivation.'

Back at the hotel, I meet Fran Millar, the 'head of winning behaviours'. Her remit was to codify what had made the team win races and then implement a culture of continuous improvement. 'We got everybody together … and put it out to the team,' explains Millar. 'What do you think it is that makes us who we are? … what sets us apart?' A framework was created for how staff and riders expect each other to act, with five key areas. 'Identifying and eradicating losing behaviours is probably more important,' says Millar. 'If you have one person exhibiting an awful lot of losing behaviours they can have a huge impact on the rest of that group.'

---

31 What are we told about food eaten by the team?

- **A** Riders are allowed as much unhealthy food as they wish on their birthdays.
- **B** Non-riders can only eat foods like chocolate when away from the riders.
- **C** Riders and non-riders usually have different meals and eat separately.
- **D** Non-riders are expected to check that riders aren't breaking dietary rules.

32 We learn that Brailsford brought Kerrison into the team because

- **A** Brailsford knew that Kerrison was an excellent motivator.
- **B** no famous cycling coach could offer the same eye for detail.
- **C** Kerrison was already known and respected by the top cyclists.
- **D** Brailsford wanted a fresh perspective on training methods.

33 Brailsford believes that, as a boss, he should

- **A** always have a clear idea of where he's going to be.
- **B** let others take control if his presence won't help.
- **C** be the one who takes pressure off other people.
- **D** always appear relaxed even when he's not.

34 The riders travel so fast on one descent that

- **A** it causes one of the bikes' tyres to fail.
- **B** several of them are affected by cold air.
- **C** one of them becomes concerned about their safety.
- **D** Kerrison can't keep up with them even though he is driving.

35 What is the writer's main purpose in the fifth paragraph?

- **A** to justify the actions of the top riders
- **B** to praise the attitude of the team's main rider
- **C** to question the role played by the other riders
- **D** to comment on the selflessness required in team cycling

36 As part of trying to find a formula for continued success, Fran Millar

- **A** tried to arrive at a set of unique values.
- **B** looked at what had gone wrong for rival teams.
- **C** invited team members to make any criticisms they wanted.
- **D** wanted the riders to focus on self-belief.

Test 4 Reading and Use of English • Part 6

You are going to read the introduction to a book about the weather. Six sentences have been removed from the article. Choose from the sentences **A–G** the one which fits each gap (**37–42**). There is one extra sentence which you do not need to use.

Mark your answers **on the separate answer sheet**.

The weather

Weather plays a huge part in our daily lives. Since the earliest times when humans scurried into their caves to avoid a storm, people have been fascinated by the weather. No doubt those same primitive people stood in front of their dwellings a few hours later to admire a rainbow or gaze at a spectacular cloud on the horizon.

What's changed over the centuries is how people interpret the weather. Most of us no longer worry, as our ancestors did, about trying to please the spirits who sent the weather to punish or reward us. Today, when the weather doesn't do what we want, we tend to look for a more scientific explanation. **37** These things have passed into the popular vocabulary.

There's still a lot we don't understand about weather. We can now predict some aspects of cold climates a whole year in advance, and yet nobody can tell you if a thunderstorm will strike at precisely 4pm tomorrow. We understand the basic physical laws that drive our atmosphere, but we can't fully observe every detail of the current weather. There's also another factor restraining our understanding. **38** The weather defies computer predictions and seems to behave with a mind of its own.

Where does that leave you, the consumer of weather information? **39** But as the wise people of the information revolution keep reminding us, data isn't the same thing as information. You might be searching for a very specific forecast, say to plan a wedding. Maybe you're heading into the countryside for a few days and want to know the weather signs that could mean trouble. Or perhaps you're travelling to a city halfway across the world and you need a sense of the typical weather at your destination.

The Rough Guide to Weather aims to help you get the weather knowledge you're seeking. **40** We also take you behind the scenes of the government forecasting centres, the TV studios and other places where your daily weather broadcast is put together.

For all the gains that forecasting has made with the help of computer guidance, humans have not yet been completely removed from the process. **41** You'll learn how the experts decide what to tell you about the upcoming weather and what they may choose to withhold due to limits of time and space, their own uncertainly, politics and other factors.

In the end, weather is what the public choose to make of it. **42** It's hoped that this book makes the weather you experience as enjoyable, understandable and as memorable as possible.

A However, the speed of computers that project weather far into the future is increasing.

B Particularly when the weather turns threatening, skilled forecasters can go a step beyond computer guidance and save lives in the process.

C Descriptions and statistics of the weather in dozens of countries and over two hundred destinations around the world have been collected in it.

D It's the fault of the jet stream, a low-pressure centre or global warming.

E Even though much is known about the individual parts of our atmosphere, the interplay between them can produce what scientists call 'non-linear behaviour'.

F Every weather forecast we see or hear passes through the filter of our own likes, dislikes, hopes and fears.

G These days, hundreds of maps and forecasts can be found on the internet and on TV.

Test 4 Reading and Use of English • Part 7

You are going to read an article in which the four presenters of a TV nature programme show an object and say why it makes them feel close to nature. For questions **43–52**, choose from the paragraphs (**A–D**). The paragraphs may be chosen more than once.

Mark your answers **on the separate answer sheet**.

Which presenter says their chosen object or combination of objects

makes them feel very privileged?	43	
might enable them to help researchers?	44	
makes them realise that what a person really enjoys can change?	45	
is relatively easy to come across?	46	
is selected from a number of possibilities?	47	
connects them with looking after an animal in an inadvisable way?	48	
shows evidence of having been used?	49	
makes them realise how incredibly clever nature is?	50	
was not in fact their original choice?	51	
is now incomplete?	52	

What makes you feel close to nature?

A **Chris Packham** – a deer's antler

I live in woodland and in early summer when I'm out walking, if I'm lucky, I will stumble upon the discarded antlers of fallow bucks, who shed them in April or early May. … I'm as excited as I would have been if I'd found them when I was eight years old. … It's like natural treasure you're honoured to possess, an immediate connection with a shy and elusive animal you've usually only seen at a distance. … Given the size and shape of this one, it has come from a mature animal of around ten years old. It has a story to tell, too: a piece at one end has been chewed off…, probably by a squirrel or another deer looking for calcium. There are scratches, too, on the polished surface where the antler has scraped the ground and trees. … So it's marked with a pattern of use, and I love that. …

B **Gillian Burke** – a 'mermaid's purse'

I have a nature table at home, an eclectic assortment of feathers, shells and crystals collected over decades. There are things I collected as a child and on my filming trips, and now my kids find heaps of things for it too. So my instinct was to take something from that table, as it represents my family's link to nature. In the end, after endless prevarication, I chose a single shark egg case, what people often call a mermaid's purse. … What I like about these egg cases is that, while on one level collecting them can be simply an enjoyable pastime, they can also feed into some real citizen science. The Shark Trust runs a campaign … which encourages people to go online and send in photos and details of any egg cases they've found that can help provide the trust with information about which species are using their waters as their nursery grounds …

C **Michaela Strachan** – my old nature books

Given that my eyes aren't as sharp as they once were, I was initially tempted to bring my binoculars: if I'm anywhere near wildlife I get so frustrated without them. … But then I remembered my old nature books, *British Wild Animals* and *What to Look for in Spring*, which I fell in love with as a child of around seven. What tickles me now is … the advice they give. In one passage we're told that if we find a newt … we're to put it in a home aquarium, which we absolutely wouldn't do now, of course. … The real point, though, is that while I loved wildlife, back then I was far more interested in ballet and gymnastics – it was only later in life that my passion for nature developed. It's a reminder to us all, but particularly to parents, that passions can change. Love of nature is something that can develop at any time.

D **Martin Hughes-Games** – the skulls of a horse and a weasel

I found this horse's skull in a ditch while out walking, and the weasel skull … was uncovered at the bottom of my garden. The disparity in size is what strikes you first, but what I like about them is what they tell us, both about what makes a mammal and about nature's infinite inventiveness.

What makes a mammal skull boils down to two bones, the articular and the quadrate. … In other animal groups they are part of the jaw, but in us mammals they've turned into the incus and the malleus, the tiny little bones in your ear. … It's a reminder that, once nature comes up with a successful design, it's incredibly plastic …

Test 4 Writing • Part 1

You **must** answer this question. Write your answer in **140–190 words** in an appropriate style **on the separate answer sheet**.

---

1 In your English class, you have been talking about food and lifestyles. Now, your English teacher has asked you to write an essay for homework.

Write your essay using **all** the notes and giving reasons for your point of view.

Is it more sensible for people to buy food that is already prepared, rather than waste time cooking meals for themselves?

Notes

Write about:

1 health

2 eating alone / eating with other people

3 .... (your own idea)

Test 4 Writing • Part 2

Write an answer to **one** of the questions **2–4** in this part. Write your answer in **140–190 words** in an appropriate style **on the separate answer sheet**. Put the question number in the box at the top of the answer sheet.

---

2 An international environmental organisation is doing research into traffic around the world. Your college principal has asked students to write a report on the situation in your town.

> Describe how the amount of road traffic has changed a place you know.

Write your **report**.

3 An English-language blogger has posted the following announcement on her website.

> *Articles wanted*
>
> *How do you think that people benefit from writing blogs? And what's the appeal of reading someone else's blog?*

Write your **article**.

4 Your town's English-language website plans to publish reviews of restaurants in your town.

> - Tell us about your favourite restaurant.
> - Describe the atmosphere and explain what kind of customer would or wouldn't enjoy going there.

Write your **review**.

Test 4 Listening • Part 1

53 You will hear people talking in eight different situations. For questions **1–8**, choose the best answer (**A**, **B** or **C**).

---

1 You hear a newsreader talking about his job.
He says that the most important thing about getting work as a newsreader is to
A practise your presentation skills.
B train to be a reporter first.
C be prepared to work unsociable hours.

2 You hear a man telling a friend about surfing.
What does he say?
A He still struggles to keep his balance.
B It was harder to learn than expected.
C He finds it less exciting to go surfing now.

3 You hear a nurse talking about healthy eating.
What is she doing as she talks?
A suggesting why some people have unhealthy diets
B describing typical health problems she sees in patients
C encouraging people to take responsibility for their health

4 You hear an advertisement for a game app.
Which feature of the game is being promoted?
A It is easy to play.
B It has multiple uses.
C It's a way to make friends online.

5 You hear two friends talking about their hobby of fishing.
What do they agree?
A Catching fish is not the most important thing.
B No two fishing experiences are the same.
C It is hard to define the perfect fishing trip.

6 You hear two friends discussing how their town has changed recently.
Why does the woman regret the changes?
A There are more traffic jams than before.
B Public transport is now less convenient.
C Journeys by car have become more complicated.

7 You hear an announcement about a TV programme.
What is the subject of the documentary?
A how to solve people's sleep problems
B why some of us have problems sleeping
C what happens in the brain when we sleep

8 You hear two teachers talking about children and reading.
What is the man's attitude to children's graphic novels?
A They help to motivate certain children to read.
B They can be used for teaching several subjects.
C They are unfairly criticised by his colleagues.

Test 4 Listening • Part 2

54 You will hear a geography student called Sam giving a talk about tea. For questions **9–18**, complete the sentences with a word or short phrase.

Tea

Sam learnt most about tea's history from the **(9)** .... he found online.

Sam gives the example of **(10)** .... being added to tea, to show how tea-drinking habits have changed.

Sam was surprised to learn that a tea plant is in fact a **(11)** ....

According to Sam, a high level of **(12)** .... is essential for all tea plants.

Sam thinks that the best tea comes from leaves that are **(13)** ....

When making a cup of tea, Sam says the **(14)** .... of the water is very important.

Sam recommends mixing **(15)** .... into tea.

Sam says he would never try **(16)** .... tea.

A relative of Sam's drinks tea to help with her **(17)** .... levels.

Sam's ambition is to see a tea **(18)** ....

Test 4 Listening • Part 3

55 You will hear five short extracts in which people are talking about astronomy. For questions **19–23**, choose from the list (**A–H**) why each speaker decided to get involved in astronomy. Use the letters only once. There are three extra letters which you do not need to use.

A I was inspired by an educational visit.

B I was looking for an interest that would challenge me.

C Something I read made me curious about astronomy.

D It gave me the chance to be part of an online community.

E My friends were already interested in astronomy.

F I realised it was something I could do while travelling.

G Astronomy can help improve life on earth.

H A relative of mine was passionate about astronomy.

Speaker 1		**19**
Speaker 2		**20**
Speaker 3		**21**
Speaker 4		**22**
Speaker 5		**23**

Test 4 Listening • Part 4

56 You will hear an interview with a woman called Natasha Green, who is talking about her job as an archaeologist. For questions **24–30**, choose the best answer (**A**, **B** or **C**).

24 What made Natasha want to work as an archaeologist?

A Several of her relatives worked as archaeologists.

B She found something ancient that was very important.

C There were many archaeological sites where she grew up.

25 What does Natasha say about digging in the Sahara Desert?

A She finds the weather to be too challenging at times.

B She is frustrated that there are so many sites to explore.

C She feels jealous of friends spending their holidays relaxing.

26 When starting a new dig, Natasha believes it's important to

A find out what remains have already been uncovered there.

B assemble the best team of archaeologists to take with her.

C be able to quickly interpret the remains that she finds there.

27 Natasha says she often meets people who are unaware that archaeologists need

A the ability to draw well.

B foreign language skills.

C a good knowledge of IT.

28 How does Natasha recommend that children can become involved in archaeology?

A by volunteering to help at a local dig

B by visiting a variety of ancient sites

C by reading widely about the subject

29 When asked what people should do if they find very old objects, Natasha

A urges people to handle them very carefully.

B expresses her anger at people who sell them.

C stresses that people should show them to an expert.

30 How does Natasha see the job of an archaeologist changing in the future?

A More time will be spent protecting sites.

B There will be fewer archaeological digs in cities.

C Remains will be identified without the need to dig.

Test 4 Speaking • Parts 1 and 2

Part 1 2 minutes (3 minutes for groups of three)

Interlocutor First, we'd like to know something about you.

- Do you enjoy using social media? ..... (Why? / Why not?)
- How often do you talk on the phone? ..... (Why?)
- How much exercise do you take a week? ..... (Why?)
- Do you play any team sports? ..... (Why? / Why not?)
- What's your favourite day of the week? ..... (Why?)

Part 2 4 minutes (6 minutes for groups of three)

Interlocutor In this part of the test, I'm going to give each of you two photographs. I'd like you to talk about your photographs on your own for about a minute, and also to answer a question about your partner's photographs.

(*Candidate A*), it's your turn first. Here are your photographs on page C14. They show **people reading in different situations**.
I'd like you to compare the photographs, and say **why you think the people are reading**.

All right?

Candidate A

1 minute ....

Interlocutor Thank you.

(*Candidate B*), **how often do you read magazines**?

Candidate B

approximately 30 seconds ....

Interlocutor Now, *(Candidate B)*, here are your photographs on page C15. They show **people dancing in different places**.

I'd like you to compare the photographs, and say **why you think the people are dancing in these places**.

All right?

Candidate B

1 minute ....

Interlocutor Thank you.

(*Candidate A*), **which of these styles of dancing would you prefer to try**? ..... **(Why?)**

Candidate A

approximately 30 seconds ....

Interlocutor Thank you.

Test 4 Speaking • Parts 3 and 4

Part 3 4 minutes (5 minutes for groups of three)

Interlocutor Now, I'd like you to talk about something together for about two minutes. (*3 minutes for groups of three*).

Here are some things people do that can be creative and a question for you to discuss.

First, you have some time to look at the task.

[Show candidates the diagram on page C16. Allow 15 seconds.]

Now, talk to each other about **how important it is to spend time doing something creative**.

Candidates

2 minutes ....

(3 minutes for groups of three)

Interlocutor Thank you. Now you have about a minute to decide **which activity needs the most creativity**.

Candidates

1 minute ....

(for pairs or groups of three)

Interlocutor Thank you.

Part 4 4 minutes (6 minutes for groups of three)

Interlocutor *Use the following questions, in order, as appropriate:*

- Do you enjoy doing creative activities?
  ….. (Why? / Why not?)
- Is there a new creative activity that you would you like to try?
  ….. (What? / Why?)
- Why do some people choose not to do anything creative in their free time?
- Are some jobs more creative than others?
  (Which ones? / Why?)
- How important is it for teachers to be creative?
  ….. (Why?)
- Is making mistakes an important part of being creative?
  ….. (Why? / Why not?)

Select any of the following prompts, as appropriate:

- What do you think?
- Do you agree?
- And you?

Thank you. That is the end of the test.

Test 5 Reading and Use of English • Part 1

For questions **1–8**, read the text below and decide which answer (**A**, **B**, **C** or **D**) best fits each gap. There is an example at the beginning (**0**).

Mark your answers **on the separate answer sheet.**

Example:

0 **A** likely **B** possible **C** hopeful **D** promising

0	A	B	C	D
	▭	▬	▭	▭

How to achieve success in difficult situations

Psychologists believe that you can give yourself the best **(0)** .... chance to be successful and happy in your life. The **(1)** .... to be successful and happy, they say, comes from within yourself. It is largely a **(2)** .... of how you react to the many problems and difficulties that will inevitably **(3)** .... your way. If you can train yourself to see these problems in a realistic, logical way, and to **(4)** .... that they are a natural part of life, it becomes easier to control and manage them when they **(5)** ....

Successful people **(6)** .... goals for themselves and have plans to **(7)** .... them to achieve these goals. They continually revisit these plans and review them. They are also very good at sensing when they need support and advice, and will seek out the best person to help them in this **(8)** .... They are also flexible and adaptable, knowing when they need to change, and welcoming change as an exciting opportunity.

1	**A** function	**B** capacity	**C** purpose	**D** operation
2	**A** situation	**B** point	**C** question	**D** concern
3	**A** come	**B** take	**C** meet	**D** stand
4	**A** tolerate	**B** approve	**C** receive	**D** accept
5	**A** obtain	**B** result	**C** occur	**D** display
6	**A** bring	**B** put	**C** turn	**D** set
7	**A** let	**B** enable	**C** suit	**D** arrange
8	**A** respect	**B** relevance	**C** reference	**D** relation

Test 5 Reading and Use of English • Part 2

For questions **9–16**, read the text below and think of the word which best fits each gap. Use only **one** word in each gap. There is an example at the beginning (**0**).

Write your answers **IN CAPITAL LETTERS on the separate answer sheet**.

Example: | 0 | F O R |

Meteorite hunter

John Birkenshaw's hobby is searching **(0)** .... meteorites – pieces of rock resulting **(9)** .... a meteor falling through the earth's atmosphere. He has a personal collection of several hundred, all of **(10)** .... he has found himself in several countries. His most successful visit was to the Sahara Desert, as he explains: 'Deserts preserve meteorites well **(11)** .... of the sand and dry conditions. But you can find them just about anywhere if you know **(12)** .... you're looking for.'

Most meteorites contain metal, so you can use either a magnet or a metal detector to find them. They are heavier than other rocks and black **(13)** .... appearance. 'Obviously **(14)** .... you've found one meteorite, there's a strong chance that **(15)** .... will be others nearby,' John says. 'You can search for meteorites on most public land and keep those you find, but it's a different matter if you're on private land, so you always need to seek permission in **(16)** .... situation.'

Test 5 Reading and Use of English • Part 3

For questions **17–24**, read the text below. Use the word given in capitals at the end of some of the lines to form a word that fits in the gap **in the same line**. There is an example at the beginning (**0**).

Write your answers **IN CAPITAL LETTERS on the separate answer sheet.**

Example: **0** | V | I | S | I | B | L | E |

Vancouver

The Canadian city of Vancouver is beautifully situated between the Pacific Ocean
and snow-capped mountains **(0)** .... from many points in the city. **VISION**
The location makes for warm, wet winters and relatively cool, dry summers.
(17) .... much of Canada, Vancouver itself rarely receives snow, **LIKE**
although skiers can easily find good conditions nearby. Vancouver has a unique
and wonderfully **(18)** .... atmosphere. This is partly because the **WELCOME**
climate makes for a laid-back feel with plenty of outdoor living, cafés and
restaurants, and partly because of its ethnic **(19)** .... **DIVERSE**

Vancouver is a great artistic and cultural centre, particularly known for its large
film **(20)** .... centre. Every September it holds the Vancouver **PRODUCE**
International Film Festival, and the city has also been the **(21)** .... for **SET**
many well-known films.

But Vancouver also has a reputation as a green city – **(22)** .... all the **VIRTUAL**
electricity is generated from **(23)** .... resources – and as a nature- **SUSTAIN**
loving place. In this respect, the annual Vancouver Cherry Blossom Festival is a
(24) .... not to be missed! **SEE**

Test 5 Reading and Use of English • Part 4

For questions **25–30**, complete the second sentence so that it has a similar meaning to the first sentence, using the word given. **Do not change the word given.** You must use between **two** and **five** words, including the word given. Here is an example (**0**).

Example:

0 The boat tour was full, so we had to wait an hour for the next one.

PLACES

There .... left on the boat tour, so we had to wait an hour for the next one.

The gap can be filled by the words *were no places*, so you write:

Example:

0	WERE NO PLACES

Write **only** the missing words **IN CAPITAL LETTERS on the separate answer sheet.**

---

25 'I really hope there are no mistakes in the letter I've written,' said Bruce.

CONTAIN

'I really hope the letter I've written .... mistakes.

26 Apart from Helen nobody in the family really loved reading.

ONE

Helen was .... in the family who really loved reading.

27 'I wish I had more talent for languages,' said Toby.

TALENTED

'I wish I .... languages,' said Toby.

28 Maria visited Luke every single day when he was in hospital.

FAILED

When Luke was in hospital, Maria never .... and see him.

29 Lynn wore the dress in spite of it being too big for her.

WRONG

Lynn wore the dress even though .... size for her.

30 The person who finally succeeded in solving the puzzle was David.

MANAGED

In the end, it .... solve the puzzle.

Test 5 Reading and Use of English • Part 5

You are going to read an article about cacti. For questions **31–36**, choose the answer (**A**, **B**, **C** or **D**) which you think fits best according to the text.

Mark your answers **on the separate answer sheet.**

Cacti everywhere!

Paula Cocozza investigates the growing popularity of the cactus.

In many countries, cacti and images of cacti are becoming the next big must-have thing inside people's houses. Cacti inside houses are one thing, but some people seem intent on remaking all their everyday objects in the image of the cactus: cactus candles, lamps and glasses are particularly popular. The world of fashion has caught on too, and the plant has spread with a speed which is inherently uncactus-like, with everything from cactus bracelets to cactus socks. Recently the UK got its first 'cactus boutique' when Gynelle Leon, 31, opened *Prick* in London.

Leon's shop, with its white walls and minimalist shelving, feels more like a gallery. It's an hour before opening time and four large cacti in the window – the ones that are most in demand – are waiting for the shutters to rise and grant them sunlight. They are very expensive but each weekend Leon sells at least one. Her theory, as far as Britain is concerned, is that lots of homeowners now in their 40s had a cactus as a child – in the 1970s there was a smaller cactus 'boom' when the prickly plant was seen as a classic beginners' item. 'They suit people of [my] generation,' she says. 'They want to do less and get more. I could put in minimal effort and a plant will thrive.'

Added to that, they photograph well. 'We're in the whole Pinterest era. You have to have nice plants as well as nice art.' It was her passion for photography that had taken Leon to Yves Saint Laurent's Jardin Majorelle in Morocco where, 'surrounded by these huge plants', she first encountered large cacti. She took some shots and, when she got back home, realised that there was a business opportunity was waiting to happen. Leon then set off on a world tour of cacti hotspots.

One of the stops on Leon's tour was Hot Cactus, 'a shoebox' of a store, according to its co-owner, 'jam-packed with plants' in Los Angeles. 'There's definitely a cactus revival,' says Carlos Morera on the phone from California. 'But I can't say how superficial it is. I can't tell whether people are into the iconography of it and maybe just having these plants as a cool sculpture . . . [or] into all the background information about the plants.' Morera would like the latter to be true. He says that with cacti, 'what you're looking at in front of you is not just what you're looking at. Yes, these plants are cool, but all this other information really makes them . . . . Most people are used to seeing the cliched two-armed emoji cactus. What we were really into was everything but that. And more so, just exposing the incredible vast variety of form and shape and attribute that existed beyond the cliché.'

Judging by the stories he tells, Morera clearly has a knack for tracking down people who are selling cacti collections without realising how valuable they are – and he needs to be, because growers cannot easily keep a cactus trend going. Fashion is all about speed. A cactus cannot be rushed. Those cute plants in 5.5cm pots that you see in garden centres and florists are already three years old. By their nature, cacti are anti-fashion. This has put a good deal of pressure on commercial growers, who are struggling to keep up with demand. This problem is then passed on to the likes of Leon and Morera.

But cacti are also brilliant survivors, adapting to adversity or change. They look as if they have mastered life, and maybe humans feel that's something they could learn from. 'I think they are a reaction to how fast everything moves,' Morera says. 'You have this plant – like a copiapoa – that will not change from the moment you get it till the moment you die. . . . They are a rebellion against modern times, efficiency, production, results. They act as testaments to the opposite.'

31 In the first paragraph, what does the writer object to most?

A keeping cacti as house plants

B having cactus-shaped objects in the house

C manufacturing clothes with images of cacti on them

D shops to open up in response to the demand for cacti

32 Leon thinks that cacti are popular with middle-aged British homeowners because

A they wrongly imagine them to be easy to maintain.

B they see them as a good financial investment.

C they already have a connection with them.

D they like the unusual appearance of them.

33 When Leon visited Morocco, she was

A investigating the possibility of setting up her business.

B on a tour of various places where cacti were popular.

C doing a work project on behalf of a company.

D on a trip not connected with cacti.

34 Carlos Morera hopes that people who are buying cacti

A are able to see the artistic appeal of them.

B are not misled by what they hear in the media.

C are genuinely interested in learning about them.

D are not going to ignore the two-armed variety.

35 What point is made about cactus shops in the fifth paragraph?

A They take a very long time to sell certain cacti.

B They have problems with the supply of their products.

C They have some customers who are very hard to please.

D They tend to sell larger cacti than those in garden centres.

36 Morera suggests that cacti appeal to people nowadays because they are seen as being

A something permanent.

B very different from other plants.

C healthy for mind and body.

D beautiful underneath.

Test 5 Reading and Use of English • Part 6

You are going to read an article about a woman who flew with migrating swans. Six sentences have been removed from the article. Choose from the sentences **A–G** the one which fits each gap (**37–42**). There is one extra sentence which you do not need to use.

Mark your answers **on the separate answer sheet.**

My journey with swans

Conservationist and adventurer Sacha Dench joined Bewick's swans on their 11,000-kilometre migration from Russia to England.

I caught sight of the south coast of England on Nov 29, from the skies above northern France. It was the first moment during my three-month paramotor journey, following Bewick's swans as they migrated from Russia's Arctic tundra to Britain, that I'd thought about coming home. Our final destination, Slimbridge Wetland Centre in Gloucestershire, was a few days away.

Adventure has always been part of my life since I grew up in the remote Australian bush. I spent a lot of time diving under water. I moved to Britain at 15 and later took a biology degree in London. It was there that I took up free-diving as a sport. Free-diving, combined with my conservation interests, took me around the world. I worked for the Environment Agency, spending time in South America looking at indigenous development projects. **37** ____ It was also in South America that I was introduced to paragliding, and after two years I tried a paramotor, basically a paraglider with a motor and propeller attached.

The link between these interests and the plight of the Bewick's swans came last year. I now work at the Wildfowl and Wetlands Trust, and attended a presentation by the top Bewick's researchers. The swans' decline had become rapid, they said, and something needed to be done urgently. **38** ____ The migration route of these birds from the Arctic across ten countries to Britain sounded amazing. How could we use it to find out what was causing the swan's decline and engage the people along the way who were possibly part of the problem?

Some months later the idea came to me. **39** ____ Whenever I'd land in Britain the questioning would be intense – Where have you come from? Why would you do that? – all the kinds of questions we wanted people to be asking about the Bewick's Swans. I realised that in a paramotor I could fly all the places the birds went, at the same speed and altitude, and thus learn a lot more about them.

40 ____ We got permission from the Russians to fly through large parts of their country. I practised water landings in case the paramotor's engine failed when I crossed the English Channel and spent time in a cold chamber testing all the kit. I launched on September 1, supported by a team of 14 people to film me and the birds, and made sure everything ran smoothly. The first time I flew with the swans was magical. They soared in a big "V" formation 50m above me, letting me get the first accurate recording of their speed – 45–50km/hour.

By the time I crossed the Channel, the size of the flock soaring over me was much smaller than it had been in Russia. To date only 150 of the 18,000 swans have made it to Slimbridge. Most of the rest of them will spend winter in the Netherlands; and some will not make it home at all. **41** ____ Alongside changing weather patterns, predation and the disappearance of wetlands are major issues.

Many people simply found it hard to believe that we cared so much. **42** ____ Perhaps next year they'll take interest in a few more of these special birds completing their journeys.

A Preparation began in earnest.

B It taught me the value of telling the stories of conservation, finding ways of involving people.

C There were lows, of course, such as when I dislocated my knee trying to take off.

D I hope my human effort will have inspired them.

E My trip has certainly brought the challenges the birds face into sharp focus.

F Paramotoring is still unusual enough that it fascinates people.

G Their action plan didn't sound like it would work quickly enough.

Test 5 Reading and Use of English • Part 7

You are going to read an article about a chef called Massimo Bottura. For questions **43–52**, choose from the sections (**A–E**). The sections may be chosen more than once.

Mark your answers **on the separate answer sheet**.

In which section does the author mention

an example of co-operation and togetherness which inspired Bottura?	**43**
the speed with which one restaurant came into existence?	**44**
residents who objected to Bottura's plans changing their minds?	**45**
Bottura being invited to act as chef for a particular occasion?	**46**
a comment on the food at The Refettorio from people who ate there?	**47**
the difference between two of Bottura's regular workplaces?	**48**
initial suspicion from the people Bottura was trying to help?	**49**
cooks needing to have a clear idea of what they are going to create?	**50**
the idea of using unwanted food to send out a message to people?	**51**
Bottura being motivated by a desire to prove others wrong?	**52**

The chef on a mission to help others

Tim Adams meets Massimo Bottura

A I am in Milan, Italy, to meet the world-famous Massimo Bottura, at the site of one of his many culinary projects: Refettorio Ambrosiano. Refettorio began as a temporary idea for the Milan World Expo show in 2015. Bottura, 54, had been commissioned to cook for various official functions, including the grand opening. The plan had been to create a kitchen at Milan's central station, in which some of the world's greatest chefs would be invited to cook alongside him for the city's homeless, with food deemed unsuitable for sale in supermarkets, making a statement about waste, and about taste. Instead, Bottura got thinking, and came up with a rather different plan. His thoughts focused on a derelict theatre in the city centre and a full-time commitment to serve Milan's homeless and refugee population every day. Bottura has subsequently set up a foundation – Food for Soul – to operate in other cities worldwide.

B Bottura leads me into Refettorio Ambrosiano, originally a very grand building from around 1930. It is far removed from his top restaurant in nearby Modena, which has 52 staff producing food for 28 guests at lunch and dinner. Here in Milan, two chefs, borrowed from one of the best new restaurants in town, have given up their day to cook at his direction for about a hundred homeless people, assisted by local volunteers. Food is donated by a supermarket – whatever is close to its sell-by date, or misshapen or damaged. The fridges and pantry are stocked with fish and vegetables and fruit, all waiting to be transformed by what Bottura calls 'every chef's key ingredient': his mental vision.

C At school, Bottura had dreams of becoming a professional footballer, but his father insisted he studied law. However, before Bottura finished his studies, he heard that a roadside café was for sale on the outskirts of Modena. He bought the building for next to nothing, renovated it, and opened Trattoria del Campazzo, his first restaurant, a week later. Having been denied the chance to follow his first passion, he was determined it would not happen again. 'Every single person in Modena said I would stay six months at this and then maybe become a mediocre lawyer,' he recalls. 'But I knew I had not to disappoint my mum. She was fighting for me with my father . . . I couldn't let her down . . .'

D The concept of Food for Soul reflects the values given to Bottura as a child. 'I come from a place, Emilia-Romagna, that is extremely social, and that expresses itself in food. That spirit is in the Parmigiano Reggiano Consortium, hundreds of small-scale cheesemakers who see the power of working together with a single voice.' Bottura sees Food for Soul as part of the same spirit. To begin with, the locals were not convinced. When Bottura announced plans to open his kitchen there were some protests from those who believed the initiative would only encourage homeless people to gather in the square. But when protesters saw the commitment of architects, artists and chefs to transforming the area, many changed their minds.

E With Food for Life, Bottura wanted to create a place where disadvantaged people could have at least one hour in a day when they could 'enjoy the pleasure of a beautiful meal in a beautiful place'. To begin with, Bottura says, Refettorio's 'customers' – who are invited as part of a social programme for three months at a time – were unsure. 'People didn't even look in your eyes. They came in, ate in 20 minutes and left immediately.' However, after a month they understood that Bottura and his team were not going away. 'We knew we were being accepted when they started complaining,' he says, with a smile. 'No more soup! We want pasta!'

Test 5 Writing • Part 1

You **must** answer this question. Write your answer in **140–190 words** in an appropriate style **on the separate answer sheet**.

---

1 In your English class, you have been talking about different things that governments spend money on. Now, your English teacher has asked you to write an essay for homework.

Write your essay using **all** the notes and giving reasons for your point of view.

Is it appropriate for governments to spend money on creating public works of art, such as statues and sculptures in parks and town centres? Why? / Why not?

Notes

Write about:

1. benefits of art which is paid for by the government
2. other things which the money could be spent on
3. .... (your own idea)

Test 5 Writing • Part 2

Write an answer to **one** of the questions **2–4** in this part. Write your answer in **140–190 words** in an appropriate style **on the separate answer sheet**. Put the question number in the box at the top of the answer sheet.

---

2 Here is part of a letter you receive from an elderly relative who lives abroad.

> *Actually, I wanted to ask you something. As you know, I haven't got a computer at home. Do you think I should buy one? Will it be easy for me to learn how to use it at my age? And how helpful do you think the internet will be for me?*

Write your **letter**.

3 You see this announcement on your college noticeboard.

> Reports wanted!
>
> Hello. I'm a sociology student in London, and I'm doing my research into how and why people give presents around the world. I want to know what kind of presents people in your country give on special days of the year such as a person's name day or at New Year, or on special occasions like weddings. How has the tradition of giving presents changed over the years?

Write your **report**.

4 You see this in a magazine.

> Articles wanted!
>
> We are going to publish a series of articles about famous people. Write about a famous person who has inspired you. What have you learned from them? To what extent are they a role model for you?

Write your **article**.

Test 5 Listening • Part 1

57 You will hear people talking in eight different situations. For questions **1–8**, choose the best answer (**A**, **B** or **C**).

---

1 You hear two TV critics talking about presenters of science programmes.
During the conversation, the woman makes the point that
- **A** criticism of current presenters is hardly ever justified.
- **B** presenters tend to lack a background in science.
- **C** TV audiences prefer presenters who are celebrities.

2 You hear a psychologist talking about friendship.
He says his best friends are people who
- **A** he works with.
- **B** he went to school with.
- **C** he shares leisure interests with.

3 You hear two friends talking about holidays.
Why does the woman choose to visit small islands on holiday?
- **A** to explore places that are remote
- **B** to escape from an urban environment
- **C** to experience a unique culture

4 You hear a man telling his wife about a product review he has read online.
How does she respond to what he says?
- **A** She questions the reliability of the review.
- **B** She revises her opinion of the product.
- **C** She is amused by the content of the review.

5 You hear a woman leaving a voicemail message.
Why is she late for her appointment?
- **A** She was held up at work.
- **B** She has been stuck in traffic.
- **C** She lost track of time.

6 You hear two students discussing their project on public parks.
What advice does the man decide to follow?
- **A** to focus on one particular park
- **B** to investigate the benefits of public parks
- **C** to look at how parks have changed over time

7 You hear a woman talking about growing up with lots of cousins.
How does the woman feel now?
- **A** sorry that she hardly sees them
- **B** envious of her cousins' achievements
- **C** convinced that it has influenced her as an adult

8 You hear a university student talking about his studies.
What does he say about his degree course?
- **A** He thinks it's easy to transfer to another programme.
- **B** He feels it could improve his employment prospects.
- **C** He will be based in the same place throughout his degree.

Test 5 Listening • Part 2

58 You will hear a man called Bradley promoting a food festival that takes place in his home town in the USA. For questions **9–18**, complete the sentences with a word or short phrase.

The Great Cheese Festival, Wisconsin, USA

Bradley says the festival takes place during what's known locally as **(9)** '..' .

The festival started because a cheese **(10)** .... opened in another region of the USA.

Every year the three-day festival starts with a special **(11)** ....

Bradley's favourite part of the festival is the display of cheese **(12)** ....

This year there will be a cheese **(13)** .... competition for all visitors.

Bradley particularly recommends the **(14)** .... for younger children.

It is essential to get **(15)** .... for the festival.

It's possible to do **(16)** .... in the mornings only.

The people from the community who organise the festival are all **(17)** ....

Money raised at this year's festival will finance a **(18)** .... in the town.

Test 5 Listening • Part 3

59 You will hear five short extracts in which people are talking about buying clothes. For questions **19–23**, choose from the list (**A–H**) what each speaker says is important to them when buying clothes. Use the letters only once. There are three extra letters which you do not need to use.

A I choose clothes I can wear to different occasions.

B I buy well-made clothes that will last a long time.

C I listen to other people's recommendations.

D I look for clothes that are discounted in price.

E I am interested in keeping up with fashion.

F I prefer my clothes to be comfortable to wear.

G I like clothes that reflect my personality.

H I care about environmental issues regarding clothes.

Speaker 1		**19**
Speaker 2		**20**
Speaker 3		**21**
Speaker 4		**22**
Speaker 5		**23**

Test 5 Listening • Part 4

60 You will hear an interview with a professor called Martin Hart and a housebuilder called Anna Peterson, who are talking about houses made out of blocks of straw. For questions **24–30**, choose the best answer (**A**, **B** or **C**).

---

24 What does Martin Hart say about using straw in the construction of houses?

A Large amounts of straw are currently wasted every year.
B The straw used is not good enough quality to give to animals.
C Enough straw can be produced to build a high number of houses.

25 When developing the technology for building straw houses, Martin added bricks to the outside because

A this meant the houses fitted with the surroundings.
B this helped to keep heat inside the houses.
C this made the walls of the houses much straighter.

26 What objection did Martin receive about the straw houses his team built?

A There were concerns about what would happen in a fire.
B People were worried about the carbon dioxide in the walls.
C The walls would not be able to support the weight of the building.

27 Anna Peterson decided to build a straw house for the first time because

A she thought they would become very popular.
B she was curious to experiment with new materials.
C she had clients who expressed an interest in straw houses.

28 When describing her current role in straw house projects, Anna explains that

A she works mainly with the site supervisors.
B she often assists with constructing the roof.
C she personally leads the team of carpenters.

29 The most important consideration for Anna in all her projects now is to

A choose natural materials.
B create unique homes.
C use simple designs.

30 When talking about the future, Anna expresses her desire to

A win an award for her work in building straw houses.
B carry out her plan for building straw houses at a reduced cost.
C teach others the techniques of building straw houses.

Test 5 Speaking • Parts 1 and 2

Part 1 2 minutes (3 minutes for groups of three)

Interlocutor First, we'd like to know something about you.

- How many hours' sleep do you usually have at night? ..... (Why?)
- Have you ever spent the night in a tent? ..... (Why? / Why not?)
- Do you enjoy staying in hotels? ..... (Why? / Why not?)
- Tell us about a book you enjoyed.
- How often do you watch the news on TV? ..... (Why?)

Part 2 4 minutes (6 minutes for groups of three)

Interlocutor In this part of the test, I'm going to give each of you two photographs. I'd like you to talk about your photographs on your own for about a minute, and also to answer a question about your partner's photographs.

(*Candidate A*), it's your turn first. Here are your photographs on page C17. They show **people doing things at home.** I'd like you to compare the photographs, and say **why you think the people are doing these things**.

All right?

Candidate A

1 minute ....

Interlocutor Thank you.

(*Candidate B*), **do you like doing housework**?

Candidate B

approximately 30 seconds ....

Interlocutor Now, *(Candidate B)*, here are your photographs on page C18. They show **how the weather is affecting people in different ways**.

I'd like you to compare the photographs, and say **how you think the weather is affecting the people in these situations**.

All right?

Candidate B

1 minute ....

Interlocutor Thank you.

(*Candidate A*), **do you dislike cold weather**? ..... **(Why?)**

Candidate A

approximately 30 seconds ....

Interlocutor Thank you.

Test 5 Speaking • Parts 3 and 4

Part 3 4 minutes (5 minutes for groups of three)

Interlocutor Now, I'd like you to talk about something together for about two minutes. (3 minutes for groups of three)

Here are some of the things people think about when deciding whether or not to start their own business and a question for you to discuss.

First, you have some time to look at the task.

[Show candidates the diagram on page C19. Allow 15 seconds.]

Now, talk to each other about **what the advantages and disadvantages of running your own business are**.

Candidates

2 minutes ....

(3 minutes for groups of three)

Interlocutor Thank you. Now, you have about a minute to decide **what might be the most difficult thing about running your own business**.

Candidates

1 minute ....

(for pairs or groups of three)

Thank you.

Part 4 4 minutes (6 minutes for groups of three)

Interlocutor *Use the following questions, in order, as appropriate:*

- If you ran a business, what kind of business would it be? ..... Why?
- What's the most effective way to advertise a new business? ..... (Why?)
- Is it a good idea to run a business with a family member? ..... (Why? / Why not?)
- Do you think working people get enough time for holidays? ..... (Why? / Why not?)
- Are people too interested in making lots of money these days? ..... (Why? / Why not?)
- Should big companies give their staff extra benefits such as free health insurance and gym membership? ..... (Why? / Why not?)

Select any of the following prompts, as appropriate:

- What do you think?
- Do you agree?
- And you?

Thank you. That is the end of the test.

Test 6 Reading and Use of English • Part 1

For questions **1–8**, read the text below and decide which answer (**A**, **B**, **C** or **D**) best fits each gap. There is an example at the beginning (**0**).

Mark your answers **on the separate answer sheet**.

Example:

0 **A** degree **B** amount **C** scale **D** step

0	A	B	C	D
	▬	▭	▭	▭

Trampolining and its health benefits

When the North American Space Agency (NASA) famously used trampolines to train astronauts to a high **(0)** .... of fitness, the sporting world **(1)** .... note. NASA claimed that trampolining was the best all-round **(2)** .... of fitness, better even than swimming, running and cycling.

Experts agree that trampolining is excellent background training for sportspeople like sprinters and gymnasts, who need their leg muscles to react very fast. It also **(3)** .... the core very well and is good for balance and co-ordination. Also, if **(4)** .... made by trampolining manufacturers are to be believed, trampolining also **(5)** .... you strong bones and produces endorphins – chemicals which make you happy.

Mini trampolines, often with a handrail **(6)** ...., are often used by sportspeople **(7)** .... from leg or foot injuries. Since you cannot bounce high on them, you can get gentle repetitive exercise for the muscles – without the strain of **(8)** .... on hard ground.

1	**A** made	**B** got	**C** took	**D** wrote
2	**A** way	**B** form	**C** manner	**D** condition
3	**A** runs	**B** plays	**C** functions	**D** exercises
4	**A** claims	**B** calls	**C** challenges	**D** concerns
5	**A** produces	**B** provides	**C** enables	**D** gives
6	**A** attached	**B** involved	**C** accompanied	**D** linked
7	**A** mending	**B** regaining	**C** improving	**D** recovering
8	**A** hitting	**B** coming	**C** landing	**D** putting

Test 6 Reading and Use of English • Part 2

For questions **9–16**, read the text below and think of the word which best fits each gap. Use only **one** word in each gap. There is an example at the beginning (**0**).

Write your answers **IN CAPITAL LETTERS on the separate answer sheet.**

Example: | 0 | M | O | S | T |

The beautiful song of the nightingale

Of all birdsongs, that of the nightingale is arguably the **(0)** .... impressive. It has been widely celebrated by poets and musicians **(9)** .... the ages. William Shakespeare referred to the bird's song in the play *Romeo and Juliet* (1595), and the early 20th-century composer Igor Stravinsky wrote an opera **(10)** .... celebration of it. Today it continues to inspire. Folk musicians still carry **(11)** .... live performances in woods, responding to the bird's song with their own voices or with musical instruments.

The bird, found in Africa, Europe and the Middle East, is small, brown and unremarkable in appearance. It likes to hide in thick bushes, **(12)** .... means it is usually easier to hear **(13)** .... to see. But when the male starts to sing, the sound is like that of **(14)** .... other bird: loud and fast with a mix of high and low notes. The best song can **(15)** .... heard at night in spring, a time **(16)** .... unpaired males sing to attract a mate.

Test 6 Reading and Use of English • Part 3

For questions **17–24**, read the text below. Use the word given in capitals at the end of some of the lines to form a word that fits in the gap **in the same line**. There is an example at the beginning (**0**).

Write your answers **IN CAPITAL LETTERS on the separate answer sheet.**

Example: | **0** | C O A S T A L |

The coffee shop that got it right

In the busy **(0)** .... town of Hastings in southern England, there are	**COAST**
many coffee shops and **(17)** .... for business is fierce. Some of them	**COMPETE**
rely heavily on the **(18)** .... of tourists in the summer, and struggle to	**PRESENT**
survive financially for the rest of the year. But one coffee shop that appears to be	
doing very well is *The Sea Cave*. Tucked away in a dark little side street with no	
view of the sea, and with space only for ten **(19)** .... at a time, at first	**VISIT**
sight it does not look very **(20)** .... from a business point of view.	**PROMISE**
But, in fact, its owners have cleverly made an advantage out of its location and	
small size. Customers are given the **(21)** .... of entering a small	**IMPRESS**
cave. Pieces of seaweed hang down at the **(22)** .... and the	**ENTER**
walls are decorated with pictures of famous sea caves from around the world.	
(23) .... the coffee is excellent, and is not made from	**FORTUNE**
(24) .... sea water!	**SALT**

Test 6 Reading and Use of English • Part 4

For questions **25–30**, complete the second sentence so that it has a similar meaning to the first sentence, using the word given. **Do not change the word given.** You must use between **two** and **five** words, including the word given. Here is an example (**0**).

Example:

0 It took James ages to repair the clock.

LONG

It took James .... the clock working again.

The gap can be filled by the words *a long time to get*, so you write:

Example:	**0**	A LONG TIME TO GET

Write **only** the missing words **IN CAPITAL LETTERS on the separate answer sheet**.

---

25 ‘Please tell me what you’ve decided in a couple of days,’ said the bank manager.

DECISION

‘Please let .... is in a couple of days,’ said the bank manager.

26 ‘If anyone needs to contact me over the weekend, they can ring me at home,’ said Mrs Harris.

TOUCH

‘If anyone needs to .... me over the weekend, they can ring me at home,’ said Mrs Harris.

27 Mark found it difficult to persuade anyone on the committee to accept his ideas.

DIFFICULTY

Mark .... anyone on the committee to accept his ideas.

28 ‘I’d love you to come to the gym one day,’ said Lucinda.

IF

‘I’d love .... to the gym one day,’ said Lucinda.

29 At first, Marie wasn’t sure whether joining the choir was a good idea.

DOUBTS

At first, Marie .... joining the choir.

30 ‘Cricket seems a pointless game to me,’ said Steven.

POINT

‘I can’t .... of cricket as a game,’ said Steven.

Test 6 Reading and Use of English • Part 5

You are going to read an article about calligraphy, a form of elaborate decorative writing. For questions **31–36**, choose the answer (**A**, **B**, **C** or **D**) which you think fits best according to the text.

Mark your answers **on the separate answer sheet**.

What beautiful writing you have: the rise of modern calligraphy

Fiona Wilson tries the art of creating elaborate decorative writing.

I'm sitting at a desk in an immaculate stationery shop named Quill, attempting to master the letter M. 'I've got this,' I think with the false confidence of the beginner, as I dip my pen into the ink and drag the tip across the page. 'Wait,' says my teacher, Quill owner Lucy Edmonds. 'You're not holding your pen correctly. Loosen your grip.' I look at my hand. I'm unexpectedly tense, holding it like a caveman might have held a spear. Lucy tells me to stop treating it like a weapon but to regard it as my friend. 'Try again.' I make a shape. Ink goes everywhere. 'Well done!' Lucy cries politely. The letter may be unidentifiable, but I feel wonderful.

I have always valued good handwriting. I spent three years of my childhood in the USA, where at school I was taught to write using D'Nealian manuscript form, an ornate style of writing that looks rather old-fashioned, and one that I've long since abandoned in favour of general, neat handwriting. With my wedding coming up at the end of the year, and invitation letters to be sent out in the post, this seemed like the ideal time to polish my writing skills. Eighty personalised envelopes to write by hand – doesn't sound too hard a task under normal circumstances. But modern calligraphy, I'm learning, is a completely different animal.

I signed up for a modern calligraphy tutorial with Lucy, a 33-year-old who opened Quill five years ago. She impresses upon me the need to change my mindset: with calligraphy you are essentially drawing a letter rather than writing it. She gives me a dip pen, which can create a finer line than any fountain pen. It's made up of a wooden penholder into which you push a special, delicate tip. Preparing this is an art in itself – you can pass it through a flame, which for me has the right amount of drama and ritual. Others use toothpaste. Then comes the hard bit: holding it correctly. Your fingers should not curl round too much and your thumb shouldn't cross them; the tip has to point to the top of the paper at all times, with the length of your pen in line with your arm.

I'm later reassured by one of Quill's former tutors, Chiara Perano, who runs her own design studio called Lamplighter, that I'm not the only one who has struggled to master this most basic of skills. 'My job is essentially teaching grown-ups how to hold a pen.' Among them, she tells me, she's had a number of primary school teachers trying to get some quality time for themselves. Their reaction is, 'Gosh I feel sorry for the kids now.' Appreciating that it's harder than it looks, the teachers get an insight into what it feels like to learn normal handwriting.

The appeal of modern calligraphy for many is that it looks attractive and requires a fraction of the years that are needed to master the traditional art. Modern calligraphy is loosely based on the ornate copperplate style, but there are far fewer rules and you are encouraged to put your personality into it. With regular practice, you can write reasonably confidently in this style within six months. Which is, mercifully, as long as I have to get my wedding envelopes right.

So why is calligraphy becoming more popular? People have always delighted in the beauty of a calligraphy script, as well as what it communicates. In an age where thankyou letters are texted and essays typed, that value is all the more noticeable. In a recent survey of people's writing habits, one in three said they had not written anything by hand in the previous six months. Is all hope lost? I'm not so sure – the revival has started!

31 What do we learn from the first paragraph?

A Lucy thinks Fiona is not treating the activity seriously enough.

B Fiona thinks calligraphy will be easier than it turns out to be.

C Lucy is pleasantly surprised by Fiona's initial efforts.

D Fiona is discouraged by Lucy's instructions.

32 When Fiona uses the words 'different animal' (line 24), she is contrasting modern calligraphy with

A regular handwriting.

B the typed out letters of today.

C the D'Nealian script she used previously.

D the highly decorative style used in wedding invitations.

33 What does Fiona say about using the dip pen?

A It looks fragile but is in fact very tough.

B It is easier to draw with than write with.

C The technical side of it is what appeals to her.

D There are several possible variations in how you can hold it.

34 Chiara Perano says that trying calligraphy has given primary school teachers

A a feeling of inadequacy.

B a great deal of enjoyment.

C ideas for their own lessons.

D a sense of sympathy with their pupils.

35 In the fifth paragraph, Fiona says that the version of calligraphy she's learning

A has to be followed very strictly.

B is ideally suited to wedding invitations.

C takes a long time to become proficient in.

D is easier to learn than ancient forms of the art.

36 What does Fiona say about the popularity of calligraphy now?

A It may be short-lived as it requires a lot of patience.

B It may return at some unknown point in the future.

C It will continue as people react against social conditions.

D It is surprising given that most people no longer write by hand.

Test 6 Reading and Use of English • Part 6

You are going to read an article about whales. Six sentences have been removed from the article. Choose from the sentences **A–G** the one which fits each gap (**37–42**). There is one extra sentence which you do not need to use.

Mark your answers **on the separate answer sheet.**

How the blue whale became so big

Scientists believe they have now discovered why the largest animal ever to have lived became so big. Blue whales can grow to 30 metres but such size is a relatively recent feature in their evolutionary history. Thirty million years ago, similar filter-feeding whales were much smaller, typically a maximum of 10 metres long. Very large whales began appearing only about two to three million years ago, according to a study of fossil whale skulls by the Smithsonian National Museum of Natural History in Washington DC, USA.

Researchers found that the increase in size coincided with the formation of glaciers in the northern hemisphere. Meltwater from the glaciers flushed nutrients from the land into the sea. **37** ____ This process changed conditions for the prey whales feed on, such as krill and other small crustaceans.

Prey became less evenly distributed around the ocean and much more abundant at certain times and places. Larger whales could make more efficient use of the dense patches of food. **38** ____ They could survive for months without eating, thanks to their vast fat stores.

Nicholas Pyenson, curator of fossil marine mammals at the Smithsonian, said studies showed that different species of whales all grew larger at around the same time. 'We see the extinction of much smaller baleen whales and the sudden appearance of very large body sizes like the blue whales and fin whales that we see today.' Other species of filter-feeding whales, such as the humpback, gray and right whale, were also now 'substantially bigger than anything we find in the fossil record,' he added. 'We live in a time of giants right now.'

While the fossil skulls have been in the Smithsonian collection for many years, scientists were only recently able to confirm that skull width was a good indicator of overall body size. **39** ____ This represents important progress.

Graham Slater from Chicago University, a co-author of the study, said: 'We might imagine that whales just gradually got bigger over time, as if by chance, and perhaps that could explain how these whales became so massive.' **40** ____ And Slater goes on to deny it: 'The only way that you can explain baleen whales becoming the giants they are today is if something changed in the recent past that created an incentive to be a giant and made it disadvantageous to be small.'

Dr Slater said the ancestors of today's filter-feeding whales were originally about three metres long and achieved a maximum size of ten metres after ten million years. **41** ____ Their huge size today results ultimately from this event.

He said the rate at which whales grew larger was 'the million dollar question that we can't answer.' **42** ____ 'We need those to really refine the timing and to understand how quickly this transition actually occurred. But whatever it was, it was pretty quick,' he said.

A It is now accepted that it can also be used to determine changes in length over time.

B They then got no bigger until the formation of the glaciers after which the largest ones trebled in length.

C They were also better able to migrate thousands of miles to find these supplies.

D Baleen whales – the group which includes the Blue Whale – have only been gigantic for the last ten percent of their history.

E This is because fossils from species that lived in the past two million years have not been found in sufficient numbers for scientists to make an accurate assessment.

F But the researchers' analysis shows that this idea doesn't hold up.

G These acted as fertiliser for phytoplankton at the base of the ocean food chain.

Test 6 Reading and Use of English • Part 7

You are going to read an article about a new popular psychology book. For questions **43–52**, choose from the sections (**A–F**). The sections may be chosen more than once.

Mark your answers **on the separate answer sheet**.

In which section does the writer

give an example of a personal goal that failed initially?	**43**
say that he's convinced of the beneficial effects of reading the book?	**44**
say that one idea in the book is backed up by an academic?	**45**
give an example of a personal goal that sounds too big?	**46**
praise the book for giving attention to various bits of research?	**47**
suggest that keeping a promise made to others can be motivating?	**48**
suggest that reading the book itself may be a personal goal some people find too hard?	**49**
say that psychology can sometimes give messages that seem very obvious?	**50**
give a jokey example of a wholly unrealistic personal goal?	**51**
suggest that bold behaviour can be helpful?	**52**

Good intentions and why we don't keep to them

Matthew Syed reports on a new book which explains why our good intentions never seem to last.

A I've always rather disliked 'self-help' books that use ideas from popular psychology to enable people to improve their lives and minds. Everything's too vague, with meaningless references to 'energy flows' and 'getting in touch with one's inner self'. You read about personal ambitions that may have been fine for the author, who's just travelled around the world on a skateboard or a wheelie bin, but don't have much relevance to the rest of us. Occasionally, however, you come across a book with a difference. *Think Small,* written by Owain Service and Rory Gallagher, is based on real behavioural science and examines experiments in different parts of the world. These are applied to practical questions in daily life, such as how to lose weight, how to stick to goals that you've set yourself.

B One trick recommended in the book is breaking a problem down into its component parts. So, if you always had a personal ambition to write a novel, don't just say, 'I'm going to write a book.' Rather say, 'I'm going to write for 45 minutes every weekday morning after breakfast.' Service says, 'When we break big problems into manageable chunks, it becomes easier to deliver. And when we link those chunks with specific aspects of our daily routine, it becomes habitualised and we're on the road to actually completing our projects.'

C Another tip is to make a public commitment. When Gallagher wanted to lose weight, for example, he joined an expensive gym. He thought that the pain of paying so much would inspire him to go but it didn't happen. His waistline kept growing while his bank account kept shrinking. This is evidently a really common phenomenon. So one morning he went into work and wrote on the whiteboard in the middle of the office: I will go to the gym twice a week for three months. He also asked one of his colleagues to referee whether he was sticking to this public declaration. This social commitment, and the subconscious desire to be seen as a man of his word, led to a change in behaviour.

D If you're thinking the tips you read in the book sound like common sense, you'd be right. Most of the insights of behavioural science, when you get down to what they're actually saying, are not unlike the things your grandmother used to tell you. The problem, however, is that we don't always apply common sense to our own lives. As Service says, 'When it comes to our own behaviour, we make too many vague personal goals, and don't have a clear way of monitoring them.'

E Service and Gallagher argue that the personal ambitions likely to make you happiest involve getting healthy and active, learning something new, being more curious, or giving to others. The last factor is particularly powerful. 'Giving your time in the form of volunteering is associated with big increases in life satisfaction' they write. 'These factors have led Harvard professor of psychology, Dan Gilbert, to suggest that helping other people is one of the most selfish things you can decide to do.'

F I don't doubt that putting these things into action will help a lot of people, improving self-reliance, discipline and the forming of good habits. However, as I completed the book, I found myself thinking that the kind of people who read it may have many of these things already. After all, they've formed the intention to buy a book, and then read it from cover to cover. It's the people who bought the book, but never got round to reading it that Service and Gallagher might wish to focus on next.

Test 6 Writing • Part 1

You **must** answer this question. Write your answer in **140–190 words** in an appropriate style **on the separate answer sheet**.

---

1 In your English class, you have been talking about the importance of learning practical skills. Now, your English teacher has asked you to write an essay for homework.

Write your essay using **all** the notes and giving reasons for your point of view.

Learning practical skills (such as cooking, managing money and mending electrical things) is just as important as studying academic subjects. But these skills aren't given enough attention at school. Do you agree?

Notes

Write about:

1 which subjects and skills should be given more / less attention and why

2 possible consequences of any changes

3 .... (your own idea)

Test 6 Writing • Part 2

Write an answer to **one** of the questions **2–4** in this part. Write your answer in **140–190 words** in an appropriate style **on the separate answer sheet**. Put the question number in the box at the top of the answer sheet.

---

2 An online magazine regularly publishes reviews written by consumers.

> Write a review of an electrical device that you bought recently. Outline its strengths and weaknesses, and value for money, with reasons.

Write your **review**.

3 Here is part of an email you have received from a language school in the UK where you once took an English course.

> *The school has had an excellent year, and has some additional money to spend on giving students a better experience. That's why we are now writing to our former students to ask for advice. This money could be spent on one of these things:*
>
> - *sponsoring one student to study here by providing a free course*
> - *taking class trips to special places around the UK.*
>
> *Which option would you recommend and why?*

Write your **email**.

4 The organisers of a public event which you recently attended have asked for feedback from people who were there. In your report you should:

> - explain how the organisation of the event affected its success
> - suggest recommendations for changes that will improve the event.

Write your **report**.

Test 6 Listening • Part 1

61 You will hear people talking in eight different situations. For questions **1–8**, choose the best answer (**A**, **B** or **C**).

---

1 You hear a shop assistant talking about buying bicycles.
What advice does he give?
A Think about what kind of cycling you do.
B Get the best bicycle you can afford.
C Choose a bike with lots of gears.

2 You hear two friends talking about skiing holidays.
What did the woman do differently on her last skiing holiday?
A She booked her holiday a long time in advance.
B She chose an alternative style of accommodation.
C She made her own arrangements regarding a hotel.

3 You hear a woman leaving a voicemail message for a friend about a job interview.
Why is the woman pleased?
A She has been offered the job.
B She was less nervous than she expected.
C She felt she gave the right answers.

4 You hear two people on holiday in Morocco talking about a camel ride they've just done.
What surprised the man about the experience?
A the beauty of the scenery
B the helpfulness of the guide
C the nature of the animals

5 You hear an IT expert talking about passwords.
She suggests that
A changing passwords regularly is advisable.
B there is an acceptable way to write a password down.
C people should avoid having the same password for different things.

6 You hear a guide on a tourist bus being asked about a tall building.
What does she say about the building?
A It offers the best views of the city.
B It's worth visiting at different times of the day.
C It's a popular meeting place for local residents.

7 You hear a local radio announcer giving a traffic report.
There are problems on the motorway because
A emergency services are working in the road.
B a broken-down lorry is blocking the road.
C current weather conditions are slowing traffic.

8 You hear a diving instructor talking to a woman who is learning to dive.
According to the instructor, how is the woman's diving improving?
A She is handling the equipment well.
B She is learning to adjust her speed.
C She is controlling her nerves before a dive.

Test 6 Listening • Part 2

62 You will hear an art student called Ella giving a talk about the history of mirrors. For questions **9–18**, complete the sentences with a word or short phrase.

Mirrors

Ella started her project by studying ancient mirrors made of **(9)** ....

Ella says the Egyptian mirrors she saw had **(10)** .... on them.

Ella was told that all the images on the ancient mirrors were related to the theme of **(11)** ....

Ella says most early mirrors weren't very large because of the **(12)** .... of the material.

Ella read about a **(13)** .... that contained a very big mirror.

Ella uses the word **(14)** .... to describe the shape of early glass mirrors.

The main problem with glass mirrors was the quality of the **(15)** .... in glass production.

During the Renaissance period, mirrors helped to start the **(16)** .... style of art.

In the 1700s mirrors became a feature used in **(17)** .... design.

Mirrors today are based on a technique that someone who worked as a **(18)** .... invented in Germany in the 1800s.

Test 6 Listening • Part 3

63 You will hear five short extracts in which people are talking about restaurants they've been to. For questions **19–23**, choose from the list (**A–H**) why each speaker recommends the restaurant. Use the letters only once. There are three extra letters which you do not need to use.

A The menu changes frequently.

B There is a lively atmosphere.

C The chef is starting to become well-known.

D It is located in a beautiful building.

E The standard of service is very good.

F It is possible to watch the chefs as they cook.

G Local dishes are served.

H The food is good value for money.

Speaker 1		**19**
Speaker 2		**20**
Speaker 3		**21**
Speaker 4		**22**
Speaker 5		**23**

Test 6 Listening • Part 4

64 You will hear an interview with a writer called Eddy Carlton, who is talking about his experience of growing oranges in Spain. For questions **24–30**, choose the best answer (**A**, **B** or **C**).

---

24 Why did Eddy decide to buy the fruit farm in Spain?
A He needed to find a way to increase his income.
B He had wanted to live on a farm for several years.
C He happened to find it for sale during a research trip.

25 What did Eddy discover when he first moved into the farm?
A The trees weren't in a healthy condition.
B The water supply to his farm wasn't adequate.
C The weather wasn't as good as he had expected.

26 What does Eddy say about the local people he met?
A They provided practical help on the farm.
B They advised him to change his working hours.
C They were happy to share their knowledge of fruit growing.

27 What does Eddy say about his writing career since he moved to Spain?
A He has found it easier to do his writing than before.
B The location has been the setting for many of his books.
C Writing has become less important to him than growing oranges.

28 What aspect of growing oranges does Eddy think could affect him?
A It's expensive to pick the oranges by hand.
B People are starting to buy other types of fruit.
C Fewer young people want to work on the land.

29 What has Eddy recently discovered about the area he lives in?
A It used to be famous for a different type of industry.
B It contains many ancient ruins that are rarely visited.
C It has been a popular holiday destination for centuries.

30 What does Eddy hope to do in the future?
A increase the size of his farm
B persuade his children to take over the farm
C convert some farm buildings into holiday accommodation

Test 6 Speaking • Parts 1 and 2

Part 1 2 minutes (3 minutes for groups of three)

Interlocutor First, we'd like to know something about you.

- What kind of music do you listen to most? ..... (Why?)
- Do you play any musical instruments? ..... (Why? / Why not?)
- What kind of job would you like to do in the future? ..... (Why?)
- Do you have any plans for next weekend? ..... (Why? / Why not?)
- Do you like meeting new people? ..... (Why?)

Part 2 4 minutes (6 minutes for groups of three)

Interlocutor In this part of the test, I'm going to give each of you two photographs. I'd like you to talk about your photographs on your own for about a minute, and also to answer a question about your partner's photographs.

(*Candidate A*), it's your turn first. Here are your photographs on page C20. They show **people working together in different places**.

I'd like you to compare the photographs, and say **why you think these people are working together**.

All right?

Candidate A

1 minute ....

Interlocutor Thank you.

(*Candidate B*), **do you enjoy working in a group**? ..... **(Why? / Why not?)**

Candidate B

approximately 30 seconds ....

Interlocutor Now, (*Candidate B*), here are your photographs on page C21. They show **people growing things in different situations**.

I'd like you to compare the photographs, and say **how you think the people are feeling about growing things**.

All right?

Candidate B

1 minute ....

Interlocutor Thank you.

(*Candidate A*), **would you like to spend your free time gardening**? ..... **(Why? / Why not?)**

Candidate A

approximately 30 seconds ....

Interlocutor Thank you.

Test 6 Speaking • Parts 3 and 4

Part 3 4 minutes (5 minutes for groups of three)

Interlocutor Now, I'd like you to talk about something together for about two minutes. (*3 minutes for groups of three*).

Here are some of the things that influence people when choosing to watch films in their free time and a question for you to discuss.

First, you have some time to look at the task.

[Show candidates the diagram on page C22. Allow 15 seconds.]

Now, talk to each other about **why people watch films in their spare time**.

Candidates

2 minutes ....

(3 minutes for groups of three)

Interlocutor Thank you. Now, you have about a minute to decide **what the most common reason is for people watching films**.

Candidates

1 minute ....

(for pairs or groups of three)

Interlocutor Thank you.

Part 4 4 minutes (6 minutes for groups of three)

Interlocutor *Use the following questions, in order, as appropriate:*

- What is the difference between watching a film at home or at the cinema?
- In your opinion, do film actors get paid too much?
- Some books are made into films. Do you think these films should follow the books exactly?
- Should films be entertaining or educational? ..... (Why?)
- Why are some films more memorable than others?
- In your country, is going to the cinema more or less popular than it used to be?

Select any of the following prompts, as appropriate:

- What do you think?
- Do you agree?
- And you?

Thank you. That is the end of the test.

Test 1

LISTENING PART 1

1 Training 1b

Man: Hi, April. What did you think of the guided nature walk we went on? I have to admit, I was really tired afterwards!

Woman: Well, the guide did warn us it'd be seven or eight kilometres. Anything shorter would've been a bit of a waste of time, as we'd never have seen those rare birds down by the lake.

Man: No, they made the walk worthwhile, I'd say. I just thought we'd spot a few other interesting creatures along the way.

Woman: Well, the weather wasn't great, was it? So that might have affected things like the butterflies coming out. I wasn't really expecting to see those, though.

Man: I guess not.

2 3 Training 3 & 4

Man: Have you been to Barnhams?

Woman: Yeah – it's a great store to browse. I spent a long time in the clothing department. The range they had was cool, all the latest stuff. The people working there were keen to help, too. Have you been?

Man: Yes, but I only got there just before they closed. I don't understand why they don't stay open later in the evenings.

Woman: Oh, they do, on Thursdays and Fridays – so that's helpful.

Man: Not for me – I'm at football practice then.

Woman: Right ... So did you find anything?

Man: No, but there were definitely clothes I wanted, and the shop assistant serving tried to find things in my size. Maybe we could go together soon?

Woman: Great!

4 Exam practice

You will hear people talking in eight different situations. For questions 1 to 8, choose the best answer (A, B or C).

1 You hear a man talking about crime fiction.

I got into crime fiction while I was doing voluntary work in Nepal. There wasn't much to do in the evenings and I quickly ran out of paperbacks to read. Someone sent me an e-reader so I downloaded dozens of crime novels. But I barely read a tenth of them. Today I read all sorts of novels but I never buy crime stories. The thing is, I lost interest in them. I'd go so far as to say they're repetitive. After I've finished one, I recall hardly any of what I've read because it was too similar to stories I've read before. I know other people find them immensely satisfying.

2 You hear two sports journalists talking about a tennis player who is retiring.

Woman: Have you heard, Jacob Meyers has announced he's retiring from tennis?

Man: Yes. I'm a bit surprised.

Woman: I suppose, with all his recent injuries, it's only sensible to give up.

Man: Well, when I interviewed him, he expressed the intention of continuing for another two years. Still, he's so committed to tennis, I suspect he's planning to come back and train the next generation of tennis stars.

Woman: There's certainly a shortage of trainers at the moment. He knows he'd be in demand.

Man: Or he might be hoping to present the tennis on television. That pays very well.

Woman: Oh, but he doesn't need the money, and he's always said he's camera-shy.

3 You hear an inventor talking about her work.

I'm often asked to visit colleges and universities to talk about my work as an inventor. I'd be a liar if I said an inventor's ideas come from moments of genius. It's actually about putting in more effort than you thought possible, messing up, and then figuring out why you messed up, and then trying something different over and over again until it eventually works. People queue up hoping to hear a motivational speech from me, inspiring them to go away and dream up the next big idea. The reality can be disappointing for them to hear.

4 You hear two friends discussing their plans for the weekend.

Woman: What are you up to this weekend, Mark?

Man: Picking up my new bike tomorrow, then taking it out on the road. I want to see how it performs on the hills.

Woman: Fantastic! I need to get out on my bike more at weekends. Cycling a kilometre into town to go shopping isn't proper exercise.

Man: Well, you're welcome to join me. I won't be going all that fast.

Woman: I still wouldn't be able to keep up with you! But thanks anyway. Perhaps you could suggest some easy rides for me to start with.

Man: OK, I'll have a think and let you know.

5 You hear a woman talking about crossword puzzles.

I've been doing crosswords on and off since I was a teenager, but, in recent years, I've started to get real pleasure from making this a part of my daily routine. Having said that, I'm not one of those people who keep going for hours until they've completed the whole crossword. I see it more as a really good way to keep fit mentally, and it improves my word power. Some people do crosswords as a way to de-stress, to switch off from everything around them. That doesn't really work for me.

6 You hear two colleagues talking about travelling to work.

Woman: Everything OK, Harry?

Man: Hmm, the train was late this morning and I nearly missed my first meeting of the day.

Woman: It's so frustrating, isn't it? I mean, we pay all this money to get to work and the train service is terrible.

Man: Quite. And it's impossible to work on the train, so you just have to sit there staring out the window.

Woman: Oh, I wouldn't say that. I make the most of my journey by reading reports and catching up with emails.

Man: I can't do that. Still, I wouldn't want to move to an apartment in the busy city centre.

Woman: Me neither. I love my neighbourhood, it's so peaceful.

7 You hear a researcher talking about social media.

Social media's such a big part of many people's lives nowadays, and there's so much discussion about whether this is a good thing or a bad thing. It's almost unimaginable that it didn't even exist only a decade ago. When you explain to younger generations that, in the past, people actually *waited* to hear from each other because there was no instant messaging, some of them think you're actually making it up. Anyway, what I'm currently investigating is the impact on friendships when communication is carried out mainly on social media rather than in person.

8 You hear a woman telling a friend about her experience of using a life coach.

Man: How are you, Karen? Still as busy as ever?

Woman: I'm fine thanks, Charlie. Actually I've just finished my last session with a life coach who's been helping me find ways to achieve my goals.

Man: Wow, sounds interesting! Whenever I give myself a new goal to achieve, I find the harder I try, the more likely I am to fail. Maybe my targets are too ambitious.

Woman: Well, perhaps you need to analyse your goal, and then divide this into a series of mini-goals that are more manageable. That's what my life coach has helped me to understand and what I'm going to do from now on.

Man: Great advice!

LISTENING PART 2

5 6 Training 2 & 4

When my friend and I arrived at the gallery, the exhibition was quite crowded, so I wasn't sure that we'd see much. I knew my friend wanted to see a painting by her favourite artist, which had a rainbow in the sky. We managed to spot that, although the one of a horse I was really keen to find was nowhere to be seen, sadly, as it had been taken away for repair. However, we did spend time looking at another picture of a castle by the same artist and that was beautiful.

7 8 Training 5 & 6

After that, my friend wanted to go to a talk by a famous artist. I thought that might be pretty dull, to be honest, as these things can sometimes be detailed and uninteresting, but I was happy to go with her. Anyway, the artist did have a lot to tell us about her paintings, and in fact the whole thing turned out to be really entertaining, and made everyone laugh!

9 Exam practice

You will hear a talk by a woman called Kelly who ran a long-distance hiking route from the top to the bottom of New Zealand. For questions 9 to 18, complete the sentences with a word or short phrase.

Hi, I'm Kelly and I'm here to talk about a long-distance run I did in New Zealand. It's called the Long Pathway and it starts at the top of North Island and goes all the way to the bottom of the South Island, that's 3,000 kilometres!

My love of running started when I was nine, when my brothers and I used to go running on my grandparents' farm. I've done marathons close to my parents' home for years, but I had to do some serious training before attempting the Long Pathway. I went to stay with a cousin who lives on the edge of a desert – an ideal place to prepare.

Before I left, my best friend set up a website for family and colleagues to follow my progress. My neighbour accompanied me on the trip. She helped with equipment, met me at various points to deliver more food, and was generally my helper. My husband loves running too, but he couldn't get time off work for this trip.

The Long Pathway takes you through varied landscapes, starting in the tropical region of the North Island and ending in the somewhat rainy south. Part of the route involves running on beaches. These were deserted, which couldn't have been more different to the beaches where I live – those are crowded with sunbathers, and noisy with people on jet-skis and those playing volleyball on the sand. It was a completely new experience for me.

It took two months to complete the run and there were a few issues along the way. One of my trainers came off in a stream. I managed to retrieve it, but my sock was very wet that day! I can't tell you how many pairs of sunglasses I broke. The most challenging thing was when I dropped my water bottle – I could have got dehydrated and been really ill, but luckily I had enough fruit to keep me going.

Normally I'm not bothered by rain, but running in the New Zealand rainforests, which were incredibly humid, slowed my progress. Undoubtedly, the highlight for me was crossing the mountains – they were so beautiful. I also had to run through some pretty muddy farmland which isn't something I'd care to repeat.

On the Long Pathway, there's a section in the North Island that's 128 kilometres long where the path disappears and the route goes down a river. At this point, some people take a canoe to cover the distance, which is what I did. Others head for the nearest road and catch a bus to pick up the route further south, but I decided against that.

People often ask me what animals I saw on my run. By far the commonest creatures I came across were sheep: they were everywhere. It was thrilling to witness parrots flying over my head and swooping from tree to tree, though the kiwi birds were nowhere to be seen, and I failed to spot any at all.

Now, you might wonder how a runner can cross from the North to South Island. Some people swim, despite the fact that the water's sometimes chilly, and the waves can get quite high. When I got to the crossing point, there were strong winds, so I crossed what's called the Cook Strait by ferry.

I've also been asked if I got injured during my run. Of course, running every day for weeks, you're bound to get bruised legs, and scratches on your arms are common. I don't really get that many blisters on my feet any more. What was an issue for me was my ankles, which became quite swollen. Thankfully that wasn't until the run was nearly over.

Running every day might seem quite boring, but you develop a routine, until it becomes something completely normal. My only emotion as my final day came to an end was feeling empty. It's funny, I'd imagined I'd feel so happy to reach the end that I might even cry. But once I'd rested, I felt delighted, and really proud.

LISTENING PART 3

10 Training 1

Speaker 1

I've always read lots of fashion magazines, but I think *Starlight* is probably the best one. Most fashion mags usually have something on the front that they're giving away. *Starlight* tends to go for giving you money off the big fashion shows and things like that, which I couldn't possibly afford otherwise, and that's the appeal for me. It does always feature things like the latest pictures of pop groups, too, which I have to admit I usually skip over to find something to read. The writing's not bad, although not many famous authors contribute to the magazine. So, I think I prefer getting absorbed in a long novel, really.

11 Training 3

Speaker 2

I find browsing through magazines, and looking at the adverts is a good way to relax after a long day. The one I buy the most frequently, *Radar,* is a local magazine, and has things like word games that make you concentrate a bit. So they're OK for passing the time on my train journey home, say, although you can find similar ones in other magazines. What attracts me to this mag, really, is reading what other readers have sent into the magazine, usually giving advice on what to do – anything from local events they've been to, to recommendations about a new writer, say. I've learnt some useful stuff from there.

12 Exam practice

Part Three

You will hear five short extracts in which people are talking about camping trips. For questions 19 to 23, choose from the list (A to H) what opinion each speaker gives about the camping trip they went on. Use each letter only once. There are three extra letters which you do not need to use.

Speaker 1

My parents and I went camping as a family for the first time this summer. I was home on vacation from college because I couldn't afford to go travelling with my college friends and didn't have anything else to do. My mom had done her research and picked a campsite near a lake and a forest with a huge network of trails and, while my parents chilled out by the lake every day, I spent the whole week mountain biking. It did wonders for my fitness levels. Still, it would have been nice to have had a hot bath in the evening.

Speaker 2

I went camping this summer as part of my holiday job accompanying a group of children from the city on a multi-activity sports holiday. I got paid for it, which was fortunate as it wasn't actually a holiday for me. I loved all the fresh air though, and cooking on the barbecue was great fun. When I next have a break, I'll be certain to go back. Only this time with my best friend, rather than a group of lively eight-year-olds. They couldn't sleep at night because they hadn't brought a proper camping mat to lie on and suitable clothes to keep them warm during the night.

Speaker 3

My children kept asking to go camping, but when I take a vacation, I just wanna do nothing. I certainly haven't the energy to put up tents and cook outdoors. Anyway, I gave in to pressure and took forever researching the best place to camp and eventually found somewhere not too far from home with tents that were already set up. I can't say it was my ideal vacation, though everyone else is asking to go again. What was great, was that it reminded me of when I used to put up a tent in the back yard with my sister, and eat candies and tell funny stories all night.

Speaker 4

Apparently we used to go camping when I was really young because my parents couldn't afford to take us to a hotel, but that was so long ago, I don't remember it. Some friends recently suggested a camping and fishing trip and I couldn't think of an excuse not to go. When we got to the campsite, it turned out my mate had chosen this amazing luxury place – with raised beds with mattresses and even heaters in the tent, which made it lovely and cosy. And to think, I'd been dreading having to sleep on bare rock by the river. It couldn't have been further from my expectations.

Speaker 5

I'm a busy person with a demanding job, and during term-time I don't spend much time with my children. Normally when we go away, we book a holiday apartment – nothing too expensive – but last summer we went camping. And do you know, all of us sharing a tent together was great. Far from getting on each other's nerves cos we weren't used to each other's company, we all became great mates. We really appreciated the quality time we spent as a family. My sons want to go again, but to be honest, it was quite a lot of hard work, and I can't say I slept brilliantly.

LISTENING PART 4

13 Training 1

Man: So, Alice, you've made some changes to your business. How do you feel about the business now?

Alice: Well, just to give you some of the background, I started by selling flowers from my own shop, and that attracted a lot of passing customers – often people who'd pop in to buy flowers when they'd forgotten someone's birthday, and they'd often stop to chat. But running the premises just became too expensive, so I was really glad when I started operating solely on the internet, which has just been so much better – I've saved a lot of time and money. So, people look on my website and choose what they'd like or, as many florists will do, I can make up a bouquet if they have something special in mind.

14 15 Training 3 & 4

Man: So do you think people really understand what your job involves?

Alice: Well, I'm sure they think it's a very pleasant job, and of course it's great to sell beautiful flowers, as they're a very special gift. But it's considerably more demanding than you might think. I mean, obviously I have to be very creative when putting flowers together, choosing colours, arranging – and customers do understand and appreciate that. But what perhaps isn't so obvious is that I have to be extremely sympathetic to my customers' needs. For example, if the flowers are for a wedding, then my customers could be in the middle of all sorts of stressful stuff, so I try to take some of the pressure off by supplying exactly the flowers they want.

16 Exam practice

You will hear an interview with a man called Jamie Cole, who is talking about his experience of writing his first recipe book. For questions 24 to 30, choose the best answer (A, B or C).

Interviewer: Today I'm talking to Jamie Cole, who's just had his first recipe book published. Jamie, thanks for coming along to talk about your experience of writing your book, *My Kitchen Recipes*.

Jamie: You're welcome, and thanks for mentioning the title!

Interviewer: What made you want to write the book?

Jamie: I was working for a food magazine, not as a writer, but as a tester of recipes – you know, trying out recipes to check they worked before printing them in the magazine. I'd always enjoyed creating my own recipes at home – not necessarily with great results! – but my job gave me an in-depth knowledge of how and why recipes work, and I felt sure I could write something people would want to buy. My co-worker Alison said, 'Jamie, it's not worth it,' but I went ahead anyway.

Interviewer: So, as a first-time writer, was it easy to get a book deal?

Jamie: I couldn't have been luckier, to be honest. The usual approach involves hiring an agent to try and get you a contract with a publisher of recipe books, but I talked to my editor at the food magazine about the concept for my book, and she was so impressed, she put me in touch with a publishing company straightaway. I was really grateful to her.

Interviewer: That was lucky! Was it hard to sit down and write a whole book of recipes?

Jamie: Well, I'd already done most of my research, which made the actual writing process shorter. It was hard sitting at a desk typing on my computer for hours. And because I had to try out each recipe several times, as a kind of quality check, I was forever making trips to the supermarket to re-stock my fridge and cupboard. That was the toughest thing, 'cos I found it so monotonous, and I was always impatient to get back to my kitchen, where I'm happiest.

Interviewer: And since the launch, you've been signing copies of your book in bookstores.

Jamie: Correct. It's been absolutely great meeting some of the people who've bought my book. They're quite curious and want to know all kinds of things about the book. A frequent question is, 'Have the photos been altered to make the finished dishes look more attractive?' The answer's 'no', by the way. Nobody's asked me yet how much of the book price I receive. And I'm still waiting for the day when someone asks whether I wrote all 175 recipes in my book myself.

Interviewer: Your book's out-selling many titles by famous chefs. Why do think that is?

Jamie: Good question. When you walk into a bookstore or look online, there's literally thousands of titles to choose from, ranging from beginner-level recipes to advanced techniques for semi-professionals. I guess I avoided using ingredients that are hard to find in food stores, and focused on tasty meals that busy individuals can put together in a hurry.

Interviewer: Interesting. Jamie, do you have any advice for someone who's considering writing a recipe book?

Jamie: Erm … whether you're a full-time chef or someone who loves to make cookies on the weekend, if you have enough recipes for a book, I'd say go for it. But I'd also say concentrate on what you do best – you might be a pastry chef, or an expert in Japanese cuisine, for example. You also have to know what you're doing in the kitchen, like how to use a knife properly. But you can teach yourself these essential skills, which is much less bother than signing up for cookery classes.

Interviewer: That's great advice. So, what's next for you?

Jamie: I have so many ambitions and plans. My schedule for next year's looking really busy – I'm filming a ten-part TV series in my own kitchen! I'd love to do a big trip, maybe around Asia, to get inspiration for my next publications, but that won't be possible yet. One thing I'm about to launch is *Jamie's Blog*, so that I can let people know what I'm doing, and get more feedback on my recipe book. That's really important.

Interviewer: Good luck …

SPEAKING PART 1

17 Training 3

Examiner: Where are you from, Ana?

Ana: I'm from Madrid. It's the capital of Spain, and it's also the largest city.

Examiner: What do you like about living in your home town?

Ana: It's a really exciting city because there are lots of things to do. For example, there are lots of cafés where I can meet my friends. There are plenty of events such as concerts and festivals, too.

Examiner: What sort of things do you do in your free time?

Ana: I spend a lot of time with my friends. I would say that I'm a very sociable person, so my friends are important to me. I'm also keen on sport, so I play tennis once or twice a week.

Examiner: In what ways do you think you will use English in the future?

Ana: Sorry, can you say that again?

Examiner: Yes. In what ways do you think you will use English in the future?

Ana: I think that English will be very important for me in my work. The reason for this is that I'd like to work for an international company, and I'd like to travel in Europe and the United States.

SPEAKING PART 2

18 Training 2

Examiner: In this part of the test I'm going to give each of you two photographs. I'd like you to talk about your photographs on your own for about a minute, and also to answer a question about your partner's photographs. Paul, it's your turn first. Here are your photographs. They show people doing exercise. I'd like you to compare the photographs and say why people might choose to do exercise in these different ways. All right?

Paul: Well, both photos show people doing exercise. In the first photo, the people are doing an exercise class, while in the second photo a group of people are playing basketball together. The people in the gym don't seem to know each other, because they aren't talking to each other. On the other hand, I think the people playing basketball are probably friends, because it looks like an informal game. The exercise class looks quite serious, whereas the basketball game looks very relaxed. The people in the gym don't look as happy as the people playing basketball. They aren't smiling, and the woman on the right looks a bit bored. I think the people playing basketball are probably enjoying themselves more because it's fun to meet your friends and do sport with them. Another difference is that the basketball is outside, which I think makes it more fun. I think people go to exercise classes because they want to get fit, and maybe it fits in with their busy lives. I think the people in the second photo do this because it's an enjoyable way to meet their friends and have fun. I'd rather do exercise in a fun way, like this, because I think just doing exercise in a gym is a bit boring.

19 Training 3

Paul: Well, both photos show people doing exercise. In the first photo, the people are doing an exercise class, while in the second photo a group of people are playing basketball together. The people in the gym don't seem to know each other, because they aren't talking to each other. On the other hand, I think the people playing basketball are probably friends, because it looks like an informal game. The exercise class looks quite serious, whereas the basketball game looks very relaxed. The people in the gym don't look as happy as the people playing basketball. They aren't smiling, and the woman on the right looks a bit bored. I think the people playing basketball are probably enjoying themselves more because it's fun to meet your friends and do sport with them. Another difference is that the basketball is outside, which I think makes it more fun. I think people go to exercise classes because they want to get fit, and maybe it fits in with their busy lives. I think the people in the second photo do this because it's an enjoyable way to meet their friends and have fun. I'd rather do exercise in a fun way, like this, because I think just doing exercise in a gym is a bit boring.

20 Training 5

Examiner: Ela, do you prefer to do exercise alone or with friends?

Ela: I'd rather do exercise with friends, definitely. Like Paul says, it's more fun if you do a sport with friends, and more relaxing, too. I wouldn't have the motivation to go to the gym on my own, for example, because I find it boring, but I often play tennis with my friends in the summer, and I really enjoy that.

21 Training 7

Examiner: In this part of the test I'm going to give each of you two photographs. I'd like you to talk about your photographs on your own for about a minute, and also to answer a question about your partner's photographs. Natalie, it's your turn first. Here are your photographs. They show people celebrating achievements. I'd like you to compare the photographs and say how you think the people might feel about their achievements. All right?

Natalie: Both photos show people who have achieved something important, and are celebrating. They are similar because both achievements involve a lot of physical effort. In the first photo, the people might have climbed for several days to reach the top of the mountain. In the second photo, the players have probably played a very difficult game to win the trophy. Another similarity is that to achieve both these things, you have to train very seriously for a long time, and be dedicated to your sport. The people in both photos look happy because they have lifted their arms up to celebrate.

I think the mountain climbers probably feel exhausted after such a long climb, and I think the football players must be really proud of themselves because they all look very happy. One difference between the achievements is that the football players have competed against other people, whereas the mountain climbers have only competed with themselves. Also, the mountain climbers can only celebrate their achievement with each other, whereas the football players can see all their fans cheering for them. Another big difference is that the football players can relax and celebrate now. On the other hand, the mountain climbers still have to get back down the mountain safely. Personally, I think that what the mountain climbers have achieved is more impressive because what they have done is dangerous, and they have to motivate themselves to continue, even when it's difficult.

22 Training 9

Natalie: Both photos show people who have achieved something important, and are celebrating. They are similar because both achievements involve a lot of physical effort. In the first photo, the people might have climbed for several days to reach the top of the mountain. In the second photo, the players have probably played a very difficult game to win the trophy. Another similarity is that to achieve both these things, you have to train very seriously for a long time, and be dedicated to your sport. The people in both photos look happy because they have lifted their arms up to celebrate. I think the mountain climbers probably feel exhausted after such a long climb, and I think the football players must be really proud of themselves because they all look very happy. One difference between the achievements is that the football players have competed against other people, whereas the mountain climbers have only competed with themselves. Also, the mountain climbers can only celebrate their achievement with each other, whereas the football players can see all their fans cheering for them. Another big difference is that the football players can relax and celebrate now. On the other hand, the mountain climbers still have to get back down the mountain safely. Personally, I think that what the mountain climbers have achieved is more impressive because what they have done is dangerous, and they have to motivate themselves to continue, even when it's difficult.

Examiner: George, which achievement do you admire the most?

23 Training 10

George: I think both achievements are very impressive. As Natalie said, they are both very difficult physically, and people need a lot of determination to do them. I would say I admire the mountain climbers more because climbing a very high mountain can be very dangerous, so I think they need to be brave and mentally strong as well as determined.

SPEAKING PART 3

24 Training 3

Examiner: Now, I'd like you to talk about something together for about two minutes. Teenagers often complain about having nothing to do and say they would like better facilities in their town. Here are some things that might improve a town for teenagers and a question for you to discuss. First you have some time to look at the task.

Sofia: Shall we start with providing parks? This sounds like a good idea. Parks are places where teenagers can meet with their friends and just hang out.

Chang: I can see what you mean, but parks are no good when the weather's bad, for example if it's raining or snowing. I think more cafés might be a better idea, because people can go there all year, even in winter.

Sofia: Yes, you're right. I hadn't thought about that. What do you think about the idea of a new cinema? A lot of young people like watching films, don't they? And the cinema is also a good place to meet friends.

Chang: Yes, that's true, but it's quite expensive to go to the cinema, and I think a lot of teenagers prefer to watch films at home, on their laptops or tablets. They might go to the cinema from time to time, but I don't think they would go every week.

Sofia: Yes, I agree. And I think the same is true for cafés. They're a good place to meet, but you need money.

Chang: Yes, and it's a bit boring, just sitting around chatting. I think the sports centre sounds like a good idea. With sports centres, you can go every day and do something different. Would you agree with that?

Sofia: Yes, I completely agree with you. And it might be a good idea to have a special low price for teenagers, so they wouldn't need much money.

Chang: That's a good idea. So, what about an annual music festival? I think that could definitely improve teenagers' lives because all teenagers love music. Do you agree?

Sofia: Yes, I do. They could watch the bands, of course, and it might also encourage them to form their own bands, so they could take part.

Chang: Yes, you're right. There would be jobs for older teenagers, too, helping with the festival.

25 Training 4

Examiner: Thank you. Now you have a minute to decide which idea would bring the most benefit to teenagers.

Chang: So, what do you think would bring the most benefit?

Sofia: Well, I think either the sports centre or the music festival. Of course, you can do sports in a park, too, but a sports centre is better, because you can use it all year and there are more things to do.

Chang: That's true, and it's also healthy to encourage young people to do sport. On the other hand, a music festival is really exciting for teenagers, and might encourage them to do music themselves.

Sofia: But a music festival is only once a year, whereas you can go to a sports centre all year.

Chang: That's true, so perhaps we should choose the sports centre?

Sofia: Yes, let's go for that.

SPEAKING PART 4

26 Training 2

Examiner: Hans, do you enjoy going to the cinema?

Hans: Yes, I do because I like films, and I enjoy watching them on a big screen. I think you get a much better experience when you watch a film on a big screen.

Examiner: And Maria, do you enjoy going to the cinema?

Maria: Yes, sometimes. There's a big cinema in my town and I sometimes meet my friends there at the weekend. But I also think it's fun to watch a movie at home with some friends, because then you can have some food at the same time, and you can also chat. What do you think, Hans?

Hans: Yes, I agree with you. It's more relaxing if you watch a film at home. I do that sometimes, too, with my friends.

Examiner: OK. Hans, what kinds of films are popular in your country?

Hans: Could you repeat the question, please?

Examiner: Yes. What kinds of films are popular in your country?

Hans: Oh, definitely American films, especially adventure films and science fiction films. They're very popular with young people in my country. In my opinion, films from Hollywood are the best, because they have the best actors, and also the special effects are very good. What about in your country, Maria?

Maria: Yes, American films are popular, of course, but there are also a lot of good Spanish films, and these are also popular in my country. I think the American films are often very exciting, but Spanish films are often more serious, so they make you think more.

Hans: Yes, but on the other hand American films are very good entertainment, and I think for most people that's the most important thing.

27 Training 3

1 I'd say that doing regular exercise is really important for your health.
2 I think that the sports facilities in my town are quite good.
3 In my opinion, towns and cities should do more to encourage people to cycle.
4 My own view is that schools should encourage young people to take up a sport.
5 What's your opinion of the new sports centre?
6 What do you think about team sports?
7 What are your views about big sporting events such as marathons?
8 How do you feel about providing outdoor gyms in towns and cities?

28 Training 4

1

Woman: In my opinion, governments should do more to encourage people to recycle things.

Man: Yes, but on the other hand, it's also up to individuals to take responsibility for this.

2

Man: I think cars should be banned in cities because they cause so much pollution.

Woman: Yes, but don't you think that some old people would suffer because they might need their cars?

3

Woman: My own view is that food companies and supermarkets use too much packaging, which is bad for the environment.

Man: Yes, but wouldn't you agree that some foods need packaging to keep them fresh?

4

Man: I'd say that flying should be much more expensive because it's bad for the environment.

Woman: Yes, but you could also argue that that's not fair because then people who have a lot of money could still fly, but poorer people wouldn't be able to.

5

Woman: I think all countries should reduce the amount of pollution they cause.

Man: Yes, but another way of looking at it would be that the countries that caused all the pollution should reduce their pollution most.

29 Training 5

1 In my opinion, governments should do more to encourage people to recycle things.
2 I think cars should be banned in cities because they cause so much pollution.
3 My own view is that food companies and supermarkets use too much packaging, which is bad for the environment.
4 I'd say that flying should be much more expensive because it's bad for the environment.
5 I think all countries should reduce the amount of pollution they cause.

Test 2

LISTENING PART 1

30 31 Training 2 & 4

Now everyone, we're currently standing in what's probably the most beautiful square in the whole city – in my view, of course! Anyway, there are certainly plenty of other nice places for you to explore and compare it with. So maybe you can decide at the end of your stay whether you agree with me, and let me know! I'm going to give each of you a map, so you'll be able to follow exactly where we are as we walk round the main sights together. And then you can have some time on your own to have a look around at the places that appeal to you.

32 Training 5

Hi, Ben. It's Karla! I'm just ringing about next week's concert – you know, the band we wondered about seeing? Well, I've just been down to the concert hall to find out about tickets 'cos their website's been down all day – and apparently they're rather more expensive than we'd been told, and I'm not sure I can really afford it, to be honest. So I'm really sorry – although I think we did agree they weren't really our first choice of band to see, didn't we? Anyway, let me know if you have any ideas about what you want to do instead, OK? I'm happy to go along with whatever!

33 Exam practice 3

You will hear people talking in eight different situations. For questions 1 to 8, choose the best answer (A, B or C).

1 You hear two neighbours talking about a new statue in their town.

Man: Have you heard about the statue that was put up in the main square last week? People are calling for it to be taken down.

Woman: Hmm, the money's been spent on it now, so that's unlikely to happen. In general, I'm not a fan of modern sculpture, but I went to see it at the weekend. Nobody can say it's unattractive to look at, but if you asked me what it's supposed to show, I'd have to say I've no idea.

Man: Well, it's created such a debate, I shall have to go and have a look.

2 You hear a music teacher talking about his job.

I'm not exaggerating when I say being a music teacher's a great job. I get to teach kids how to create music, I have lots of time off for vacation, and the pay's not bad either. And I have the privilege of introducing young people to the music that means so much to me, and hopefully create a new generation of music lovers. That being said, it saddens me when I hear so many people say that our job is nothing but fun and games. They should try coming into one of my final year classes – they'd see how demanding the work is then.

3 You hear two journalists talking about driverless cars.

Woman: I've just done a report on driverless cars.

Man: Well, they do say that's what we'll all be using in the future.

Woman: Hmm … *I* wouldn't want to go around the city in a driverless car, would you?

Man: Of course. I'd love the chance to test one out.

Woman: You'd be in the minority, according to my research. People are worried about whether driverless cars would stop for other cars. And, more to the point, who'd be responsible if a driverless car bumped into another car?

Man: That's something the government will have to create a whole new set of regulations about.

Woman: I couldn't agree more. And they'll have to start work on this soon.

4 You hear a doctor talking on the radio about colds.

It always surprises me how many patients still make appointments to see me when they're suffering from colds. Some public health messages *have* got through, and I'm hardly ever asked for antibiotics any more – people understand they're not a cure for a cold – but I find myself having to give people advice about hand washing and the importance of staying away from others who have a cold, in order to keep well. It's amazing how many times patients say they'd never heard that made a difference. But at least people seem to know that a diet rich in fruit and vegetables can help you to get over a cold more quickly.

5 You hear a brother and sister talking about a musical they have seen.

Man: Did you enjoy that?

Woman: Yes, it's the third time I've seen this musical and it was just as good as the first.

Man: Ah, that's why you knew the words and were singing along to everything.

Woman: Well, I've had the CD for years, but I don't know *all* the words. I wouldn't compare myself to the main character and I don't always understand the reasons for her behaviour, but the story's basically about friendship and family, and what brings people together – things I care deeply about. I find it a really touching story.

Man: Yes, it's quite emotional.

6 You hear a woman talking about horse riding.

I took up riding again recently, after a break of more than ten years. I'd had an accident while I was out running one day. And after that, I didn't feel physically strong enough to control a horse and keep myself upright in the saddle. And then I got a really busy job and was away travelling a lot, and I just didn't go back to riding for ages. I'm so glad I have now though, as I've got a fantastic social life out of it. I seem to have so much in common with the people I've met recently through riding.

7 You hear a customer complaining in a department store.

Woman: Can I help you?

Man: Yes. I bought this sweater last week and wore it once, and it's shrunk in the wash. I can hardly get it over my head, it's so small now. I followed the washing instructions properly.

Woman: Oh, I'm sorry about that. Would you like to swap it for a new one?

Man: Actually, I don't want another one, but I would like to buy something in your shoe section. Could you give me a credit note and I'll use that for some new trainers?

Woman: Well, I can give you your money back on the jumper. We don't do credit notes any more, I'm afraid.

Man: OK, that's fine.

8 You hear a food critic talking about a chef called Peter Tinney.

The award-winning chef Peter Tinney has just been voted Chef of the Year by the readers of *Great Food* magazine. Peter's been well known for his inventive approach to every dish he creates for the menu at his chain of fine-dining outlets. His announcement that he plans to shut these in the new year, and move on to become a presenter of food programmes on satellite TV, has been met with disbelief by the public and food critics alike. But as Peter himself said, he wants to be able to give his full attention to his new project. This makes complete sense to me, even though the public will be disappointed.

LISTENING PART 2

34 Training 2

Hello everyone! Today I'm here to tell you all about a type of food that you probably eat a lot, but don't really know much about – honey! Now, did you know that honey has been used all over the world for centuries? And people have used it for very different purposes. For example, some scientists believe that it can boost people's ability to fight diseases, such as ones that affect the heart. It's also common practice for people all over the world to try and make their skin better by drinking milk and honey. And some athletes also use it to give them extra energy and help their performance.

35 Training 5

Of course, when you're thinking about what honey to buy, there are a lot of different types to choose from! And the flavour can vary enormously, depending on the types of flowers the bees have visited, and the methods used to produce it. Of course, you may want to ensure you get the best quality of honey available, and sometimes you can tell that from the colour, but just because it's expensive, it doesn't always mean it's the best.

36 Exam practice 2

You will hear a cameraman called Chris giving a talk about filming a wildlife documentary in Gabon, Africa. For questions 9 to 18, complete the sentences with a word or short phrase.

Hi, I'm Chris and I work as a cameraman. I've just come back from Gabon in Africa, where I've been filming a wildlife documentary.

I'd never been to Gabon before, and my knowledge of the country was very limited. I don't remember ever seeing any other documentary about it before. Come to think of it, I'd never read anything about the country in the newspaper either. But one day I happened to spot a crazy advert that showed hippos swimming in the sea, and I thought, I have to go there!

So, when I was asked to go on a film trip there, I jumped at the chance. I checked on a website that gave me lots of statistics about the country, but it was a guidebook that told me what I really needed to know. I read it from cover to cover. I was also given a file of research notes to read, but it wasn't very detailed.

My boss, Maria, helped with preparations. I've been to other African countries and had already had the injections you need if you're travelling there. But Maria said I should make sure I applied for a work visa, not an ordinary visitor visa, otherwise they wouldn't let me in the country. Luckily, I didn't need a mosquito net or special clothing – I had those already.

When I arrived in Gabon, I was met by a driver, who took me to my hotel in the capital. There I was introduced to a biologist who I thought had come along to give me some background information. But it turned out he'd volunteered to accompany me for the duration of my trip. I was so happy because it was like having a teacher with me the whole time. I learnt lots.

Filming was mostly to take place in Loango National Park, on the coast. Getting there involved a flight in a small plane during a storm – not something I'd recommend. I was grateful for the helicopter that covered a vast area of forest, as that spared me hours travelling in a safari jeep on a dirt road. Finally, we took a short, but not very pleasant, ride in a speedboat, to reach our destination, the beach.

The first animals I spotted on the beach at Loango were forest elephants. My guide explained they're shy creatures that hide in the forest where they get most of their food, typically leaves, fruit and bark. Occasionally though, they leave the forest alone or in small groups, in search of salt, which is plentiful on the beach.

After that, I got some great shots of buffalo going for a walk on the beach. And then to my amazement, several of them headed off into the water. To me they seemed to be surfing, and my guide laughed when I told him that. They were probably just cooling off rather than swimming properly.

We spent several weeks at this location because there was so much to see. I spent hours looking though my camera at hippos, and various kinds of birds, and even managed to catch a few seconds of a gorilla. Every morning there were tracks left by leopards that had passed through in the night, but they never appeared during the day.

After the beach, we headed to one of the few villages in this region, to stay in a traditional house. The locals were very welcoming, and cooked lots of delicious food for us. It was really curious meeting them as they weren't used to strangers. I had expected them to be shy or nervous around us, which wasn't the case.

The Loango National Park takes conservation seriously, and animal numbers have increased steadily in the last decade, which is great news. However, despite the building of a new road and several luxury hotels, tourism has hardly increased at all. Hopefully films like mine'll help.

LISTENING PART 3

37 Training 3

Speaker 1

Starting a new job can be stressful. I remember feeling nervous the night before, and not being able to sleep that well. But by the time the first day was over, I was really wondering what I'd been so worried about! I soon made friends with my new work colleagues, and luckily I'd done some research on the company beforehand, so I knew who the boss was, and who her team were. Sounds really obvious, but that's pretty important, I'd say, so that you know exactly who it is you might be talking to. Anyway, I'm pleased to say, I'd chosen the right kind of clothes to put on that morning, so I didn't stand out because of the way I was dressed!

38 39 Training 5 & 6

Speaker 2

I can clearly remember my first day in my first ever job. I'd practised the route to the office the day before, and set off an hour before I needed to, as I was determined not to be late that morning! A bit silly, really! Anyway, the first day was pretty confusing, as I'd expected it would be – loads of information to take in. But I was prepared for that, and no-one expects you to know it all on the first day. That's something you really should bear in mind, I'd say. Anyway, everyone was really helpful, and told me that it was OK to ask, rather than pretending I knew things I didn't, although I know that's not the situation in every company.

40 Exam practice 2

You will hear five short extracts in which people are talking about their experiences of doing part-time courses. For questions 19 to 23, choose from the list (A to H) how each speaker says they benefited from doing a part-time course. Use each letter only once. There are three extra letters which you do not need to use.

Speaker 1

My boss sent me on a part-time course about marketing for small businesses. I was a bit surprised actually, because it wasn't an area of activity I normally have anything to do with. But it cost nothing *and* it took place during the week, so it didn't take up any of my free time. And it crossed my mind that it might help me get a better job. Anyway, the course was quite interesting, but I don't think marketing's for me, really. But it did give me a push to sign up for other classes if I'm offered the chance again. Who knows, another course might lead to a career change!

Speaker 2

I used to be a drama teacher. It was a stressful job, but I loved it, especially when I became head of drama and was responsible for the annual school play. When I retired, I wasn't prepared for how dull everyday life can seem when you have hardly anything to do. So I enrolled on a part-time French course, which I really got into and soon found I was doing loads of extra homework. There wasn't a moment to be bored any more. Most of the other participants were students taking extra classes to help with their exams, which meant we were there for different reasons, but that didn't matter.

Speaker 3

I'd been working for an investment bank for twelve years, and had climbed my way up the company ladder. The salary was amazing and I had a great social life, but the work wasn't rewarding. By chance, I saw a sign language course advertised, and I thought how fantastic it would be if I could communicate with deaf people, and maybe do some voluntary work. The course was stressful to start with, but I knew I'd found a new purpose in life. It didn't lead to a certificate or anything, but I'm now an assistant in a deaf school. The salary's tiny, but I no longer care about that.

Speaker 4

I'm currently doing a physics degree at college, but I've always loved reading literature during my leisure time, especially science-fiction novels. Last summer vacation, I took a part-time course in writing fiction for children. I think I've always had a lot of imagination and it was great the course allowed me to exploit that. The course was all done online, so I never actually got to meet the other participants, but we used the course blog and reviewed each other's stories. You get all kinds of people on these courses. I was the only one writing sci-fi stuff, all the others were doing teen romance. How weird is that!

Speaker 5

When I graduated with a degree in architecture, I'd had enough of studying and got a job with a private firm. After a few years, I was desperate to go for a higher position in the company. But when a vacancy came up, I was turned down because the company said they wanted someone with project management skills. That's when I signed up for a part-time vocational course to gain the skills needed. There was no formal qualification at the end, but that didn't matter, as it got me the result I wanted. Working and studying at the same time was exhausting, but it was only for six months.

LISTENING PART 4

41 Training 1

Int: So you started playing the piano at an early age, didn't you? How did you feel about learning to play?

Dennis: Well, you're right – I started learning to play the piano when I was about four, I think. I come from a very musical family, where everyone played some instrument or other – my father's a professional violinist, my mother's a music teacher, and my older brother was a brilliant guitar player from an early age. As time went on, though, I came to see that the piano just wasn't my thing, and that I'd much rather be outside playing football with my mates – something that I guess never occurred to my family. But for the sake of peace, I just kept quiet and carried on practising.

42 43 Training 3 & 4

Int: But you eventually turned to sport instead of the piano. Did you ever wish you hadn't given it up?

Dennis: Well, as soon as I was able, I managed to persuade my parents that music really wasn't for me, and that I'd be much better off devoting my time to sport. Teachers at school were already recognising that I had talent. But then I attended a concert that my brother was playing in – and it was brilliant. The audience went wild watching the band, and at that point I really did regret my decision about music. If I'd kept going, that could easily have been me on the stage.

44 Exam practice 2

You will hear an interview with a retired sportswoman called Gemma Porter, who now runs her own business. For questions 24 to 30, choose the best answer (A, B or C).

Interviewer: And on this week's *Ask the Expert* programme, I'm talking to retired athlete Gemma Porter. Gemma now runs her own recruitment business, helping other retired sportspeople to find new careers. Gemma, welcome.

Gemma: Thanks.

Interviewer: Could I ask, first of all, why you retired from athletics?

Gemma: I'd been moderately successful in my athletics career, and had been lucky enough not to pick up too many injuries. I'd achieved several medals for coming second and third in world events and felt I had the ability to keep on going, and possibly even set a world record in my event. But the truth was, I was fed up with living out of a suitcase. I was lucky I'd been all over the world for my job, but I'd had enough.

Interviewer: Fair enough. And was it easy to adjust to life after retirement?

Gemma: Initially, no. I missed the support of the other athletes, and when I thought of them all setting off to the next competition without me, I felt left behind. It was lovely to take a few weeks off and have a break from training though, and after I'd had a rest, I started applying for paid jobs. I originally thought about taking a year off, but I needed something to do to distract me from thinking about the good things about being an athlete.

Interviewer: So, was it easy, with your background, to find a job?

Gemma: Not at all. I sent in loads of applications and didn't even get an interview. Some of the vacant jobs were simple office work that I could have done with my eyes closed, but my CV let me down. You see, I left school at sixteen, before taking my final exams, so that I could compete in the national championships. When employers looked at my CV, there was no evidence that I was capable of doing the job they were advertising. Of course, *I* felt that my training routine as an athlete would show I could be committed to a job, so that was all very frustrating.

Interviewer: But eventually someone took you on, and then five years later, you set up your own recruitment company to help retired sportspeople. What made you want to do that?

Gemma: There were only a handful of other agencies providing this service, but I was convinced that my background in sport put me in a unique position to be able to help others after leaving the sporting world. My family told me to go for it, and my best friend even helped me with various practical things, like setting up my website.

Interviewer: And was the business an immediate success?

Gemma: Not in the very early days, but very few businesses take off straight away. But I didn't give up because I was confident that I would succeed. I always had a reputation for being a strong person when I was an athlete. What kept me going most of all was the knowledge that my business would meet a real need. I wish I'd had that sort of guidance when I first gave up being a sportswoman.

Interviewer: And can I ask, do you think it's easy for retired sportspeople to adapt to life in a company?

Gemma: In general, the move from sport to business is a natural fit, but not everyone finds it easy to start with. Sportspeople are committed and determined and have bags of energy, and they can get a bit cross with others who don't have the same values as them, especially when it comes to rules in the workplace. Disagreements can happen if their workmates feel they're being criticised.

Interviewer: Very interesting.

Gemma: Yes, but that doesn't happen in every case. And I'd even go as far as to say that in the future, companies will recruit *more* people who've retired from sport because they possess the desire to set and achieve their aims, just like businesses. That's an important quality in today's rapidly changing world, and one of the ways for companies to ensure they stay in business.

Interviewer: Well, thanks …

SPEAKING PART 2

45 Training 1

Well, both pictures show people taking photos, but for different reasons. The two people in the first photo look like tourists because they're taking a picture of themselves in front of a historic monument. I think they probably want to remember their trip, and this photo will help them. Or maybe they're going to send the photo to their friends and family, to show that they're having fun. On the other hand, the man in the second photo looks like a professional photographer because he's got some special equipment to help him take a good picture. He seems quite serious because he's concentrating on his camera. I guess he might be taking this photo for a newspaper or a magazine. So, I think they will probably have quite different feelings about their photo. I'm sure the tourists will feel happy when they look at their photo, because it will remind them of their trip. On the other hand, the professional photographer might feel proud if it's a good photo, and he might also be pleased if he can get some money for it.

46 Training 5

So, both these photos show people playing music in a group, but the situations are quite different. In the first photo the people look like professional musicians. They all look quite serious, and they're all concentrating on playing. I think they're probably playing classical music, and they're in a theatre or something like that, so maybe they're practising for a concert. On the other hand, the teenagers in the second photo look very relaxed. They're outside somewhere, so maybe they're at a kind of summer camp. I think they're playing just for fun because they're smiling and chatting, and they don't look very serious. I think playing music with friends is a great way to relax and have fun together, especially if you like the same kind of music. I don't think I'd enjoy playing music as a job because there would be a lot of pressure to play perfectly every time.

SPEAKING PART 3

47 Training 3

Woman: So, we have to decide on the best form of accommodation for the group. What do you think?

Man: Well, I'd suggest either a hotel or staying with friends. I think they're the two best options. Are you happy with that?

Woman: Yes, I agree with you. My choice would be the hotel because I think it would be a lot of work for your friends to have a whole group to stay.

Man: OK, so shall we choose a hotel?

Woman: Yes, let's go for that.

SPEAKING PART 4

48 Training 3

1

A: I think having shops in town centres is good because it provides jobs for people.

B: Yes, that's an interesting point. But online companies provide jobs, too.

2

A: If we had no shops, our city centres would be very empty.

B: Yes, I hadn't thought of that. But there would be cafés and restaurants, of course.

3

A: Online stores can offer much more choice, so they're better for customers.

B: Yes, I see what you mean. There's no limit on their space, so they can show customers a huge range of items.

4

A: I think most designer brands are definitely too expensive.

B: Yes, I think I agree with you about that. I never buy them!

5

A: I think it's wrong that our clothes are made in developing countries where people aren't paid much money.

B: Yes, I can see your point of view about that. I think everyone should get a fair wage.

Test 3

LISTENING PART 1

49

You will hear people talking in eight different situations. For questions 1 to 8, choose the best answer (A, B or C).

1 You hear a man talking about flying long distances.

I travel abroad a lot for my work and I regularly take flights that are at least twelve hours long. That can get boring, but I keep busy on the plane and I usually travel business class. The thing that really gets to me is how exhausting it is to adapt to different time zones, especially when you're only there for a few days. I've tried loads of techniques, like, when I get on the plane, I set my watch to the time zone in the country I'm flying to, so I establish a new routine from the start of my journey. But nothing seems to make much difference.

2 You hear a woman telling her friend about a jewellery-making course she did.

Man: That's a lovely necklace you're wearing, Becky.

Woman: Thanks, I made it myself at a jewellery class I did in the evenings.

Man: Really. That sounds like a very relaxing activity to do after work.

Woman: Mmm … I just shut myself off and got on with my creations. There were about fifteen of us on the course altogether, but everyone worked really quietly. That's what made it such a pleasurable experience. Some of the people are now selling their pieces at the craft market and asked me to join them, but that's not really my thing.

Man: Well, I'd buy your necklace if it was for sale. My sister would adore it.

3 You hear a woman talking about moving home.

I've just moved into a new apartment on the other side of the city. It's not near any of my friends, which is a real shame, but the upside is my commute to work is now under twenty minutes. I didn't enjoy the process of moving though: it seemed to take weeks to pack everything up, and then even more time to unpack and sort through it all when I got to the new place. I ended up throwing away loads of stuff I didn't need any more. I won't make that mistake next time. I can't believe I paid the removal company to transport all that old stuff.

4 You hear two film critics discussing a film starring an actor called Tania Fry.

Man: What did you think of Tania Fry's latest film, *In the Park*?

Woman: Well, I've only given it two stars in my review. I mean, Tania did the best job she could, given the plot was so predictable and the dialogue uninspiring.

Man: She's a brilliant actor with a particular talent for comedy, but this production didn't bring out that side of her.

Woman: Well, I suppose there were a few funny moments, but essentially yes, that was the main issue – this role didn't stretch her in the slightest. But I do think it's great there are so many more parts around now for older actors.

Man: Mmm … it's a welcome development.

5 You hear a football referee talking about his job.

As a professional football referee, I make sure I take plenty of exercise and eat healthily. I prefer refereeing top league games, or even international matches, but so do most of my colleagues, and there's quite a lot of competition between referees. But we're also each other's support network, so I always have someone to talk to about what went wrong in a game. I couldn't do without this, as refereeing can be really stressful. Don't get me wrong, football's come a long way, and standards of refereeing have improved, but there are still disagreements on the pitch between players, and some of them question the referee's decisions.

6 You hear two friends discussing a photography exhibition they have just been to.

Woman: I really enjoyed the exhibition. Thanks for asking me to come.

Man: That's OK. I know you're a keen photographer yourself.

Woman: Yes, but not in the same league as that. I've been following the photographer's work since I saw an article about him online. It's great to see how he's developed over the years, but I am a bit envious of the amazing landscapes he manages to capture so beautifully. It's really made me want to track down the locations he used, so I can go and photograph them too.

Man: What a good idea.

7 You hear a travel and tourism student talking about a project she is doing about pop-culture tourism.

For my project, I'm looking at pop-culture tourism – that is, people who travel to destinations featured in literature, movies, TV shows, etc. All these forms of entertainment have huge numbers of devoted fans who get really excited at any chance to go and visit where the action happens. This presents the tourism industry with many new opportunities, but at the same time it's proving hard to deliver what fans expect once they arrive in the destination. Pop-culture tourism providers have been working with local people and experimenting with what to offer visitors, but more work needs to be done on this growing sector of the industry.

8 You hear two friends discussing a local market.

Man: Do you ever go to the local market? I've started shopping there since it re-opened.

Woman: No, but I'd heard the building looks lovely now they've put a glass roof on it. I wouldn't really call myself a fan of markets, to be honest. I can't bear being squashed into the narrow gaps between the lines of stalls.

Man: You might give it a try one time, I think you'd be impressed that only goods from this region are sold there, which is great for the economy around here. It might be a bit dearer than shopping elsewhere, and it is getting really popular, but I think it's worth it.

Woman: OK, thanks for the tip.

LISTENING PART 2

50

You will hear a man called Pete talking about a cycling holiday in the UK that his company organises. For questions 9 to 18, complete the sentences with a word or short phrase.

Hello. My name's Pete and I'm here to tell you about a cycling holiday in the UK that my company organises. The trip involves cycling the length of England and Scotland – a journey of around 1,600 kilometres.

Incidentally, the fastest time anyone has ever made this journey is one day and 20 hours, but the shortest trip *we* offer is nine days long and is what we call 'Extreme' level. We find that most cyclists choose our 'Challenging' level, which is 15 days long. But if you're fairly new to cycling, I'd recommend our 'Beginner' or 'Regular' levels – they're 28 and 21 days long.

We offer this holiday twice a month during June, July, August and September. We call these our 'Supported' option, meaning you are accompanied throughout the trip. We also have an 'Independent' option, which involves us making all the arrangements for you but you do the cycling on your own. This option appeals to people who want more dates to select from.

Some people start the trip from the top of Scotland and cycle southwards, but *we* begin in the south-west of England. Whichever way you go, there's more rain at the start and end of the trip, with generally dry weather in the middle. We set off very early in the morning, as soon as the sun comes up, and are often helped along by the wind.

You may see a few other companies offering this holiday, but *ours* is the only one that's been given an international award for the past three years in a row. We believe the value for money that our trip provides is outstanding, but it's been our trip leaders who've been recognised by the award organisers, probably because they have most interaction with customers.

If you book one of our holidays, you'll be well looked after, and you'll have delicious food to help you keep your strength up! We stop at roadside cafés during the day, and eat at restaurants at night. From this season onwards, we're offering even more accommodation options than before. That's because we generally stay in towns overnight, where there are places to suit all budgets.

So, what do our holidays include? Basically, you bring your bike to the starting point, and we provide the rest, except for personal belongings, cycling clothes and personal medical kits, of course. People often purchase maps of the route, but please don't bother with this unless you particularly want to, as we provide them for you, together with daily briefings and route updates.

When people see that the route has a lot of hills, one question I'm often asked is how difficult the cycling is on this holiday. Overall most hills are gentle, and the views of the countryside below are beautiful. There are some sections which consist of some very steep climbs, and the cliffs near the start can be hilly.

Naturally, on a long-distance route like this, there's bound to be times when we're in busy cities. Wherever possible, we avoid busy main roads, especially dual carriageways, and in the biggest urban centres, we direct you onto cycle paths, as that's the most sensible way to avoid the worst traffic.

Other things that are important to know about this holiday: obviously fitness is essential for all participants. Cyclists can use the services of our support vehicle, so luggage is carried for you, and our driver can do bike repairs if necessary, and he or she carries spare bottles of water, too. But you don't get any rest days so you do need to be fit, and training beforehand is recommended.

The trip ends will a farewell celebration, though not everyone can always stay for that. There's a certificate for everyone who completes the trip, and just for fun we award prizes like a T-shirt for the person who gets the most injuries or who tells the best jokes.

Are there any questions?

LISTENING PART 3

51

You will hear five short extracts in which people are talking about learning to drive a car. For questions 19 to 23, choose from the list (A to H) what advice each speaker gives. Use each letter only once. There are three extra letters which you do not need to use.

Speaker 1

The majority of adults can drive a car, so in theory, it should be possible for almost *anyone* to learn, shouldn't it? Well, that's what I thought when I first went to a driving school. They said I had to learn the theory first, so I worked through the advice and practice questions in a book, and that was all fine. But you have to be aware that the practical side of learning to drive is completely different, and it can take loads of sessions before you're good enough to pass the driving test. Now I have passed and have got my own little car, the freedom's great.

Speaker 2

Leading up to my first lesson, whenever I was being given a lift in someone else's car, I studied closely what the driver was doing with the pedals and the gears. So when my turn at the wheel came, I didn't *feel* like a beginner. That's a real advantage. I passed my driving test in 15 lessons which I was thrilled about as my older brother needed 25 before he got his driving licence. I had a great instructor, who was so calm with me, even once when we were at a crossroads and the car just stopped.

Speaker 3

I remember the first time I got in my own car and drove off by myself. It was so weird not having my instructor sitting next to me, reminding me of the things I was doing wrong. I even had trouble getting the car into gear at one point. It was at traffic lights on a really busy road. Thank goodness that didn't happen when I was doing my practical driving test as I'd never have passed. You have to accept that being an accomplished driver is something that you build up over years of driving experience.

Speaker 4

My first few driving lessons were in my mum's big car on my uncle's farm. It was a really stressful experience. Even though there were no other cars around, I found it impossible to keep the car going in a straight line with my mum calling out more instructions than I could possibly take in. What I'd say to other people is get yourself a patient instructor, ideally at one of the large driving schools because they're more likely to offer a discount if you sign up for, say, 20 sessions when you enrol. Some people can practise with a relative, but it didn't work for me.

Speaker 5

Learning the theory of driving is quite straightforward and you can do that in your own time. But I think it's always worth finding out who your friends have learnt successfully from and then checking who gets the best online reviews. Then you can book with that person. Driving lessons aren't exactly cheap, so the aim is to learn in the shortest space of time possible. You absolutely want to maximise your chances of passing the test first time, and then get out on the road in a car of your own. That's what I think, anyway.

LISTENING PART 4

52

You will hear an interview with a woman called Helena Best, who has been a contestant on three TV quiz shows. For questions 24 to 30, choose the best answer (A, B or C).

Interviewer: Now, welcome to Helena Best, who's been on several television quiz shows. Helena, is it three shows you've appeared on?

Helena: Yes. The first one was called *Full Marks*, about ten years ago.

Interviewer: How did you find that?

Helena: Exciting, but scary. I remember walking out onto the stage – the spotlights were so bright, you could hardly see the studio. The cameras were noisy, but that didn't bother me once the show started. There was a group of people watching – friends of another contestant – who kept talking when it was my turn to answer questions. It made it harder to stay focused on the questions, and I remember feeling quite cross about it. I did OK, but I didn't win.

Interviewer: Oh. And what about the second show?

Helena: That was *Great Minds*. I'd tried to get on it, but was originally turned down. Then one day the show's producer called me saying another contestant had suddenly dropped out and could I stand in. I'd watched the show loads of times and knew how it worked, so I said yes as I thought I'd be OK. But really it wasn't a very sensible decision, as it was a general knowledge quiz and everyone else had been revising hard. They knew far more of the answers than me and weren't very friendly, as they clearly felt they had nothing in common with me. I felt quite uncomfortable and was happy to go out in the first round.

Interviewer: Then came *Brainbox*. Congratulations on winning the recent final!

Helena: Thanks! In a way, that was harder than the other shows. It was a team competition and I should have felt less pressure, and, unlike the other shows I'd been on, it wasn't going out live. The thing was, my team-mates were terribly nervous, which made it stressful. When it was my individual round, all the questions were about tennis – my perfect subject – and all the stress I'd been feeling just disappeared.

Interviewer: How lucky. Apart from winning, what did you enjoy about being a contestant?

Helena: Erm … everyone's charming to you and you're escorted everywhere as if you're someone well known and important. That was the highlight for me. You're picked up from home in a posh car and your hair and make-up are done by a professional! They tell you what to bring to wear, so I had to go clothes shopping beforehand. The host of the show was having his make-up done the same time as me, and we had a nice chat, which was lovely, as there wasn't time for that later.

Interviewer: How do people get picked to be a contestant? Presumably there's an application process?

Helena: That's right. You fill out an online form – just like applying for jobs, really, except there's more questions about family, hobbies and personal experiences than qualifications and career history. You have to let them know if you've done other programmes because if you're not open about that, they'll find out. They don't want the same people popping up on quiz programmes, as it looks unfair.

Interviewer: Yes.

Helena: Actually, what some people might not know is that you have to sign a legal contract before the show.

Interviewer: I suppose there's a risk some people might put the questions on social media before the programme's actually been shown.

Helena: You won't get into trouble for talking about the questions, but it is a matter of confidentiality. Some contestants earn money by selling their story to newspaper reporters, which *is* allowed according to the rules. But the issue is, you're under strict obligation to stay silent about the outcome – even to family and closest friends.

Interviewer: And finally, do you have any tips for anyone who's going to appear in a TV quiz show?

Helena: Forget you'll be watched by millions of people, for a start. You don't have to be a genius, but it really helps if you know the format of the show, so nothing comes as a surprise. Study all the previous series to get familiar with the kinds of questions they ask and how they ask them. Above all, remember it's a privilege to be part of these shows, and that matters more than setting out to win.

Test 4

LISTENING PART 1

53

You will hear people talking in eight different situations. For questions 1 to 8, choose the best answer (A, B or C).

1 You hear a newsreader talking about his job.

It wasn't my ambition to be a newsreader, I just happened to be offered a presenting job after being a correspondent for a daily paper for 13 years. I'd say that, before anyone can sit in a studio and present news, it's essential to build up practical experience of researching a story and preparing a piece on it. Of course, you need to be able to present in a clear and professional way, but the main job's about journalism. Some people think because I read the news at 11 o'clock at night, I turn up for work at 10.30, but *hours* of writing and editing go into the late night broadcasts.

2 You hear a man telling a friend about surfing.

Woman: You've been going surfing for ages, Ben, haven't you?

Man: Yes, it must be over ten years. I went to a surf school to learn how to do it properly.

Woman: Sensible. In theory, standing on a board *should* be simple, but in reality it's really tough. When I watch surfers at the beach, the main thing I notice is how often they end up falling into the water.

Man: Don't laugh. That's me quite a lot of the time too. It's incredibly hard to keep upright, but it's worth it for the excitement you get when you do finally catch a big wave.

3 You hear a nurse talking about healthy eating.

I work as a nurse at a health clinic and I find my job really satisfying. But it's such a shame that a lot of patients who come to me are suffering from things that are entirely preventable. If only they would adopt a more sensible approach to healthy eating and exercise. I mean, we all have to look after ourselves, don't we? Of course, it's really rewarding when I can make a difference to people's lives. And I like it that I get to meet all kinds of people of all ages and with a variety of medical conditions.

4 You hear an advertisement for a game app.

Allpower is a brand new educational game for children of all ages. It began as a collection of classroom quizzes that were entertaining and educationally beneficial, but the *new* app goes beyond that. Parents, teachers and classmates can now enter quizzes on the *Allpower* app, and either share these or set permissions for a group.

There's a team mode for group quizzes, a single player mode, and it's possible for anyone to select quizzes created by others. Creating a quiz is straightforward, and students stay focused and are constantly challenged with new questions.

5 You hear two friends talking about their hobby of fishing.

Man 1: When I think of the fishing trips we've been on – day time, night time, sea fishing, river fishing – I think I've enjoyed every single one of them. Even when there are no fish around all day.

Man 2: Absolutely. Or even when the weather's cold or rainy, I hardly notice it.

Man 1: Yes, that moment, when you're standing in the shallow water, out in the open air and without a care in the world. It's just the best feeling there is.

Man 2: Yeah, for me, it's essentially about getting outside and being able to enjoy nature.

6 You hear two friends discussing how their town has changed recently.

Man: I'm so glad the roadworks around the town have come to an end. The queues of cars aren't nearly as long as they have been recently.

Woman: Yes. The thing is, though, there's a road I have to drive along sometimes that's now closed to private vehicles. So I have to find an alternate route that takes me out of my way. And it's not like I can catch a bus instead.

Man: Oh dear, that's not good. In general though, it was time for them to put in special lanes for buses.

Woman: Yes, people do need to leave their cars at home and use forms of public transport.

7 You hear an announcement about a TV programme.

Do you ever feel you should be getting more sleep? Do you ever wonder why we need to sleep? Sleep is certainly a common topic of discussion nowadays. A brand new documentary explores this topic that has preoccupied scientists for centuries and offers clues as to why we need to sleep. The presenter is a doctor who suffers from a lack of sleep himself. He explains recent research findings that sleep doesn't just help the cells in the body to recover. It also clears our mind of information we no longer need and supports learning and memory. So that's *The facts about sleep*, next Tuesday at 8.30pm.

8 You hear two teachers talking about children and reading.

Man: I recently ordered a set of graphic novels for my class, but, do you know, I had to justify to my head-teacher why I needed them. When I explained that I was basing the term's literature, history, art *and* drama projects on this one book, my request was approved straightaway. That's why I think they're so good to have in class. It's funny that some people look down on them.

Woman: I know. Most of my pupils love reading cartoons, and when I gave them some graphic novels to read for the first time, they absolutely loved them.

Man: I read graphic novels myself sometimes.

LISTENING PART 2

54

You will hear a geography student called Sam giving a talk about tea. For questions 9 to 18, complete the sentences with a word or short phrase.

Hi, I'm Sam, and I've been finding out about tea. The history of tea-drinking dates back nearly 5,000 years, when it was discovered by a Chinese Emperor. It's said he discovered the drink when tea leaves accidentally blew into his pot of boiling water.

Today, tea is one of the most popular drinks in the world, and I found out loads about its history online. There are millions of internet articles on tea and I didn't know where to begin, but luckily I came across a documentary that covered everything I wanted to know about tea's origins. There are books about tea for sale, but I didn't buy any of those.

Tea's been drunk in South-east Asia for centuries, but it didn't really reach Europe till the late-1500s. The reason why it's remained popular is the number of varieties – around fifteen hundred – *and* also the way it's served has evolved to suit consumers. In 1904, a tea merchant in the USA, who couldn't sell his product in the hot weather, put ice in tea, to produce a more refreshing drink than hot tea with milk.

Tea comes from the *Camellia Sinensis* plant. The drink is generally made with the dried leaves, though the flowers or flower buds may be used. We've probably all seen pictures of a tea bush, but what I hadn't realised was that tea's actually a tree. It can grow to 17 metres high, but the plant is cut to waist-height to make the leaves easier to pick.

Tea grows best in mountain areas, at least 1,000 metres above sea level, though there are exceptions. For example, the Portuguese Azores Islands, an island off the coast of South Carolina USA, and the far South-west of the UK. Wherever it's cultivated, it's true to say there must be a lot of rainfall for the plants to grow well. Rich soil and sunshine are much less important.

There are four main types of tea plant: green, black, white and what's known as oolong. But the huge variety of aromas, flavours, and colours that tea comes in is determined by how it's processed. However, it's probably true to say the leaves have to be hand picked in order to obtain the highest quality product.

So, how to make the best cup of tea! Firstly, I recommend using an electric kettle or saucepan to boil the water. Some people use microwaves, but I think it's harder to control the water temperature in them *and* you risk damaging the flavour of the tea. Some people say water quality matters, but I think you can make a great cup of tea with water from anywhere.

Next, the all-important question of whether to add anything to your tea. Here in Britain, most people add milk or lemon to their tea. Fewer people here put sugar in their tea nowadays, but have you ever tried it with honey, I wonder? It's worth giving it a go, as it's a lovely flavour combination.

Experts say you should always use loose tea, not teabags, though personally I find teabags convenient. As for instant tea, there's no way I'd drink that – the list of ingredients on the label puts me off. There's also canned tea – if you haven't seen it before, it comes in tins or cartons. It's a nice drink, but I wouldn't call it proper tea.

Some people say tea has many health benefits. Some people insist green tea is good for controlling their weight, and my aunt claims tea gives her more energy. Given that tea contains caffeine, that's almost certainly true. Whether tea reduces blood pressure or the risk of other diseases, I don't know, but compared to fizzy drinks, it seems a healthy choice.

Now I've completed this project, I'm keen to learn more about tea culture. Obviously I live nowhere near China or India, so visiting a tea plantation is out of the question. However, someone at a café told me about a place where you can watch a traditional tea ceremony, which is something I'd definitely love to do one day.

LISTENING PART 3

55

You will hear five short extracts in which people are talking about astronomy. For questions 19 to 23, choose from the list (A to H) why each speaker decided to get involved in astronomy. Use each letter only once. There are three extra letters which you do not need to use.

Speaker 1

I first got into astronomy in a big way when I heard a radio advert for a company that was offering an online preparation course leading to a qualification in astronomy. It was just the kind of thing I needed – something serious to keep my mind active. I don't know how many other people were on the course, but the tutors were great, always so enthusiastic about the subject. I've never actually met a proper astronomer, but I do enjoy looking at the stars. In some countries I've been to, the levels of pollution are so low that, at night-time, galaxies millions of kilometres away are visible through a telescope.

Speaker 2

My local university runs something called a dark skies project, which is where ordinary members of the public are encouraged to look at the sky at night. They then compare what they witness with a 'star map' produced by astronomers for that part of the night sky. People upload their observations to a website, and everyone comments on them. I really liked the idea of blogging, so that's how come I joined. And my interest in astronomy grew from there, really. I'm looking forward to discovering a new star one day and telling my friends on the blog about it.

Speaker 3

I came to astronomy by accident when I watched a science-fiction film about black holes for a project we were doing at school. What started my fascination with everything to do with astronomy was that I realised it asks the biggest questions of all: 'What's the universe made of?' and 'Is there any other life out there?' But more than that, I realised that if you can answer some of those questions, it will provide solutions to problems we face here on our planet. Of course, I knew I could never come up with those answers myself, but I wanted to keep up with what professional astronomers are working on.

Speaker 4

My grandfather had a telescope and when we went to stay with him, he'd make us look through it while he explained how far away the stars were, and how long it took for light to travel from the stars to Earth, and so on. As a child, I didn't take any of it in. I didn't come back to astronomy 'til I became a teacher. I took my class to a space centre and they were so excited by everything they saw and read. And I thought, actually they're right: astronomy *is* a fantastic subject, and I've been reading about it ever since.

Speaker 5

I've been interested in astronomy for a few years. I go away a lot for work and rarely have time for hobbies. But then I got the idea that I would be able to combine astronomy with my business trips. It actually started with a camping trip I went on with friends. As soon as the sun went down, it was so dark, you couldn't see your hands in front of your face. So we just sat there staring at the sky, gazing at the patterns made by billions of stars. Fantastic! I've tried to get my daughter involved in my hobby as well. She even has her own telescope.

LISTENING PART 4

56

You will hear an interview with a woman called Natasha Green, who is talking about her job as an archaeologist. For questions 24 to 30, choose the best answer (A, B or C).

Interviewer: Today I'm talking to Natasha Green, who's an archaeologist. Welcome Natasha. Could I start by asking what made you want be an archaeologist?

Natasha: I was interested in the dinosaur remains that were being dug up in Australia when I was growing up there, though none of them were discovered near where I lived. But my aunt and uncle, who loved the outdoors, took me on a camping trip and I came across a stone tool that looked fascinating. It turned out to be 80,000 years old, and archaeologists got really excited about it because it suggested people had been in Australia longer than previously thought. From that day on, there was only one career for me.

Interviewer: You have a special interest in the archaeology of the Sahara Desert. What's it like digging there?

Natasha: It's not everyone's dream to spend the summer vacation working in the baking sun in temperatures of over 40 degrees – my friends think I'm mad – but I love the desert. There are places where you can dig almost anywhere and be guaranteed of finding something. Sometimes it drives me mad because I just don't know where to investigate next. But I find the desert beautiful, especially at night-time when it's cooler and so quiet.

Interviewer: What kind of preparation goes into a new dig? Presumably you want to know whether another archaeologist has already dug there before.

Natasha: Well, that doesn't require *too* much effort to find out. There are written records for digs going back over 100 years. When I'm on a project and someone digs something up out of the ground, it's important that I can immediately identify what it is. That way, the other archaeologists assisting me know what to do with the object – how to process it, as we say – in order to keep it in the best possible condition.

Interviewer: So, what particular skills would you say an archaeologist needs?

Natasha: I don't imagine anyone would be surprised to hear me say IT knowledge is vital, as that's the case in most research type jobs. What's less widely known is that we still produce drawings of every site as a way to record where we find the objects. If you're on a dig, you have to be able to take your turn at doing that. Depending where your archaeological project is taking place in the world, you may need to be able to speak a foreign language, but I suppose that's self-evident, really.

Interviewer: Can children get involved in archaeology?

Natasha: Absolutely. It's a great way for even very young children to start learning about the past. Even if you don't have archaeological sites near you, all libraries have archaeology books for youngsters. There are also lots of websites on the subject for kids, too. I'd encourage anyone, young or old, to learn all about this fascinating subject. Maybe there's a dig in your area you could go and see, but health and safety regulations mean they couldn't let you join in just like that.

Interviewer: What should people do if they find something in the ground that looks very old?

Natasha: Well, not just keep it for themselves, definitely. Objects from the past are part our shared culture, so they need to be examined carefully by a specialist and put on display for the public to see. It makes me furious to hear stories of people not taking things they find to a museum.

Interviewer: Do you think there'll be less need for archaeologists in the future? After all, so much about the past is already known.

Natasha: There are layers and layers of the past beneath our feet that haven't yet been discovered. Every city construction site has to be investigated by archaeologists to see what ancient remains are there, and that'll carry on. Remains that are open to the public are exposed to weather and pollution. This means we're going to have to devote more effort to making sure they stay in the best possible condition, to preserve them for future generations.

Interviewer: Natasha, thanks …

Test 5

LISTENING PART 1

57

You will hear people talking in eight different situations. For questions 1 to 8, choose the best answer (A, B or C).

1 You hear two TV critics talking about presenters of science programmes.

Man: I think science programmes have got so much better recently.

Woman: In terms of content, definitely. And also in the way that complex scientific information is communicated by the scientists to TV audiences.

Man: Well, that's down to the individuals who are presenters, some of whom are celebrities.

Woman: It's one thing to be a scientist in a research lab, and another to be able to present your subject to non-experts. That's why *this* generation of presenters deserves such praise. It's rare nowadays to watch a science programme on TV that's so abstract you can't understand a word.

2 You hear a psychologist talking about friendship.

Friendship plays a crucial role in our lives, so it's not surprising that there are so many songs about friends. Like many people, my closest friends have been an important part of my life over decades. The people whose company I enjoy most are those that I have a shared past with, going back to childhood. Together we remember the trouble we got into in class, games we played and things we celebrated together. That connection remains strong today, even if we don't share the same hobbies now. In my mind, I always make a clear separation between work colleagues and close friends.

3 You hear two friends talking about holidays.

Man: Where are you going on holiday this year, Samantha?

Woman: To Melville Island in the Northern Territories. It's about 80 kilometres north of Darwin.

Man: Do you always visit islands on holiday? Or does it just seem that way?

Woman: No, you're right. There's something I find absolutely fascinating about visiting small islands. It's true to say island life is calmer and quieter than life in the city, but for me, no two islands are alike – they all have their own customs and traditions developed over time, and that's their appeal. Anyway, I can't wait for my holiday to come around.

4 You hear a man telling his wife about a product review he has read online.

Woman: Have you found any online reviews for the phone you want to get?

Man: I'm looking at one now that says don't buy it 'cos it's the worst phone on the market.

Woman: That's got to be someone playing some kind of a joke, surely? Maybe a dissatisfied customer, or someone who hasn't even bought one of these phones. I mean, this phone is just an upgraded version of your current model, so it doesn't make sense to say the new one's inferior. Maybe check out a few other reviews before making your mind up.

Man: Exactly.

5 You hear a woman leaving a voicemail message.

Hello. This is Lauren Ray. I have an appointment at 2.30 today. I'm calling to let you know I may be a few minutes late. I'm on my way from work now and the freeway's pretty clear, so hopefully I won't be too late. I don't know what happened, I left my office really early, but on the way to the parking lot, I ran into a former co-worker, and before I knew it, half an hour had passed. I'm so sorry for any inconvenience. See you soon.

6 You hear two students discussing their project on public parks.

Man: Sally-Ann, could I ask you about the project on public parks? I was going to choose my favourite park, and analyse how important the artworks in it are to people who go there. I'm wondering if that's a good choice.

Woman: Interesting topic, but I'd say go for something broader, like the historical development of parks, and pick at least one other park to compare it with.

Man: Yes, good idea. I can still use my local park as one example. Is my topic different enough from yours?

Woman: Yeah, I'm looking into the social function of public parks, you know, what role they play and how useful they are as community spaces.

7 You hear a woman talking about growing up with lots of cousins.

My parents both had brothers and sisters, and my aunts and uncles all have children. So when we were growing up, family gatherings were huge. You can imagine how long it took to get everyone organised for family photographs. Sometimes there were disagreements – no, that's too strong a word – but there were little jealousies over who had the best toys. Overall though, I have happy memories of growing up with my cousins and I sometimes wish we didn't all live so far apart. It'd be great to catch up with them all and find out what they've all achieved as adults.

8 You hear a university student talking about his studies.

I'm in the second year of my four-year degree course. Next year, I'll be working in industry or in a research laboratory, which is something all science undergraduates here are offered the chance to do. I'm really looking forward to it, as it might lead to a great job once I graduate. This placement is unlikely to be in my university town, so I'll need to relocate. I originally got accepted to do a general science degree, but as soon as I got here and started a module on biochemistry, I knew that was what I really wanted to specialise in. Luckily, the university let me switch courses. That's not always guaranteed.

LISTENING PART 2

58

You will hear a man called Bradley promoting a food festival that takes place in his home town in the USA. For questions 9 to 18, complete the sentences with a word or short phrase.

Hi, I'm Bradley and I'd like to tell you all about a food festival that's really important to us in my home town of Little Chute in Wisconsin. It's called The Great Cheese Festival, and I hope you all like the sound of it enough to want to come and see it for yourselves. The festival takes place during the first weekend in June, and it's a huge event for celebrating what we refer to as 'Dairy Month'. That's because our state is famous for cheese-making.

The festival's been going since 1988 and it's gotten bigger and bigger every year. The mayor at the time set up this event after reading that a museum all about cheese had been set up nearly a thousand miles away in New York. He thought that was totally unfair, as they have nothing to do with cheese making there, whereas we have a cheese factory in practically every town here.

So, for three days a year we celebrate our local cheese-making industry, and our festival's so well-known people come from miles around to join in. It's basically a three-day carnival, with a live music programme, and lots of eating, of course, and it all kicks off with our very own song, which was written just for this event.

The three days are packed with events, for example a fun-run, pony rides, a cheese market, and an exhibition of sculptures which are all carved out of cheese. That's the one event that I never miss because they are amazing, and they seem to get more and more sophisticated as every year goes by.

There are various competitions taking place over the weekend: every year there's a painting competition just for teenagers. Anyone who attends the festival this June is welcome to join in our cheese tasting contest, and there's a cheese eating competition for adults only. There's also a fancy-dress competition, but that's just for locals.

The festival really is an event designed for all the family. I always remember going to the magic show every year when I was a little kid – it's the best fun ever. But there are other things for young kids to do, such as spending a few hours at the funfair, or there's also the woodland walk.

As I said before, the festival's become so well known that people come from far and wide to visit it. The hotels in town are usually full, and the town authorities have had to limit the number of visitors. It used to be possible to buy day tickets when you arrived but now you won't be allowed in unless you buy advance tickets. There are never any left once the festival starts.

So, what else can I tell you about? Most of the events are held around the centre of town. They start early in the morning and go on till close to midnight. There's a barbecue all day, and farm tours, but they're only up until midday, and the shops are open all afternoon and evening.

There are hundreds of people involved in the organisation of the festival, from local store owners, to high-school students, to cheese producers, and of course the mayor and his staff too. The people who help before, during and after the event are all volunteers, which I think is great, seeing as how it's an important event in our town.

You might wonder what happens to the profits from the festival. In the past, the money's been spent on improving public facilities, and the next thing for the town to benefit from is the construction of a skateboard park. Hopefully, that should be open well in time for next year's festival. A playground was built in only a few months last year, and a new public garden in the town opened the year before that.

LISTENING PART 3

59

You will hear five short extracts in which people are talking about buying clothes. For questions 19 to 23, choose from the list (A to H) what each speaker says is important to them when buying clothes. Use each letter only once. There are three extra letters which you do not need to use.

Speaker 1

I've never been really interested in fashion. Don't get me wrong though, I do regularly buy quite a lot of new clothes. I try to ensure my purchases are suitable for various situations, so for example, at weekends I tend to wear smart casual trousers that are equally appropriate for an average day in the office when I don't have any important meetings. Admittedly shopping for clothes isn't one of my favourite activities. That's why it's great when you come across an online store that has all the styles you like and that doesn't cost a fortune.

Speaker 2

I think of myself as quite an organised, efficient person, but you probably wouldn't guess that from my appearance. I never read clothes magazines, and I couldn't care less about what the latest styles are. I choose fabrics that are warm and feel good next to the skin. I have a lot of baggy jumpers and I always wear soft shoes wherever possible. I suppose when I finish studying and get a job, I might have to invest in some smart things for work, but for the time being, I'm more than happy with my wardrobe.

Speaker 3

If you asked me to define my favourite style of clothes, I'm not really sure what I'd say. I do have a few designer label items, and my friends sometimes comment on that, because they get most of their things in the sales. My response is that buying cheap clothes is actually a false economy – sometimes they can get worn out surprisingly quickly. My ten-year old winter coat looks as good as the day I bought it. OK, it's not this season's colour, but so what. It's not like I'm particularly interested in clothes.

Speaker 4

I've heard people suggest that your clothes can communicate what kind of person you are. For example, if you're into high fashion, you might be a changeable character. Or if you go bargain hunting in the sales, this might mean you're careful with money, or if you like bright colours, then you're an extrovert. When I'm at the mall, I go for things that are made from organic, natural materials as that's better for the planet. Not that my clothes look any different to anyone else's. And actually, I don't think my clothes would tell you anything about me as a person.

Speaker 5

My rule when it comes to buying clothes is never to get anything at the start of the season. By holding back a few months or sometimes only a matter of weeks, you can take advantage of special offers. The longer you wait, the better, in my experience. That's what I always tell my friends to do. If I look in my wardrobe, I'd say the clothes I buy represent a whole range of styles. I love the outrageous prints from nature from the 1970s, but equally I have some very smart designer jackets and shoes.

LISTENING PART 4

60

You will hear an interview with a professor called Martin Hart and a housebuilder called Anna Peterson, who are talking about houses made out of blocks of straw. For questions 24 to 30, choose the best answer (A, B or C).

Interviewer: My guests today are Anna Peterson, a builder who makes houses out of blocks of straw, and Professor Martin Hart, who's researched using straw as a building material. Professor Hart, could I ask you about your research first?

Martin: Oh, please call me Martin. I'd been aware for some time that a few eco-friendly houses had been built using straw. Straw normally serves as animal bedding, but I discovered that not all of it is used for that purpose, and that there's potentially sufficient straw for a million new homes every year. So I set up an engineering research project with the aim of discovering whether this building material could be brought to the wider housing market. It's one thing building a single property, but bigger construction firms need millions of tonnes of material.

Interviewer: I read you built a row of straw houses. But they don't look like they're made of straw, do they?

Martin: No. The exterior walls are brick. The building method was to put up a wooden frame, then fill it in with blocks of straw. We could've added an outer layer of wood or plaster – whatever you use, the straw walls themselves are great at making sure the house stays warm. The interior walls are just as straight as a conventional house. The bricks are there in order to resemble the style of housing already in place on the street where they were built. From the outside you wouldn't know they're straw houses.

Interviewer: Not everyone was happy with your team's straw houses.

Martin: Mmm. All the relevant fire safety tests had been done and had demonstrated beyond doubt the houses weren't a fire risk, so you'd have thought no-one would've objected. We were open about the fact that the walls contained carbon dioxide, but people assumed that was a risk, whereas in fact, it's an advantage. You see, the carbon produced during the growing process is locked away in the straw, so that's actually good for the environment. Anyway, we'd tested the buildings' ability to support the weight of the floors and knew they were strong enough, so there were no concerns raised about that.

Interviewer: Thank you, Martin. Now Anna, you've used straw as a building material for some time. Why's that?

Anna: I turned to straw about eight years ago. My customers were all very happy with the wooden and stone houses I'd built for them, and I had no plans to change. Then one day I read about a woman in the USA who built her own house out of straw really cheaply. I thought the idea of straw houses could potentially go down really well with house buyers. And I've been proved right. At any one time I can have multiple projects on the go.

Interviewer: And you do the building work yourself.

Anna: Well, the first few I built, I was involved in everything, from start to finish. Now I'm building 15 to 20 at a time, I have a wider role. But I'm actually a qualified carpenter, and on almost every house I build now, I work alongside the roofers. It makes me feel I've made a personal contribution to every house, and, quite frankly, I'd rather do that than discuss how the project's going with the site supervisors.

Interviewer: Right. What's the main consideration for you when you're building houses?

Anna: Well, if you'd asked me a decade ago, I'd have said to build people a home with eye-catching features that were different to anything else. But my current focus is on making sure I employ only architects who produce plans that are completely straightforward. For me personally, the fact that my houses use renewable materials is just a bonus, to be honest.

Interviewer: So, what's next for you, Anna?

Anna: My intention is to pass on the skills I've learned to other house-builders, so that they adopt this style of house-building. The award I've won for my work has certainly created a lot of publicity for me nationwide. I'm confident people'll be interested to learn, and then, who knows, maybe one of them will find a way to make straw houses even cheaper.

Interviewer: Anna and Martin, …

Test 6

LISTENING PART 1

61

You will hear people talking in eight different situations. For questions 1 to 8, choose the best answer (A, B or C).

1 You hear a shop assistant talking about buying bicycles.

With literally hundreds of models on the market, it's tough for people to know where to start looking for a new bike. Customers often ask me, 'Which bike is best to buy and should I go for the most expensive one?' But what I think actually matters is what you want to use the bike for; for example, an expensive bike isn't necessarily the most suitable for doing off-road riding. And similarly, what's the point in paying out hundreds of dollars on a top-of-the-range racing model with 18 gears, if you're just gonna take a gentle ride around the park once a week?

2 You hear two friends talking about skiing holidays.

Man: I'm off on holiday next week. Can't wait. I'm going skiing again.

Woman: Fantastic. I went last month. If skiing trips weren't quite so expensive, I'd go several times a year.

Man: I know what you mean. But you go during school holiday time, don't you? The prices always go up then.

Woman: True, and the holidays always seem to sell out fast, so I've never been able to take advantage of last-minute deals. Mind you, I managed to save myself some money this time by booking accommodation direct, rather than through my usual tour operator's website. The hotel even threw in lift passes as part of the deal.

Man: That's good to know.

3 You hear a woman leaving a voicemail message for a friend about a job interview.

Hi Catrina, just to let you know I had my interview this morning, for the hotel manager job. It went OK, I think. Well, I was shaking like a leaf before I went in – I don't know why because I was well prepared – but once I got into the room, I think I replied to everything they asked clearly and confidently, and they seemed satisfied with what I had to say. They said they'd let me know within the next three days, so I'll just have to wait and see. I'm keeping my fingers crossed. See you soon. Bye.

4 You hear two people on holiday in Morocco talking about a camel ride they've just done.

Man: Wow, what an unforgettable experience!

Woman: I got loads of photos. Including some of our camels looking really grumpy!

Man: Luckily, I couldn't see their faces for most of the ride.

Woman: Well, camels aren't exactly known for their friendliness.

Man: And anyway, Ismail, the guide, made it clear to my camel that *he* was in charge. He wouldn't have put up with any nonsense. You know, the sight of the sand dunes and the shapes of desert rocks took my breath away – I hadn't been prepared for that.

Woman: I was so pleased we paid extra for the guide to take a different route to the other groups.

Man: Yes, that was good thinking on your part.

5 You hear an IT expert talking about passwords.

The thinking on passwords keeps changing. We once advised people to choose passwords that mixed up words, for example by adding capital letters, numbers and symbols, and to change their password every 90 days. But when people changed their passwords, they made only minimal alterations, so panda1 became panda2, for example. So, passwords like these got easier for cybercriminals to crack. Some people keep a note of their password by inserting it into the middle of what looks like a phone number. That's something we're told not to do, but I find it works for me, though the password's never actually stored on my cellphone.

6 You hear a guide on a tourist bus being asked about a tall building.

Man: What's that building on the skyline there? It's huge – I bet you can see the whole city from up there.

Woman: That's the City Hall. Its nickname is The Icicle, because of all the glass used in its construction. I love going there at sunrise and sunset because the light reflected off the glass is amazing. You can see the river from the top, but you don't get a panorama of the whole city – the clock tower's better for that. And The Icicle gets really busy outside, as it's where a lot of tour groups get dropped off and meet up again.

Man: OK, thanks.

7 You hear a local radio announcer giving a traffic report.

And now a traffic update. I'm pleased to report that traffic is moving smoothly in and around the city centre this afternoon, despite the icy conditions earlier in the day. But for drivers on the motorway, please be aware that traffic is at a standstill in both directions between junctions nine and ten. A lorry carrying tins of paint tipped over onto its side several hours ago. The vehicle has now been removed, but fire crews are in the process of clearing up the spilt load. The police are advising finding alternative routes in the meantime.

8 You hear a diving instructor talking to a woman who is learning to dive.

Man: Well done, Fliss. That was a great dive.

Woman: Thanks. I'm always terrified about jumping in backwards.

Man: Well, we can work on technique. But you've clearly listened to my advice about moving underwater. I don't know if you noticed but you didn't frighten off the fish because you were going at a much gentler pace. One thing I did spot today was you need to check the needle on your tank. Even though we're only doing short dives, it's an important habit to get into, as it's crucial to be aware of how much air you have left at all times.

Woman: I'll try and remember that.

LISTENING PART 2

62

You will hear an art student called Ella giving a talk about the history of mirrors. For questions 9 to 18, complete the sentences with a word or short phrase.

Hi everyone. I'm Ella and I'd like to tell you about the project I've just finished, which was about mirrors. I chose this topic because mirrors have a very long history and are important to us in both art and photography.

Early humans probably looked at their refection in rivers or streams, so you could say the very first mirrors were made of water. The earliest *man-made* mirrors were cut from stone, and I went to look at some of these at the Ancient Treasures Museum, which was a really exciting way to begin my project. Some ancient mirrors were made using a very shiny volcanic glass, which was black, but I didn't see any of those.

The museum has a room filled with Ancient Egyptian objects, including a collection of mirrors. They were flat, round discs and I had to pick them up wearing gloves to keep them free from scratches. They were made of polished copper and attached to handles, which would have made them easier to use. Despite being 4,900 years old, I could sort of see my face reflected.

Elsewhere in the museum, there were mirrors from Ancient Rome, Japan and China. They must have taken ages to make, as every single one of them had symbols carved on them. I couldn't decide if these illustrations represented nature, or possibly love, but I later learnt from the museum's researcher that they symbolise beauty, something that we in the art world are very concerned with.

The researcher lent me a book that contained pictures of early mirrors that have been found in different parts of the Roman Empire. No matter whether they were made from copper, gold or silver, they were really small – less than 20 centimetres in diameter. It occurred to me this must have been due to the cost of the metal, but then I read it was actually a question of weight, which made complete sense.

However, when I did some research online, I discovered that not all mirrors were small, and fragments of much larger mirrors have been uncovered. Although no remains survived from it, written records describe a lighthouse whose large mirror reflected sunlight during the day and a fire at night. This was to signal to ships they were approaching a harbour.

Mirrors made from glass didn't become widespread till the Middle Ages, from the 5th to the 15th centuries. They still weren't all that large, the glass had a slight colouring and was also curved, rather than flat like our mirrors today. This was a result of the manufacturing process, and the glass was backed with a sheet of metal.

These glass mirrors were very fragile, and the glass often broke as the hot metal was applied to the back. Even worse, the technique for making glass involved melting sand, but this wasn't pure enough, and the finished product was a poor reflector.

It wasn't until the Renaissance in the 15th century, when glass producers in Florence in Italy invented a new process, that modern mirrors started to appear. These mirrors were clearer than anything that had gone before, and were used by artists to enable them to show greater depth and scale in many paintings. And they gave rise to the self-portrait, a form that became incredibly popular.

From the 1700s onwards, mirrors were found in the houses of the wealthy, either on the walls or as portable objects. Round, square and oval mirrors were also added to furniture, and decorated with patterns that matched textiles and floor coverings.

Mirrors today are produced by fixing a thin layer of aluminium to a piece of glass. But this process was actually based on one developed by a chemist. He got his assistant to coat glass with a thin layer of silver in his workshop in Germany in 1835, and this made it possible for mirrors to be produced commercially by factory workers. For the first time in history, ordinary people could afford a mirror.

LISTENING PART 3

63

You will hear five short extracts in which people are talking about restaurants they've been to. For questions 19 to 23, choose from the list (A to H) why each speaker recommends the restaurant. Use each letter only once. There are three extra letters which you do not need to use.

Speaker 1

When I eat out, I usually book places I've never eaten at before, especially ones serving international food. For a recent family party, I booked a restaurant that's only been open a month. What I didn't realise was that it's had some fantastic reviews online, and the place was packed out. There was a band playing, and there was lots of noise from the chefs in the kitchen. But, do you know, that's what made it just right for a celebration dinner, and why I'd recommend it to anyone booking a similar event, even if the prices are a bit higher than elsewhere and the service is a bit slow.

Speaker 2

To celebrate the end of term, my friends and I ate at a fantastic restaurant last week. It's located in an old bicycle shop, so there are bike wheels hanging on the walls which is a bit different, but otherwise there's nothing particularly interesting about the place. But we spent half what you'd normally expect to pay and the portions were huge, and it was all fresh, healthy stuff. You order your food at the counter and then they bring it to your table, which some people might find a bit strange for a restaurant. I'm surprised it wasn't busier, but I've added a positive review on social media.

Speaker 3

I recently had a great lunch at a fish restaurant down by the harbour of my town. It took us forever to decide what to eat 'cos the menu was huge and everything on it was based on traditional recipes from this region. I guess the service was a bit slow, and the chef prepared the wrong starters for us, so it was lucky we weren't in a real hurry. I think it's definitely worth a visit though; you can sit outside and enjoy watching the boats go by. Everything we ate was so tasty. I'm sure I'll go back and try something different next time.

Speaker 4

My family took me to a really smart restaurant for my birthday. It's quite new and I'd never been there before because it's the kind of place you'd only go to on special occasions; it's not cheap to eat there. But the food was beautifully presented, there was so much attention to detail in every single dish. And the head chef came out and spoke to us personally, which I thought was a really nice gesture. Since our visit, he's been in lots of newspapers and magazines. I've heard it's already harder to get a table as people want to try his food for themselves.

Speaker 5

We had dinner at a popular restaurant in an area of our town where there are lots of narrow streets with really interesting old houses. The head chef trained at a top hotel in the Caribbean and everything on the menu was seafood, which is my favourite. Throughout our meal the waiting staff couldn't do enough for us – basically nothing was too much trouble – so that's why I'd encourage you to go. Unfortunately, there happened to be some noisy people at the table next to us, which was really annoying, so we asked to move and we were given a different table.

LISTENING PART 4

64

You will hear an interview with a writer called Eddy Carlton, who is talking about his experience of growing oranges in Spain. For questions 24 to 30, choose the best answer (A, B or C).

Interviewer: Today, I'm thrilled to welcome best-selling author Eddy Carlton, who's back in the UK promoting his new novel. Before we talk about your novel, Eddy, I'm sure our listeners would love to know why you left Scotland and moved to Spain where you bought a fruit farm.

Eddy: Well, my farm's in Southern Spain, in a beautiful valley where people have been farming for centuries. A couple of years ago, I was there looking for background information for a novel and I walked past a picture of the farmhouse in an estate agent's window. It was love at first sight! I knew I had to buy it. It wasn't cheap, but I had enough income from the sale of my books, and I'd grown up on a farm, so I knew a bit about how to run an agricultural business.

Interviewer: Fantastic. So you bought the farm, moved in, and then what?

Eddy: Well, the day we moved in there was a tremendous storm, which I knew happens there sometimes, but which I'd never experienced in my life before. Luckily, the heating was working and we had enough food, so we stayed indoors for a few days. When we finally came out and were able to make a tour of the orange trees, we noticed that many of them were diseased and had to be cut down. It's taken a good few years to get to the stage of producing enough good fruit to sell.

Interviewer: And how were you received by the locals?

Eddy: Everyone was really welcoming. None of them knew who I was, so I wasn't given any special treatment, which was a relief. I think they thought I was a bit mad going out into the midday sun to work, but they kept their thoughts to themselves. They *were* willing, however, to give me plenty of guidance on how to look after orange trees. It proved invaluable to learn from their experience of running their own orange farms.

Interviewer: I'm amazed you had time to carry on writing, with so much to do on the farm.

Eddy: Well, both sides of my life are of equal significance to me. I don't think I could give up either. In Scotland, I used to stare out the window for hours, desperately searching for inspiration, but now, I only have to glance up at the sky or take a quick walk through the trees and the ideas start to flow. Having said that, I'm yet to base any of my novels in Spain. I don't know why.

Interviewer: So, how's the orange farm doing now?

Eddy: We're producing plenty, and luckily I sell everything I grow to a local co-operative. There are plenty of students around to help with the picking, and I've had loads of family and friends come over for a free holiday in exchange for doing some work. There's less demand for oranges in some markets – shoppers are tending to go for smaller, more tropical fruit – so that might mean I won't do so well in the future.

Interviewer: You mentioned the area where you live has been inhabited for a long time.

Eddy: That's right. Since the Romans settled there and built a military base, a theatre and baths. You'd expect the place to be crowded with tourists, but hardly anyone goes sightseeing there. The remains are everywhere, but you have to look hard to find them. Perhaps I shouldn't say this, but I'm not sure I'd appreciate seeing hotels being built in our lovely valley.

Interviewer: Quite. So are there any other plans for the farm?

Eddy: Well, I won't be able to carry on doing this forever, and I'm delighted my sons and their families have agreed to come over and share the running of the farm. There are a couple of cottages on the estate, so I'll move into one and they're going to have the main farmhouse. I'm having discussions with a neighbour to see if I can buy some of his land and that'll mean we can start growing other things.

Interviewer: Fantastic. So, your new novel …

Keys

Test 1

Reading and Use of English

Part 1

Training

1 **1** from **2** to **3** in **4** for **5** to **6** of **7** on **8** with **9** from **10** to

2 **1** Why don't you apply ~~to~~ for the job? **2** I don't believe ~~of~~ in telling lies, even to be kind. **3** The match resulted ~~with~~ in a draw. **4** Mary dealt ~~from~~ with the problem really well. **5** What can you contribute ~~for~~ to the discussion?

3

verbs followed by nouns	**verbs followed by infinitive with *to***
assist support accept imagine achieve appreciate	manage agree pretend struggle

4 **1** D **2** B **3** D **4** A **5** C **6** C **7** A **8** B

5

make	**take**	**put**	**hold**	**keep**	**have**
use of your way the most of	into account responsibility a risk advantage of an interest charge/control the opportunity something seriously	pressure on an end to	your breath	an eye on someone waiting pressure on	responsibility a word the opportunity

6 **1** to hold her breath **2** to take into account **3** made their way **4** take anything seriously **5** kept waiting **6** have a word **7** putting pressure on **8** keep an eye on

7 **1** D **2** B **3** C **4** A **5** D **6** B **7** B **8** A

8 **1** fault **2** raise **3** valuable **4** definitely **5** support **6** rise **7** error **8** valued **9** assist **10** absolutely

9 **1** f **2** h **3** e **4** b **5** c **6** d **7** g **8** a

10 **1** takes after **2** catch up with **3** fell through **4** get away with **5** came across **6** lived up to **7** give away **8** sort out

Exam practice

1 **D:** 'Typically' means that train stations and airports are the most common places to put pianos.

2 **A:** 'In theory … but …' is a common expression. The pianos may be played by anybody but in fact it's capable pianists who tend to use them.

3 **C:** 'from memory' means the same as 'by heart', i.e. without needing to read the music.

4 **A:** The crowd will be 'attracted' to the area. The sound of the piano cannot 'invite' or 'welcome' them.

5 **B:** The meaning of 'quiet thoughtful moment' is 'time to reflect'.

6 **A:** This is the grammatical phrase 'get somebody doing something'.

7 **B:** This is a fixed phrase. None of the others fit with these prepositions.

8 **C:** Only one of these has the right meaning here of 'in different circumstances'.

Part 2

Training

1 **1** –; the; a; – **2** an; a; –; The; a **3** The; the; the **4** this; a; these **5** the; a; –; the; the **6** This; an; a; the; –

2 **1** lot **2** few **3** the **4** more **5** Every **6** many **7** most **8** a **9** none **10** any **11** lots **12** no **13** one **14** a **15** an **16** Both **17** some **18** a **19** an

3 **1** who / that **2** which / that **3** who(m) **4** where **5** who **6** which **7** whose **8** which

4
1 Let me introduce you to Barbara, ~~her~~ whose mother you know quite well.

2 The train, ~~that~~ which was five hours late, finally arrived at its destination.

3 correct

4 My cousin, ~~that~~ who lives in America, is coming to visit me next month.

5 correct

6 I went back to the café ~~which~~ where I thought I'd left my umbrella.

7 Rita was the colleague ~~which~~ who/that helped me the most when I started here.

8 There aren't many people that/who have worked here as long as I have.

5 at least; at all costs; at risk; at first sight
on behalf of; on balance; on average; on condition that
for the sake of; for real
in any case; in doubt; in a way; in view of; in theory; in due course; in the first place; in need of; in conclusion
with respect to
by heart; by far

6 **1** in due course **2** for the sake of **3** in need of **4** by heart **5** at least **6** with respect to **7** for real **8** on behalf of

7 **1** d **2** e **3** g **4** a **5** c **6** f **7** h **8** b

8 **1** Despite **2** as **3** Not **4** Nevertheless **5** no **6** top **7** long **8** not

Exam practice

1 A

2 **9** for: a person can be 'famous for (doing / having done) something'.

10 came: a three-part phrasal verb frequently used with 'idea'.

11 of: 'over the course of' means 'for the duration of' or 'throughout'.

12 one: The 'it' rules out answers like 'some', 'many', etc.

13 him: The grammar of the verb is 'provide somebody with something'.

14 in: A very common linking phrase.

15 been: The full infinitive is 'be able to' and the meaning is 'managed to'.

16 as: It's important to know the 'as … as' grammatical structure, and it's also very common with 'long', 'well'.

Part 3

Training

1 **2** noun **3** adjective **4** adverb **5** adjective **6** adjective **7** adverb

2 **1** noun; impression **2** adjective; impressed **3** verb; impresses **4** noun; impressions **5** adverb; impressively **6** adjective; unimpressive

3

noun(s)	creation creativity	addition	mystery	enjoyment
verb(s)	create	add	mystify	enjoy
adjective(s)	creative	added additional	mysterious	enjoyable
adverb(s)	creatively	additionally	mysteriously	enjoyably

noun(s)	appearance apparition	care carelessness	energy
verb(s)	appear	care	energise
adjective(s)	apparent	careful careless caring	energetic
adverb(s)	apparently	carefully carelessly caringly	energetically

4 **1** mysterious **2** careless **3** creatively **4** apparent **5** additions **6** enjoyable

5 **1** beautifully **2** advertisements **3** similarities **4** convincing **5** accidentally

6 **1** disorganised **2** misunderstanding **3** impatience **4** unrecognisable **5** irresponsible

Exam practice

17 courageous: This adjective fits with *heroic*.

18 jewellery/jewelry: Note the spelling change required if you write the British English version. *jewels* would not be correct, because of the words *items of*. You can say *pots and jewels* but you have to say *pots and items of jewellery*.

19 fearless: There are two possible adjectives: *fearless* means 'without fear', and *fearful* means 'frightened', which doesn't apply to the Amazons!

20 birth: *at birth* means 'when they were born'.

21 truth: This is the noun form of *true*. It's uncountable, so it goes with *some*.

22 neighbo(u)ring: There are two adjectives from *neighbour* – the other (*neighbourly/neighborly*) applies to people and means 'being helpful and friendly'.

23 evidence: The only other word you could form from this word would be *evidently*, which is clearly not the correct part of speech here.

24 unusually: This one needs both a prefix and suffix change. The sense of this refers back to their tallness in the first paragraph.

Part 4

Training

1 **1** play tennis as well as **2** deal less than **3** the most boring film **4** speak as confidently

2 **1** to take **2** to catch **3** walking **4** missing **5** to give **6** to get

3 **1** a **2** b **3** b **4** a **5** b **6** a

4 **1** agreed **2** admitted **3** persuaded **4** denied **5** demanded **6** refused **7** advised

5 **1** wishes he lived in a **2** knew his number I would/I'd **3** wishes she had enough **4** time **5** find the recipe I'll

Exam practice

25 can't / cannot come out until: *only when* means 'not … until', and the negative is formed with *can't*.

26 apologised for making / having made: The grammar of the verb is *apologise (to somebody) for doing / having done something*. Note that *upset* is a verb in the first sentence and an adjective in the second.

27 be too busy: In this instance, *too* means 'not enough' and that idea is present in the first sentence.

28 made the/a decision not: With *decide* you can have: *decide (not) to do something*, or *decide against doing something*.

29 been sent a number: *several* is the same as *a number of* NOT 'lots of'.

30 had more experience: You can say *was more experienced* or *had more experience*.

Part 5

Training

1b she tried to ignore the thoughts that had been bothering her for the last few weeks: Was this place really for her? Should she have picked somewhere less grand? Her friends had all assured her she'd have a fabulous time there, but how could they possibly know?

1c D

1d **1** B **2** C **3** A

2a ending

2b Key: C

A is wrong because *too many* indicates a problem. There were a lot of students there, and most of the seats were already taken when Nora arrived.

B is wrong because the other students didn't know Nora was going to be there.

D is wrong because the other students were happy and talking, but not about Nora.

Exam practice

31 A: Tom wonders why such a strange-looking sport should have a regular place in the sporting calendar and be watched worldwide with such huge interest. B is tempting because of 'Everyone picks a side' but B means that the public have strong opinions that it is either a good thing or a bad thing.

32 D: As a boy, Tom thought the crews should simply go faster, but we can infer from this that he was just too young to understand that this would be impossible to do. Tom didn't at the time have any thought of being in the race himself, nor was he playing a game imagining to be a coach.

33 B: The whole paragraph is about this, but the words 'the alarm always tested my resolve' gives the answer in particular. C is tempting but Tom does not actually say this – he doesn't comment on the nature of what he's eating.

34 A: This comes from *heavily-favoured Oxford crew*. The Cambridge crew seem well prepared but there's no comment from Tom about this being perfect. The injury was only to their best rower.

35 C: The Cambridge crew were already upset by the injury, and then the weather conditions seem to demoralise them further. Oxford started fast and then kicked again later. The river conditions did not suddenly change.

36 D: This is clearly stated in *Head to head ... Them or us ... This is why it matters* Tom seems to like the psychological challenge but doesn't describe it as *complex*.

Part 6

Training

1 **1** Nevertheless; them **2** Others; here **3** As a result; his **4** This was because **5** the latter

2 **1** f **2** a **3** i **4** c **5** h **6** e **7** g **8** b **9** d

Exam practice

1 **1** It's an introduction to a book, and it's about the approach the writer has taken in the book when writing about his research into polar bears.

2 **Suggested answers**

1 the polar bear symbolising the Arctic

2 the Arctic being the polar bear's natural home

3 the polar bear and the ocean

4 the background to the writer's research

5 the polar bear as an important part of the polar marine ecosystem

6 how the polar bear conserves energy

7 the polar bear as a unique individual

2 **37** G: In G, *it is simply where it belongs* links backwards to the main idea of the first paragraph. After 37, G links forwards to the idea of *home* for a polar bear.

38 A: links backwards to the idea of *marine mammal* and forwards to the idea of confusion between the animal's status in different North American countries.

39 E: This sentence is the only one that says what the writer is trying to do in his book as a whole.

40 F: There is a clear link between *other species* in F and *the arctic seal* after the gap.

41 D: The idea of *next meal* in D, fits backwards with obtaining energy and forwards with success as predators.

42 C: The idea of *inquisitive* in C links very strongly forwards to the polar bear behaviour described.

Part 7

Training

1 **1** c **2** e **3** d **4** a **5** b

2 **1** determined **2** convinced **3** ashamed **4** disappointed **5** delighted **6** astonished **7** relieved **8** amused

Exam practice

43 C: This is at the end of c: *He did concede later ...* .

44 B: This is Baird's quote about people not going to *places of entertainment*.

45 A: *The first broadcast ... No recording exists ...*

46 E: This is in the last sentence of E.

47 B: This is the reference to the BBC trialling a new TV service.

48 A: This is Lord Reith writing criticisms in his diary. It's not C – the programme Gander is critical of is one he hasn't yet seen but has read a preview of.

49 C: This is the beginning of C and Gander's complaint in a newspaper about the broken window programme.

50 D: This is from *the announcers could not ...* .

51 D: This is from the first two lines of D.

52 A: This is in the words of the singer Adele Dixon.

Writing

Part 1 (essay)

Training

1 **1** I would argue that; It seems to me that **2** whereas; It could be argued that **3** On the one hand; For example; rather than; Additionally **4** despite; In my opinion **5** In my view; On the other hand; In conclusion

2 Whether or not you think the internet has changed our lives including something about the benefits of the internet and how it has affected personal relationships. You also have to write about an idea of your own.

3 Students' own ideas

4 **1** d **2** c **3** e **4** a **5** b

5 I agree; On the one hand; it could be argued that; Additionally; It seems to me that; In my view; I would argue that; rather than; In my opinion; In conclusion

6 **1** Studying abroad to learn English **2** how you can learn English abroad; where you can stay while you're doing it, and an idea of your own

7 Students' own ideas

8 **1** Yes, each paragraph has a different purpose **2** I think; I would argue that; despite; In my opinion; I seems to me; To conclude **3** Paragraph 2 **4** Paragraph 3 **5** Paragraph 4 (importance of experiencing culture) **6** Paragraph 5

Exam practice (essay)

1 **1** your English teacher **2** giving opinions and reasons; you can also include examples of your own experience from your childhood **3** You could add something about your own childhood or experience. Alternatively, you could mention the importance of a healthy lifestyle. Or you could say how time outdoors helps people become interested in sports, which is good for health and developing relationships.

2 **Sample answer**

Childhood for many people was a time of adventure. They spent a lot of time out in the fresh air, running around, climbing trees and playing games. But it's known that these days, children don't spend as much time outside, and some people are concerned that this is becoming a problem.

It's true that when children are outside, they do lots of physical activity like sports, and this is good for their health. It helps their muscles get stronger, and it can also help them make friends. On the other hand, children often fall and hurt themselves. It's also true that the 'fresh air' probably isn't very fresh at all because of traffic pollution.

Personally, I don't think that schoolteachers and parents should be too worried if children are spending more time indoors. Many children and teenagers spend a lot of time looking at screens, but this has a lot of benefits. It's also wrong to assume that time spent outdoors is healthy and that time spent indoors is unhealthy. Over time, lifestyles change, and we need to accept that this is true.

Notes

- *A successful answer which fully addresses the question*
- *Both content points and the writer's own idea (changing lifestyles) are discussed*
- *Clearly doesn't agree with the statement, and gives reasons for this view*
- *Uses a range of phrases to begin sentences: 'But it's known that'; 'On the other hand'; 'It's true that'; 'Over time,'*
- *No grammar mistakes; verbs formed correctly (although almost all verbs are in the present simple tense)*
- *Some repetition: 'true' is used three times*

Part 2 (article)

Training

1 angry – furious big – enormous hot – boiling
interested – fascinated good – awful
frightened – terrified cold – freezing small – tiny
happy – delighted bad – fantastic

2 **1** awful **2** enormous **3** fantastic **4** delighted **5** tiny **6** freezing **7** boiling **8** fascinated **9** terrified **10** furious

3 **1**d **2** b **3** a **4** c

4 and 5 **1** a: *mean a lot, stay in touch, feeling down*

2 a: use of rhetorical questions, giving examples, exclamation marks.

3 b: exclamation marks – *even if we can't sing in tune!; luckily for me they all feel the same way!*

rhetorical questions – *Have you ever wondered …?; How many friends have you met …?*

6 **1** Homes of the future; **2** Describe in what ways homes will be different and what ways they will be the same.

7 **1** Science fiction or reality? **2** Devices control the house **3** The same as usual

8 **1** Fine: 189 words (with headings)

2 Yes, three paragraphs. The first paragraph introduces and contextualises the exam question; paragraph 2 provides advantages; paragraph 3 explains that the writer doesn't think things will change
3 Yes, it has an informal tone similar to a magazine article.
4 Yes, paragraph 2 describes the differences in the future and paragraph 3 describes what will be same.
5 Rhetorical questions: *Science fiction or reality?; Will robots take over?; Will we build houses using different materials?* Informal language: *click of your fingers; super-clean*

Exam practice

1 **1** to interest the people who have requested articles for the website, and to make them want to publish your article there **2** three
3 There are many ways to make your answer interesting. For example, you could express a strong opinion (either in favour of or against learning music) throughout your article. You could begin with an anecdote, or with a question for the reader.

2

Sample answer

Music in education

I'm a huge fan of music, and always have been. I'm in a band (I play the guitar), and for a time I was also in my college orchestra (I used to play the flute too, and we rehearsed every day). I've benefitted a lot from being musical – performing at concerts has helped me to be more confident. Music has always been an important part of my social life, as my band members are also my closest friends.

But does that mean that everyone should be taught music? No, not necessarily. I think everyone should have the choice. Learning music involves a lot of time. Plus, paying for lessons and buying an instrument can be expensive, and for some people, that can be a waste of money.

For me, music is a passion, and I'm glad that I can play an instrument, as it helps me appreciate when I hear other people play music. But other people aren't musical, and I don't believe that music should be imposed on them.

Notes

- *A clear answer*
- *All questions answered (though not in the same order)*
- *The writer addresses the question from their own perspective; also talks about music education generally*
- *The writer's main point ('I don't believe that music should be imposed') is well expressed*
- *More varied sentence structures would be better: the first three sentences all start with 'I*
- *Some appropriate vocabulary related to music: 'band member'; 'perform'; 'rehearse'.*

Part 2 (review)

Training

1 General: *I found/felt that …; I have used it for …; In my opinion …; One thing to consider is …*

Negative: *I felt let down by …; On the downside, this device …; I was disappointed by …; Unfortunately, one of the minuses is …*

Positive: *One of the positive features of this device is …; I was extremely impressed by …; The big advantage of this device is …; I'm really delighted by …*

2 **1** *One thing to consider is* the battery life of the mobile phone.
2 *In my opinion,* there are lots of similar mobile phones on the market at the moment.
3 *I'm really delighted by* the special filters included on the camera.
4 *One of its positive features is* that it's very light.
5 *I felt let down by / I was disappointed by* the headphones; they were very uncomfortable.
6 *Unfortunately, one of the minuses is* its short battery life.

3 **1** The writer has organised them into clear paragraphs and used headings for each paragraph. **2** The writer used an asterisk (*) to indicate these. **3** five paragraphs. **4** Yes, they mention a recent gadget, give information about the features and make a recommendation. **5** The writer has included some useful language to include in the review.

4 Students' own answers

5 **1** visited, a new restaurant, your areas, your opinion, describe, food, staff, recommend to other people **2** eating at a restaurant **3** describe the food, staff, prices **4** a recommendation

6 No, the writer felt that the service and food was very poor.

7 **1** I was given excuses ranging from being too busy, or running out of food. I had to wait for an hour for my burger. When it did arrive, the burger was too well done and the chips were cold. I complained to the waiter but he said nothing. **2** restaurant: modern, large (windows), relaxed; menu: extensive, reasonably priced; food: awful, overcooked, cold. **3** Contrast links: although, but; Other linking expressions: Also, as well as, overall, as **4** I was impressed by …, On the downside …, I felt that …,

Exam practice (review)

1 **1** This is up to you. Many reviews contain both positive and negative comments. **2** The review needs to be well planned and well written. It doesn't matter what film you have written about, or whether anyone has seen or heard of the film. You can make up the film if you wish!

2 **Sample answer**

I recently watched Kenneth Branagh's film version of Shakespeare's great tragedy *Hamlet*. Many of the central characters are related to Hamlet, such as his mother the queen, his stepfather Claudius, and his father, the old king Hamlet.

The film is beautifully shot and brilliantly acted. It is very faithful to Shakespeare's original text, meaning that it is four hours long, which may be excessive for some people.

It's probably fair to say that most families are loving groups of people, who support each other. Tragically, Hamlet's family is different. Hamlet suspects that his father was murdered by Claudius. This suspicion drives Hamlet wild, as he is torn between his love for his mother and hatred of his stepfather.

I don't want to reveal what happens in the end, but the film is certainly worth watching. After seeing *Hamlet*, it made me realise how lucky I am to have the family that I have! Poor Hamlet wasn't so fortunate.

Notes

- *A successful answer, with some advanced vocabulary used well: 'central character'; 'faithful to'; 'excessive'; 'torn'*
- *Appropriate focus on Hamlet's family in the answer*
- *Good balance between summarising the story and explaining the role of the family members*
- *Gives a personal reaction to the film*
- *No title – although it's not compulsory, a well-chosen title would have been a good idea*
- *Correct length*
- *Sensible division into four paragraphs*
- *No errors of grammar, vocabulary, spelling or punctuation*

Part 2 (email)

Training

1 I couldn't believe it! I
I could not believe it. F
I would be grateful if you could explain … F
I want to tell you … I
I would like to put forward … F
I'm writing about … I
It would be advisable to … F
Can you tell me about …? I
to think about I
to consider … F
Hi David! I
Dear Mr Simpson F
Please try to … I
Approx.: I
approximately F
It's a good idea … I
It was advisable to F
I am writing in response to … F

2 **1** *I am writing in response to* the job vacancy advertised in the local newspaper. **2** *I would be grateful if you could explain* where you plan to build the new car park? **3** *It was advisable to* postpone the plans until next year. **4** You should *consider* about the impact on the environment. **5** *I would like to put forward* our new initiative. **6** *It would be advisable to* remember the local residents in your plans.

3 **1** scholarships are being offered to overseas students **2** fees, accommodation and food **3** write an email explaining why they should get a scholarship

4 Yes **2** In the first paragraph **3** No, so he uses *Dear Sir/Madam* **4** Yes **5** Yes **6** Dear Sir/Madam; Yours faithfully **7** Yes **8** I am writing in response to; I would be grateful; consider

Exam practice (email)

1 **1** to ask for your help with a college research project about parks **2** Your email will just focus on parks *in your country*. **3** a) What problems do parks face in your country? b) What can be done to improve and maintain them? c) Who should be responsible for this work?

2 **Sample answer**

Hi Steve,

What a surprise to hear from you after all this time! It sounds as though you're busy with your course, and of course I'm glad to answer your questions.

Basically, the parks in my country are in poor condition on the whole. New plants and trees are rarely planted, and the grass isn't cut very often. It's such a shame, because most parks are used quite a lot, especially by families at weekends, and people play a lot of football there.

According to the law (as far as I know), the government owns the parks and is responsible for the maintenance. But the thing is that there isn't really enough money to pay for all the schools, roads and hospitals, as well as keeping the parks in good condition.

What I'd like to see is community action, and people offering to clear up the parks in their own time, plant trees and that sort of thing. Oh well, maybe one day!

Anyway, good luck with your research, and stay in touch.

Say 'hi' to your family from me.

All the best,

Diana

Notes

- *A friendly email, with appropriate opening and closing; the first and last paragraphs are basically 'chat' with Steve*
- *All the information Steve has asked for has been provided*
- *Paragraphs are used appropriately*
- *No language errors*
- *Correct length*
- *Some good vocabulary is included: 'trees are rarely planted', 'grass isn't cut, 'responsible for the maintenance'.*

Listening

Part 1

Training

1a **1** A conversation **2** Two friends **3** They are talking about a nature walk they both went on.

1b C

2 The underlined section matches the key – C. They were both impressed by the rare birds they saw.

A isn't correct. The man says he thought they would see *a few other interesting animals and birds,* but the woman points out that the bad weather didn't help. For example, she … *wasn't really expecting to see* any butterflies, for that reason.

B isn't correct because, although the man is tired after the walk, the woman says *the guide did warn us it'd be seven or eight kilometres.*

3 B The man thinks the later opening times aren't helpful to him, as he's playing football when the store is open later.

4 A They both like the fashions. The woman says that *the range they had was cool, all the latest stuff,* and the man says there were *definitely clothes I wanted.*

C They both agree about the staff. The woman says they were *keen to help,* and the man says *the girl serving tried to find things in my size.*

Exam practice

1 C **2** B **3** A **4** C **5** C **6** A **7** A **8** B

Part 2

Training

1 a noun

3 horse – The cue for the answer is *the one (painting) I was really keen to find.* The distractors are *rainbow* and *castle.*

5 entertaining

6 The cue was *and in fact the whole thing turned out to be* and the distractors were *dull, detailed* and *uninteresting.*

Exam practice

9 cousin **10** neighbour/neighbor **11** deserted **12** water (bottle) **13** (beautiful) mountains **14** canoe **15** parrots **16** (strong) wind(s) **17** (swollen) ankles **18** empty

Part 3

Training

1 **1** *Starlight* tends to go for giving you money off the big fashion shows and things like that, **2** The distractors are B, D and F. **3** G The distractors are: A – *things like word games,* C – *looking at the adverts is a good way to relax,* and H – *local events they've been to,* although they're not *what attracts me to this mag* (G)

Exam practice

19 F **20** B **21** G **22** A **23** C

Part 4

Training

2 B – Alice says that she *was really glad* when she started operating on the internet, which *has just been so much better* than running her shop, as she's saved time and money.

A – isn't correct – she used to chat to customers, but she doesn't say she misses it.

C – She may be proud of the service, but it isn't *unique* – she says that other florists will do the same thing.

3 A – Alice says she has to be *extremely sympathetic to my customers' needs.*

B is wrong because although she has to be creative, she says *that customers do understand and appreciate that.*

C is wrong because it's not the job that is stressful for Alice. She's trying to make her customers' situations less stressful, by trying to *take some of the pressure off.*

Exam practice

24 C **25** B **26** A **27** A **28** B **29** A **30** C

Speaking

Part 1

Training

1 To add extra information: and, as well, too

To give a reason: because, the reason for this is

To give an example: for example, for instance, like, such as

To give your opinion: I think, I would say that

To ask the examiner to repeat: Could you repeat that, please? Sorry, can you say that again?

2 **1** also **2** because, For **3** such, too **4** would **5** think **6** reason

3 Ana asks examiner to repeat: In what ways do you think you will use English in the future?

Part 2

Training

1 2, 3, 5, 6, 8, 9, 10

2 **2** Well, both photos show people doing exercise.

3 In the first photo, the people are doing an exercise class, while in the second photo a group of people are playing basketball together.

5 The people in the gym don't seem to know each other, because they aren't talking to each other. On the other hand, I think the people playing basketball are probably friends, because it looks like an informal game.

6 The exercise class looks quite serious, whereas the basketball game looks very relaxed. … Another difference is that the basketball is outside, which I think makes it more fun.

8 The people in the gym don't look as happy as the people playing basketball. They aren't smiling, and the woman on the right looks a bit bored. I think the people playing basketball are probably enjoying themselves more.

9 I think people go to exercise classes because they want to get fit, and maybe it fits in with their busy lives. I think the people in the second photo do this because it's an enjoyable way to meet their friends and have fun.

10 I'd rather do exercise in a fun way, like this, because I think just doing exercise in a gym is a bit boring.

3 **1** Both **2** other **3** whereas **4** as **5** more **6** difference

4 **1** rather **2** enjoy **3** prefer **4** more **5** not

5 2, 3, 4

6 **1** c **2** b, f **3** d, g, h **4** a, e

7 Students' own answers

8 b

9 Students' own answers

10 Students' own answers

Part 3

Training

1 **1** The topic is improving a town for teenagers. **2** You should discuss all the ideas. **3** No, you shouldn't try to reach agreement until the examiner asks you to.

2 **1** c **2** a **3** d **4** b

3 **1** sounds **2** see **3** idea **4** right **5** think **6** true **7** agree **8** completely

4 They agree that a sports centre would bring the most benefit.

Part 4

Training

1 1 T 2 T 3 F 4 F

2 1 B 2 B 3 H 4 H

3 **1** say **2** think **3** opinion **4** view **5** opinion **6** think **7** views **8** feel

4 **1** b **2** e **3** a **4** c **5** d

5 Students' own answers

Test 2

Reading and Use of English

Part 1

Training

1 **1** arose **2** occurs **3** happened **4** appearing **5** risk **6** danger **7** uncertainty **8** threats **9** guide **10** control **11** directed **12** conducted **13** idea **14** attitude **15** view **16** Opinions

2 **1** drew **2** bear **3** delivered **4** crossed **5** raised **6** play **7** Leave **8** put

3 **1** D **2** B **3** B **4** D **5** A **6** C **7** A **8** B

Exam practice

1 D: This is a very useful fixed phrase to remember: *an extremely popular destination for/with* + a group of people.

2 C: This is a collocation, but the meaning might also help you a little: 'closely guarded' suggests you keep a secret close to yourself.

3 A: The grammar of the verb is *praise something for (its)* + some quality it has (or *praise somebody for (doing) something*).

4 B: This is the right word in the situation – it is one of the many uses of *achieve*.

5 D: *cater for* + *(the tastes of)* is a common expression.

6 C: This is a useful collocation – something has a *(very/highly) distinct flavour*.

7 D: You can say: *The café is hard to reach / find* or *The café is hard to get to*.

8 A: A very useful fixed phrase, but the meaning might also help you a little – if it's hard to get to, it suggests visitors have had to put in some *effort* to do so.

Part 2

Training

1 **1** Could you send me some more information about the place where you're living?

2 That was a strange thing to say!

3 There aren't any biscuits left.

4 Correct

5 There's an interesting course I'd like to do in the evenings.

6 My two sisters ~~all~~ both like coffee ice cream.

7 Where's the best place to have coffee in this area?

8 A l~~L~~ot of people at the meeting said they rarely used public transport./Lots of people at the meeting said they rarely used public transport.

9 Correct

10 Lucy's doing a college project on the history of film.

2 **1** are **2** had **3** have **4** is / was **5** been **6** was

3 **1** enough **2** than **3** whichever **4** through **5** Whose **6** whether

4 **1** in time **2** As soon as / Once **3** until **4** yet **5** In the meantime **6** already **7** By the time **8** since

5 **1** By the time **2** already **3** in the meantime **4** until **5** since **6** As soon as **7** once **8** yet

Exam practice

1 C

2 **9** of: *the truth of the matter* is a very common and useful phrase.

10 being: *being* here is a gerund – a word ending in *-ing* that is made from a verb and used like a noun.

11 this / that: *this category* refers back to people who can write equally well with either hand.

12 comes: as with many fixed phrases, there is only one possible answer.

13 an: Grammatically, this clause requires an article.

14 to: You *train somebody to do something*, for example a coach trains a runner to become faster.

15 same: Another very useful fixed phrase: *the same can be said of*

16 less: The context should rule out *more* – so this gap shows you the importance of reading the text carefully.

Part 3

Training

1 **1** -y, bravery **2** -ible, visible **3** -ship, relationship **4** -or, operator **5** -ism, criticism **6** -ish, foolish **7** -er, supplier **8** -ist, motorist

2 **1** foolish **2** operator(s) **3** relationship **4** bravery **5** motorists **6** invisible **7** suppliers **8** criticism(s)

3

adjective	noun	verb	adverb
free	freedom	free	freely
hot	heat	heat	hotly
strong	strength	strengthen	strongly
wide	width	widen	widely
long	length	lengthen	
anxious	anxiety		anxiously
deep	depth	deepen	deeply

4 **1** strength **2** anxiety **3** widened **4** freely **5** depth **6** heating **7** lengthen

Exam practice

1 A

2 **1** a verb **2** a noun, (t)ion **3** there's a spelling change, the final *e* is lost

3 **17** pleasure(s): This is the noun in this word formation *family*; *simple pleasure* is a well-known collocation.

18 entertaining: This is a common adjective to describe books, often occurring with *highly*.

19 desperate: Note the spelling changes. Also, *desperate* as an adjective can be quite positive, as in: *I'm desperate to see you after all this time*, whereas *despair* is very negative.

20 excitement: This is the noun from *excite*, the adjective being *exciting*.

21 careful: The other adjectives from *care* are *careless*, *caring* and *carefree*.
22 reference: A reference guide / book / manual is one that you refer to when you need some information.
23 something: The following *it* rules out *somebody* or *someone* as an answer.
24 explanation: Note the loss of the *i* from *explain*.

Part 4

Training

1 **1** had done **2** should have checked **3** had **4** hadn't **5** might have had **6** must have thought **7** I'd been **8** could have got

2 **1** has shown Anna **2** had ever seen **3** is preparing **4** couldn't have **5** were given **6** must have been told **7** actually seen leaving **8** the staff uniforms kept

3 **1** d **2** h **3** g **4** f **5** b **6** a **7** e **8** c

4 **1** pointed out **2** coming down with **3** call off **4** face up to **5** hit it off **6** give in **7** run out of **8** came up with

5 **1** to have **2** knew **3** taking **4** have been **5** to go **6** to **7** getting **8** having

Exam practice

25 prevented Lizzie (from) training for: The grammar of the verb is *prevent somebody from doing something*.

26 to leave most / much: If you only eat a little of something, you leave most of it.

27 haven't / have not done as much: *less* in this context means 'not as much as'.

28 had become a mother: The word *become* is prompting you to come up with *mother*, and there's no need to say *for the first time* as this would take the answer to well over five words.

29 keep it to: *Don't shout it out* and *keep it to yourself* are both useful expressions, and different ways of saying the same thing.

30 change your mind about (wanting): Changing your mind is the same as deciding not to do something or deciding not to have something.

Part 5

Training

1a C

1b The value of research into risk taking and the people who take part in extreme sports has been questioned by some. Given the limited funds available, is it really worth spending time and money investigating this particular aspect of human nature? I think this is a fair question, and it also seems to me that extreme sports tend to attract those with less concern than most not only for their own safety, but also for that of others; when things go wrong, rescuers are frequently put at risk because someone else was deliberately putting themselves in danger. Thrill-seeking and a wish to escape from everyday routine hardly excuses an outcome such as this. Even relatively well-established sports such as snowboarding and paragliding entail a level of risk-taking that many would consider unacceptable.

1c A: The value of research into risk taking and the people who take part in extreme sports has been questioned by some. Given the limited funds available, is it really worth spending time and money investigating this particular aspect of human nature? I think this is a fair question

B: Thrill-seeking and a wish to escape from everyday routine

D: relatively well-established sports such as snowboarding and paragliding

2a A

2b **Suggested answer**

Looking for thrills and *wishing to escape from everyday routine* are the grammatical subjects of the verb *excuses*, so they cannot be the object of the verb, too. *People deliberately putting themselves in danger* is not an outcome (result). *Rescuers being put at risk* is a result, and the writer is saying there is no excuse for this happening, so *this* refers to option A.

Exam practice

1 **1** T **2** F **3** F **4** F

2 **31** B: This comes from *This is not always the case*. Usually he's brain dead after long plane journeys. He isn't late or apologetic, although these are tempting ideas in the circumstances.

32 D: This comes from *career depends on profitable live shows* and also in Porter's quote beginning *to be the most streamed artist …* . If you try to work out the answer just from your knowledge of *slim* then you might be tempted by B or C.

33 A: This comes from *sort of half off-duty, half on*, as well as the rest of the paragraph. Porter hasn't had a marketing image created for him and the use of the cap suggests he plans his own individual image.

34 C: This comes from lines 4–5 in the paragraph. Porter did keep up his singing. No comment is made about the jobs he tried.

35 D: This is the point of the paragraph but in particular the words: *Some people have settled in their discontent*. C is particularly tempting but this is not the point that Porter is making.

36 B: This is the main point being made by Porter. D is particularly tempting but in a way the opposite is true – he uses car travel as work time.

Part 6

Training

1 **1** D **2** A **3** C

2

A great deal of research has been done on memory. There are apparently many reasons why we remember certain things but forget others. **1…** One of the conclusions they have come to is that much of this happens while we are asleep.

The quality and duration of our sleep appears to affect whether or not our brains can successfully convert experiences and knowledge we have acquired whilst awake into long-term memories. To do this, our brains rely on regular periods of sleep every day. **2…** That is one of the reasons why sleep has become such an important area of research.

In the future, sleep experts may finally understand all the connections between sleep and memory. **3…**

A This means that interruptions to these patterns matter.

B As a result, interest in sleep research has increased significantly.

C Until they do, much of what happens after we have closed our eyes at night will remain a mystery.

D Scientists are also interested in how we process what we have seen or has happened to us.

E So our memories are formed in ways that are still not fully explained.

In paragraph 1, *they* in the text refers to *scientists* in option D.

In option A, *these patterns* refers to *regular periods of sleep every day*.

In paragraph 2, *That* refers to *interruptions to these patterns matter*.

In option C, *They* refers to *sleep experts*; also link from *In the future* and *Until they do*.

Exam practice

1 **1** Yes, the text has an 'I' voice (and this comes into one of the items).
2 Caroline Schefuele, co-president of a jewellery company
3 The name Caroline gives to the original diamond she bought.
4 a collection of jewels cut from the diamond

2 **37** F: The information in F refers to the diamond rather than the finished jewellery, and the *it* in F refers to *something* that's been found.

38 D: In D, *the only question was, what to do with .....* links very strongly with *There were various possibilities* after the gap.

39 A: The computer modelling in A is how Scheufele managed to figure out the best possible combination.

40 G: This speaks of *the impact of the jewels* and after the gap we have the writer's reaction to what she sees.

41 E: This gives an example of the collection's versatility and how it can be worn differently for different occasions.

42 C: This fits strongly in both directions. *This* after the gap refers to the fact that almost everybody in the workshop worked on the jewellery.

Part 7

Training

1 **1**g **2** f **3** e **4** b **5** d **6** c **7** h **8** a

2a **1** A **2** B **3** neither A nor B **4** A

2b A

Question 1: local councils frequently say these have been approved following extensive consultation amongst the local residents. However, in the case of policies designed to reduce the impact of traffic in cities, this is frequently not the case.

Question 4: It would be in the interests of all concerned if the views of residents were adequately researched, preferably by an agency approved by those on all sides of the debate.

B

Question 3: This idea was excellent, and aimed to encourage car sharing and increased use of public transport.

Question 2: Unfortunately, because of local opposition, this initiative had to be abandoned. In my view, the council should not have backed down. If they had kept the policy in place for longer than a couple of weeks, residents, including drivers, would have had the chance to experience the benefits, and would, I believe, have ended up in favour of the scheme.

Exam practice

1 **1** The same person – the runner is writing about his own experiences.

2 Initially he is indifferent to the dog, but by the end he feels sympathy / a sense of responsibility.

2 **43** C: from the last line of this section.

44 E: *I put her in my arms, warily, in case she bit me.*

45 D: This is from the second and third lines of D.

46 A: This is the writer's reaction to seeing other racers feed the dog and also in *There's no way I'm feeding it.*

47 B: *Normally my wife runs alongside me and we're quite sociable, but when it's just me I concentrate more on the race.*

48 E: *But flushed with happiness, towards the finish we raced past the others.*

49 C: This refers to his worries about the dog getting squashed.

50 D: This is the second half of D, when the writer sits and reflects on the dog's incredible loyalty.

51 E: From the first lines of E where the writer stops to help Gobi across the river.

52 A: This is referring to the 'self-sufficiency' regarding food and equipment.

Writing

Part 1 (essay)

Training

1 *Introductions:* I would argue that …; The question of …; First of all …

Contrasting linkers: However; Although; in contrast to; Nevertheless; Whereas …; in spite of

Conclusions: Lastly …; To sum up, there are arguments …; I have come to the conclusion that …; In conclusion (I believe that) …

2 **1** in contrast to **2** Nevertheless **3** The question of **4** In conclusion **5** in spite of

3 **Suggested answers**

Paragraph 1: introducing the topic - First of all, young people love gadgets and technology, whereas they see science as uninteresting.

Paragraph 2: write about television programmes - One way to make science more attractive is to have television programmes presented by celebrities, with subjects which are relevant to young people.

Paragraph 3: write about interactive museums - Another idea would be to set up interactive science museums in every town, where parents could take their children.

Paragraph 4: Explaining how to make science more attractive - Of course, it would help if scientists were better paid and young people were made aware of the range of jobs available.

Paragraph 5: conclusion - In conclusion, it is vital that more young people are attracted to science, since society's future depends on scientific progress.

4 **1** The writer's opinion is that (young people) see science as uninteresting and that the number of young people following a career in science has dropped. – paragraph 1

2 Television programmes – paragraph 2; Interactive museums – paragraph 3

3 The author also discusses scientists' salaries and job availability in the science sector in paragraph 4.

4 Television programmes = making science programmes with celebrities, with subjects relevant to young people; children identify with well-known people

Interactive museums = better to teach children about science through hands-on experiments rather than teach them in a classroom

Science jobs and salaries = young people are put off a scientific career because they think it means working in a badly paid job in a boring laboratory.

5 First of all; whereas; I would argue …; In conclusion…., in spite of

Exam practice (essay)

1 **1** This is up to you. You are free to agree, disagree, or partly agree, as long as you provide convincing reasons for your opinion.
2 You could refer to the changes in a town you know, and use this as evidence for your opinion.

2

Sample answer

The last few years have seen the centre of Lansford, where I live, change dramatically. When I was growing up, the town centre was thriving, with a number of shops and restaurants which always seemed to be busy. Nowadays though, several of these once successful businesses have had to close, and many of the streets in town contain boarded up buildings, especially where clothes shops used to be.

I suspect that the boom in online shopping may be to blame. When people can order products from their own home, there's no need to drive into town and look for a place to park. As a result, physical shops on the high streets are suffering.

However, it's hard to say whether this is definitely true. Trends in shops and shopping have always evolved, and this was the case long before the internet arrived in the late 20th century.

So perhaps it's a bit unfair to blame the internet. Time will tell whether our town centres will recover.

Notes

- *Agrees with the statement and gives reasons*
- *Also expresses doubt, saying that certainty about the cause isn't possible*
- *A range of tenses*
- *No language errors*
- *Appropriate length*
- *Ends by mentioning the future of town centres*

Part 2 (report)

Training

1 **1** Conclusions **2** Description and findings **3** Introduction
4 Recommendations and suggestions

2 **1** The main aim / purpose of this report is to give …
2 It has been suggested that / It would appear that most …
3 I would recommend / I would suggest that the council …
4 In conclusion, the council …
5 The council may lose the next election, according to a recent poll.

3 Key words: teacher, asked you, write, report, sports, local area, the views of visitors/local people, recommendation

4 **1** After a class discussion, the writer has to write a report.
2 Your English teacher **3** Either formal or neutral
4 Include the views of visitors and local people; make a recommendation.

5 **1** D **2** C **3** B **4** A

6 **1** I wanted to write a report; People were saying that; are rubbish; Why don't …?
2 *equipement* = equipment; *swiming* = swimming; *fasilities* = facilities; *counsil* = council
3 *local residents was asked for their views* = were asked; to enjoying themselves = to enjoy themselves.
4 Paragraph 1: … *facilities As part of…* → … facilities. As part of (missing full stop); Paragraph 2: *We, are also fortunate* → We are also fortunate (comma not required); Paragraph 4: … *themselves and get fit as well?* → themselves and get fit as well. (a full stop is required instead of a question mark).
5 Paragraph 1 – *It was very interesting to do the survey.* Paragraph 2 – *at lunchtime with school children and office workers in the evening* Paragraph 3 – *I don't like using them.*

Sample text

Introduction

I wanted to write a report to give an overview of the town's sporting facilities. As part of the survey, both tourists and local residents were asked for their views.

Available facilities

There are a number of good quality gyms in the area, which are modern and have a good range of equipment. There are also two swimming pools which are open every day of the year, apart from public holidays. We are also fortunate to have several football pitches, which are very popular.

Problem areas

It was reported that in recent years most gyms have increased their membership fees by 20%. It would appear that the swimming pools are often dirty and crowded, especially in the summer months. According to three school principals, the football pitches are in poor condition and the floodlights are hopeless.

Conclusion

In conclusion, the two main areas of concern among the people interviewed were the rising prices and the poor condition of some of the facilities. I would strongly recommend that the council repair the facilities and subsidise the gym membership fees. This will allow more people in the area to enjoy themselves and get fit as well.

Exam practice

1 **1** You need to describe three aspects of a new building or construction project: 1) its strengths; 2) its weaknesses; 3) its likely future impact on the area. **2** It should be in reasonably formal language, and the same register used throughout.

2

Sample answer

A report on Zatira's new road system

Zatira's new road system

For many years, the town of Zatira suffered from high levels of road congestion and pollution. For this reason, the town council took the decision to build a ring road, so that long-distance traffic could pass around the outside of Zatira instead of going through it.

Construction lasted five years, and work was finally completed in 2017. As soon as the new ring road opened, there was less traffic coming through the centre of the town. Air quality was also said to improve slightly, and many people were very pleased about the road, as they will be able to travel more quickly.

How I have been affected

However, for me personally, it is not so simple. My flat is on the outskirts of Zatira, and from my flat, you can hear the sound of the traffic. On hot days, when the windows are open, it gets really quite noisy. For people living nearer to the road, the situation is worse. I think they should have considered building a wall alongside the road to deal with the noise issue. Hopefully, this will be added soon.

Notes

- *An effective answer, outlining strengths and weaknesses of the road system*
- *Clear title and effective use of headings, making the structure clear (first description of the project, then evaluation of its success)*
- *Appropriate division into paragraphs*
- *No language errors*
- *Good range of grammatical structures: 'so that'; 'was said to'; 'should have'; 'will be added')*

Part 2 (letter)

Training

1 **1** Giving news **2** Requests **3** Making suggestions and recommendations **4** Apologies **5** Thanking someone

2 **1** Your English-speaking friend, Joan.

2 Joan wants to know about the birthday party you organised for your brother.

3 *What kind of party did you organise? Who did you invite? How did it go?*

3 **1** A **2** F **3** G **4** E **5** C **6** B **7** D

4 **1** Yes, it has four paragraphs with a clear structure in each.

2 Yes. She organised the birthday party at a club (para 2); She invited her brother's work friends (para 2); *It was fantastic* (para 2) and *we had a great time* (para 3)

3 To tell Joan about the party (para 1).

4 She uses the phrase: *Hope to hear all your news soon.* (Para 4)

5 *Hi Joan, How's it going?; It's good to hear from you.* (contractions); *I picked my brother up; His face turned bright red* (exclamations); *Anyway, I've got to run; Lots of love*

Exam practice

1 **1** They are English-speaking friends who are coming to stay in your home while you are away. You may wish to invent some details about them to include in your essay (e.g. where they live normally, etc.). **2** You could say that you will be visiting your own family during the friends' visit, or that you are on holiday. **3** You could write about any appropriate jobs you would like your friends to do for you, such as watering your plants, taking the rubbish out, etc.

2

Sample answer

Dear Jon and Patsy,

Welcome to my flat! I've left some food in the fridge for you, so do help yourselves, as I'm sure you're hungry after the journey. Hope your flight wasn't delayed.

It's such a shame that I'm not able to be there to welcome you and show you round the city myself. Unfortunately, I'd already bought my ticket to the conference before I knew you were coming. Anyway, I'll be back in four days, so will see you then.

In the meantime, can I ask a favour? The rubbish is collected every Thursday morning. So, on Wednesday night, would you be able to take the bins out for me, and leave them by the entrance to the building? You'll see everyone else's, so it'll be obvious where. There's also a green box for the recycling. It lives under the kitchen sink, and needs to go out too. Thanks a lot!

Anyway, I hope you'll make yourselves at home. Look forward to seeing you soon.

All the best,

Andrzej

Notes

- *A helpful and welcoming letter*
- *Friendly beginning and ending*
- *Suitable chatty informal style, including appropriate ellipsis: 'Hope your flight wasn't delayed' instead of 'I hope your flight wasn't delayed'*
- *No language errors*
- *Appropriate division into paragraphs*
- *Request for help is made politely*
- *Clear explanation of what the guests need to do*

Part 2 (article)

Training

1

Involving the reader: Have you thought about …?; Are you one of those people who …?; Just imagine …; How would you feel if …?

Adding interest: I was absolutely terrified when I …; More importantly, it was something …; Unsurprisingly, I ended up …; It was the most amazing experience I have ever had.

Developing your points: Another advantage of …; On top of that, …; You also have to …

Making suggestions: Go online and find out about …; Give it a try!; Take my advice and …

2 **1** *Unsurprisingly, I ended up arriving* two hours late.
2 *I was absolutely terrified when I* did my first bungee jump.
3 *On top of that,* I had left my passport at the hotel.
4 *Take my advice and* stay at one of the recommended hotels
5 *Have you thought about* going on a round-the-world trip?

3 **1** A very special holiday you've been on.
2 The readers of a travel magazine.
3 Write about where you went and what you did on holiday.
4 The instructions don't say but it's a good idea to include a title.

4 **1** *Imperatives:* Live the dream! Give it a try! *Rhetorical questions:* Have you ever thought about the perfect holiday? Why worry about that though?

2 Have you ever…? (para 1); If you're looking to (para 4); Give it a try! (para 4)

3 I quickly got used to the food, humidity and even tried some of my Japanese, although it's not very good! (para 2); Japan was very clean (para 3); everyone was really friendly, (para 3); hotels were superb (para 3); I took the bullet train (para 3); slept on a matted floor (para 3); bought a Kimono (para 3); did a sushi making class (para 3)

4 *Final paragraph:* If you're looking to spend amazing time while completely changing your outlook,

5 *Using a title with impact:* Fabulous Japan – Live the dream!; *Start the article with a rhetorical question to address the reader directly:* Have you ever thought about the perfect holiday?

5 **1** Yes, it has four paragraphs with a clear structure. Paragraph 1: gives the introductory information about the holiday; Paragraph 2: explains more about the holiday; Paragraph 3: gives examples of impressions and activities; Paragraph 4: conclusion and suggestion

2 Yes, the writer explains that it was a special holiday (Paragraphs 1 & 4), where he went (Paragraph 1) and what he did (Paragraphs 2 &3).

3 Yes, the writer uses an informal style and tone throughout, with personalised examples, rhetorical questions, exclamation marks, phrases to make the article more interesting.

4 *Have you ever thought about …?* (Para 1); Just imagine (Para 1); *It was the most amazing experience I have ever had.* (Para 1); *Unsurprisingly, I ended up* (Para 3); *Give it a try!* (Para 4)

Exam practice

1 **1** describe a skill that you have learned; describe the challenges you faced while learning it; explain the benefits of having this skill; give advice for others learning the same skill **2** You can choose something that you can or cannot do. *Suggested examples:* driving a car; speaking a foreign language; playing the piano, etc. **3** This depends on the skill, but you need to demonstrate that you can use vocabulary which is appropriate for the level and topic. For example, if your skill was driving, the following phrases might be useful: *change gear smoothly, get used to reversing, gives me greater independence, don't underestimate the time needed to learn*

2

Sample answer

One lesson I'm glad I learned

My father taught me lots of useful things when I was a kid. But one of the most useful was carpentry.

Making his own furniture was always a favourite hobby of my dad's. He'd always prefer to build something himself rather than just get something ready-made from a shop. And so when I was about 9, he decided that I was old enough to learn.

He had some small tools which he showed me how to use. And before long, I was making things myself. Most of it was pretty basic. For example, I remember making a wooden box to keep my toys in. This helped me keep my room tidy, as I wanted to put things back in the box I was so proud of!

It wasn't all easy though. I cut myself a couple of times. And I always found it hard to saw in a really straight line. But the thing you have to remember is that with practice, you get better, and jobs get easier.

Notes

- *Answers all parts of the question: skill = carpentry; challenges = not hurting himself, and cutting in a straight line; benefits = being proud of what you've made; advice = practise*
- *Opening sentence creates interest, but the reader must read on to find out what the skill is*
- *No language errors*
- *Appropriate vocabulary related to topic: 'hobby'; 'tools'; 'saw'*
- *Each paragraph develops the idea from the topic sentence (first sentence of paragraph)*
- *The right length*

Listening

Part 1

Training

1 It's a tour guide, talking to a group of visitors about a city.

2 The key is B – you can decide whether you agree with me, and let me know!

3 & 4

Guide Now everyone, we're currently standing in what's probably **(C)** the most beautiful square in the whole city – in my view, of course! Anyway, there are certainly plenty of other nice **(A)** places for you to explore and compare it with, so maybe you can decide at the end of your stay whether you agree with me, and let me know! **(B)** Anyway, I'm going to give each of you a map, so you'll be able to follow exactly where we are as we walk round the main sights together, and then have some time on your own to have a look around at the places that appeal to you.

A is wrong because although he mentions that there are other nice places to explore, he doesn't say what they are.

C is wrong because they're already in what is probably one of his favourite places – he hasn't had to persuade them to go there.

5 Why is she phoning?

6 The key is B. She's explaining that the concert tickets are more expensive than they'd been told, so she's correcting some information. A is wrong – she's asking for ideas, not giving suggestions. And C is wrong – they *weren't really our first choice of band to see,* so she's not disappointed.

Exam practice

1 **1** two speakers talking about a statue **2** a male music teacher talking about his job **3** two speakers discussing cars without drivers **4** female doctor on the radio talking about colds **5** a woman and a man talking about a musical they have seen **6** a woman talking about horse riding and the benefits it gives her **7** two speakers; a man complaining in a shop and a shop assistant replying to his complaint **8** a woman talking about a chef

2 **1** the statue **2** something the speaker is sad about **3** an opinion both speakers agree on **4** a doctor explaining something that many of her patients don't know about **5** what the woman likes about the musical **6** how the woman has benefitted from going riding **7** what the shop assistant agrees to do in answer to the customer's complaint **8** explaining what she knows about Peter Tinney

3 **1** B **2** A **3** C **4** C **5** A **6** A **7** B **8** C

Part 2

Training

1 The answer could be a part of the body, for example.

2 The key is *skin – it's common practice to do this* = many people do it.

3 *energy* and *performance* are distractors, but only *some athletes* not *many people*, use honey to improve these.

4 Students' own answers

5 The key is *flavour.* The main distractors are *price, colour* and *quality*.

Exam practice

2 **1** a talk **2** filming a wildlife documentary in Gabon **3** a man **4** 9 noun 10 noun 11 adjective 12 noun; probably a person 13 noun; form of transport 14 probably a noun; something they can only get at the beach 15 verb 16 plural noun 17 adjective for describing people 18 noun, probably a kind of animal

2 **9** advert/advertisement **10** guidebook **11** work **12** biologist **13** helicopter **14** salt **15** surfing **16** leopard(s) **17** welcoming **18** tourism

Part 3

Training

2 **1** 'And luckily I'd done some research on the company beforehand so I knew who the boss was, and who her team were. Sounds really obvious, but that's pretty important I'd say,'

2 The key is G – Learn all you can about your employers.

4 The speaker also refers to B, D and H. However, B is wrong because although he made friends with colleagues, he doesn't give this is a piece of advice. D is wrong because he just happened to be wearing the right clothes – he doesn't advise others

H is wrong because he only mentions that he couldn't sleep the night before.

5 **1** Speaker 2 says *no-one expects you to know it all on the first day – useful to bear that in mind, I'd say.* **2** Don't pretend to know everything. **3** The key is E, but she also refers to options A and C.

A is incorrect because although her colleagues told her to ask for help, this wasn't her advice – and she admits that this doesn't happen in every company.

C is incorrect because although she did her best not to be late for work, setting off an hour early, she admits this is *a bit silly.*

Exam practice

1 **1** part-time courses **2** A: if anyone got promoted because of doing a course B: if anyone changed their priorities following the course C: if anyone used it as a way to use their spare time D: if anyone met similar thinking people during the course E: if it helped anyone to wind down after work F: if it gave anyone the opportunity to be creative G: if anyone got a qualification H: if it persuaded anyone to do more courses

2 **19** H **20** C **21** B **22** F **23** A

Part 4

Training

1 & 2 The answer is B – he realised that he preferred football to the piano, but *for the sake of peace, I just kept quiet and carried on practising.*

3 A is correct – *at that point I really did regret my decision about music.*

4 B isn't correct – Dennis doesn't suggest that he felt jealous of his brother.

C isn't correct – as far as we know, he hasn't performed in public at all.

Exam practice

1 **1** an interview **2** an ex sportsperson runs a business **3** an interviewer and a woman called Gemma Porter

2 **24** B **25** C **26** A **27** C **28** B **29** A **30** B

Speaking

Part 1

Training

1 **1** T **2** F **3** T **4** T **5** F

2 **1** present **2** future **3** past **4** future **5** present **6** past

3 **1** B **2** C **3** B **4** A **5** C **6** B

Part 2

Training

1 **1** e **2** c **3** g **4** f **5** a **6** h **7** b **8** d

2 2, 3, 4, 6

3 special **2** like **3** something **4** kind

4 Students' own answers

5 Students' own answers

Part 3

Training

1 **1** with a partner **2** different possibilities **3** all of these **4** three minutes **5** reach agreement **6** one minute

2 **1** That's because **2** For one thing **3** After all **4** The reason for this

3 **1** either **2** happy **3** choice **4** choose **5** go

Part 4

Training

1 **1** your opinions **2** examples and reasons **3** can **4** should **5** might

2 **1** I'd say that … **2** I think that … **3** In my opinion, … **4** correct **5** What's your opinion about … **6** correct **7** What are your views about … **8** How do you feel about …

3 **1** d **2** a **3** c **4** e **5** b

Test 3

Reading and Use of English

Part 1

1 D **2** B **3** C **4** A **5** B **6** A **7** B **8** D

Part 2

9 off **10** myself **11** have **12** One **13** take **14** which **15** not **16** up

Part 3

17 involvement **18** untrained **19** revolutionised / revolutionized **20** suitable **21** intention(s) **22** chosen **23** shortage **24** emotional

Part 4

25 since my sister got married **26** whether / if he had / he'd recovered **27** ever been I allowed to **28** so / as long as Dad is / Dad's **29** warned everyone not to get OR warned everyone to avoid getting OR warned everyone against / about getting **30** is more important to / for Brian OR matters more to Brian

Part 5

31 D **32** B **33** C **34** C **35** A **36** C

Part 6

37 B **38** E **39** A **40** F **41** G **42** D

Part 7

43 B **44** C **45** D **46** A **47** C **48** A **49** C **50** D **51** B **52** A

Writing

Part 1

Sample answer

No school, college or university would be as effective without a library. Libraries are essential in these places, as are public libraries in our towns and cities. But we have to accept that times are changing, books are cheaper to buy, people spend less time reading books, and so as a result, libraries aren't as busy as they once were.

Besides that, the internet provides us with so much to read, that old books in libraries now have some serious competition. But despite this, I think that we still need libraries, and they must adapt in order not to disappear. They already have new services. Most libraries now have public computers, but even that seems a bit old-fashioned now, as almost everyone has a smartphone.

I think that libraries should develop new services, for example allowing people to browse their books online, and order books for loan and delivery. They could hire out their rooms as meeting rooms, or open a café. It's a testing time for libraries, and we should all support them.

Notes

- *A successful answer, addressing all parts of the question*
- *Limited use of tenses (present simple), but this is appropriate for the task*
- *Wide range of modal verbs used effectively*
- *No language errors*
- *Linking phrases are used appropriately: 'as a result'; 'besides that'; 'despite this'*
- *The right length*

Listening

Part 1

1 A **2** C **3** B **4** B **5** B **6** C **7** A **8** C

Part 2

9 challenging **10** independent **11** rain **12** (trip) leaders **13** accommodation **14** maps / a map **15** gentle **16** (cycle) paths **17** rest days **18** certificate

Part 3

19 E **20** D **21** H **22** C **23** A

Part 4

24 B **25** A **26** B **27** C **28** A **29** C **30** C

Test 4

Reading and Use of English

Part 1

1 B **2** B **3** A **4** B **5** C **6** B **7** D **8** A

Part 2

9 it / this **10** too **11** get / be / go **12** up **13** like **14** unable **15** At **16** having

Part 3

17 undivided **18** anxious **19** Another **20** unsure **21** frightened **22** relaxed **23** tendency **24** sociable

Part 4

25 have / get something to **26** to / would take such a **27** if / whether (s)he objected to **28** doesn't / does not annoy me any **29** thanked everybody for making her / the **30** was / felt desperate to win

Part 5

31 B **32** D **33** B **34** D **35** D **36** A

Part 6

37 D **38** E **39** G **40** C **41** B **42** F

Part 7

43 A **44** B **45** C **46** A **47** B **48** C **49** A **50** D **51** C **52** A

Writing

Part 1 (essay)

Sample answer

Ready meals saved my life!

If I ever cooked a meal for you, you would never forget the experience. I am not boasting. But I am being honest. I am probably the worst cook in the world. If I make toast, I burn it.

That's why I almost always go for ready meals. My local supermarket has a good supply of pre-cooked portions, which just go into the microwave. Two minutes, and it's done. It's tasty too – even when I microwave things! And the takeaways near my home are great too!

Some of my friends laugh at me because I never cook. Actually, I laugh at them because they waste hours chopping up vegetables into tiny pieces. What a waste of time! People say that ready meals and fast food are bad for you, but actually, eating them can be just as healthy if you have a balanced diet, not the same thing all the time. Plus, my flatmates and I often eat together, so ready meals and takeaways can be sociable too.

Notes

- *Good choice of title, which exaggerates, but summarises the writer's point*
- *Starts by addressing the reader which grabs the reader's attention successfully: 'If I ever cooked a meal for you'*
- *Uses a mixture of short and long sentences in the first paragraph which creates interest, and seems to express the writer's personality*
- *Covers all the points in the instruction, as well as the writer's own idea (their inability to cook)*
- *Suitable length*
- *Paragraphs used appropriately*
- *No language errors*

Listening

Part 1

1 B **2** A **3** C **4** B **5** A **6** C **7** C **8** B

Part 2

9 documentary **10** ice **11** tree **12** rain(fall) **13** hand(-)picked **14** temperature **15** honey **16** instant **17** energy **18** ceremony

Part 3

19 B **20** D **21** G **22** A **23** F

Part 4

24 B **25** B **26** C **27** A **28** C **29** C **30** A

Test 5

Reading and Use of English

Part 1

1 B **2** C **3** A **4** D **5** C **6** D **7** B **8** A

Part 2

9 from **10** which **11** because **12** what **13** in
14 when(ever) / if / once **15** there **16** that / this

Part 3

17 Unlike **18** welcoming **19** diversity **20** production
21 setting **22** virtually **23** sustainable **24** sight

Part 4

25 doesn't / does not contain (any) **26** the only one
27 was / were more talented at **28** failed to go
29 it was the wrong **30** was David who / that managed to

Part 5

31 B **32** C **33** D **34** C **35** B **36** A

Part 6

37 B **38** G **39** F **40** A **41** E **42** D

Part 7

43 D **44** C **45** D **46** A **47** E **48** B **49** E **50** B **51** A **52** C

Writing

Part 1 (essay)

Sample answer

Spending money wisely – or wasting it?

For the last several hundred years, governments all over the world have spent money building monuments to themselves. The reason was simple – to make themselves look good. I think that when governments nowadays spend money on an art festival, or on a new statue in the park, it's the same. They think they can buy popularity.

But even in wealthy countries, public institutions like schools and hospitals rarely have enough money. If the government then decides to pay for a mural on the town hall, they'll have even less. You could argue that paying for public works of art does more harm than good.

I would suggest that anyone who is in favour of public artworks should be able to donate money to the local government for that purpose. When there's enough money, the people who have donated could have a say in choosing what kind of artwork gets created. I think that would be much fairer.

Notes

- *A successful answer*
- *Clearly states opinion in first paragraph*
- *Fully addresses the question*
- *Makes own recommendation in final paragraph*
- *Appropriate length*
- *Uses range of tenses and modal verbs*
- *Uses complex sentences: 'I would suggest that anyone who is in favour of public artworks should be able to donate money to the local government for that purpose.'*

Listening

Part 1

1 A **2** B **3** C **4** A **5** C **6** C **7** A **8** B

Part 2

9 Dairy Month **10** museum **11** song **12** sculptures
13 tasting **14** magic show **15** advance tickets
16 farm tours / (a) farm tour **17** volunteers **18** skateboard park

Part 3

19 A **20** F **21** B **22** H **23** D

Part 4

24 C **25** A **26** B **27** A **28** B **29** C **30** C

Test 6

Reading and Use of English

Part 1

1 C **2** B **3** D **4** A **5** D **6** A **7** D **8** C

Part 2

9 over / through(out) **10** in **11** out **12** which **13** than
14 no **15** be **16** when

Part 3

17 competition **18** presence **19** visitors **20** promising
21 impression **22** entrance **23** Fortunately **24** salty

Part 4

25 me know what your decision **26** get in touch with **27** had difficulty (in) persuading **28** it if you came / would / could come
29 had (her / some / a few) doubts about **30** see / understand the point

Part 5

31 B **32** A **33** C **34** D **35** D **36** C

Part 6

37 G **38** C **39** A **40** F **41** B **42** E

Part 7

43 C **44** F **45** E **46** B **47** A **48** C **49** F **50** D **51** A **52** C

Writing

Part 1 (essay)

Sample answer

Too academic – and not practical enough

Like many people, I learned lots of things at school that I will never need. In maths, I learned how to calculate the exact lengths of the three sides of a triangle. This is perhaps the most useless skill I have ever learned. I remember my physics teacher getting us all to learn the names of the planets in our solar system. She needn't have bothered, as I don't plan to visit any of them!

But I also left school without knowing a lot of really basic stuff about life, like how to open a bank account, or how to change an electrical fuse. It's the little things like these that make a real difference later in life. People waste millions each year on plumbers, electricians and builders, paying for simple repairs that they should be able to do themselves.

And school is the place to learn these skills. Every week, why not have a lesson where one professional comes in and talks to the students? It could be a bank manager one week, and an electrician the next. It would really help.

Notes

- *Appropriate title, which summarises the writer's opinion*
- *Entertaining use of anecdotes from the writer's own schooldays*
- *All aspects of the question fully addressed*
- *No language errors*
- *Effective use of paragraphs*
- *Correct length*
- *Chatty informal style, which is acceptable, as it used consistently: 'She needn't have bothered, as I don't plan to visit any of them!'; 'why not have a lesson where …'*
- *Writer's opinion is clear throughout*

Listening

Part 1

1 A **2** C **3** C **4** A **5** B **6** B **7** A **8** B

Part 2

9 stone **10** handles **11** beauty **12** weight **13** lighthouse **14** curved **15** sand **16** self(-)portrait **17** furniture **18** chemist

Part 3

19 B **20** H **21** G **22** C **23** E

Part 4

24 C **25** A **26** C **27** A **28** B **29** B **30** A

Reading and Use of English

38926

OFFICE USE ONLY - DO NOT WRITE OR MAKE ANY MARK ABOVE THIS LINE

Cambridge Assessment English

Candidate Name		Candidate Number	
Centre Name		Centre Number	
Examination Title		Examination Details	
Candidate Signature		Assessment Date	

Supervisor: If the candidate is ABSENT or has WITHDRAWN shade here ○

First Reading and Use of English Candidate Answer Sheet

Instructions

Use a PENCIL (B or HB).

Rub out any answer you want to change using an eraser.

Parts 1, 5, 6 and 7:
Mark ONE letter for each question.

For example, if you think A is the right answer to the question, mark your answer sheet like this: 0 A B C

Parts 2, 3 and 4: Write your answer clearly in CAPITAL LETTERS.

For parts 2 and 3, write one letter in each box. 0 EXAMPLE

Part 1

	A	B	C	D
1	○	○	○	○
2	○	○	○	○
3	○	○	○	○
4	○	○	○	○
5	○	○	○	○
6	○	○	○	○
7	○	○	○	○
8	○	○	○	○

Part 2

	Answer	Do not write below here
9		9 1 ○ 0 ○
10		10 1 ○ 0 ○
11		11 1 ○ 0 ○
12		12 1 ○ 0 ○
13		13 1 ○ 0 ○
14		14 1 ○ 0 ○
15		15 1 ○ 0 ○
16		16 1 ○ 0 ○

Continues over →

OFFICE USE ONLY - DO NOT WRITE OR MAKE ANY MARK BELOW THIS LINE

Page 1 of 2

38926

Reading and Use of English

38926

OFFICE USE ONLY - DO NOT WRITE OR MAKE ANY MARK ABOVE THIS LINE

Part 3	Do not write below here
17	17 1 0
18	18 1 0
19	19 1 0
20	20 1 0
21	21 1 0
22	22 1 0
23	23 1 0
24	24 1 0

Part 4	Do not write below here
25	25 2 1 0
26	26 2 1 0
27	27 2 1 0
28	28 2 1 0
29	29 2 1 0
30	30 2 1 0

Part 5				
31	A	B	C	D
32	A	B	C	D
33	A	B	C	D
34	A	B	C	D
35	A	B	C	D
36	A	B	C	D

Part 6							
37	A	B	C	D	E	F	G
38	A	B	C	D	E	F	G
39	A	B	C	D	E	F	G
40	A	B	C	D	E	F	G
41	A	B	C	D	E	F	G
42	A	B	C	D	E	F	G

Part 7						
43	A	B	C	D	E	F
44	A	B	C	D	E	F
45	A	B	C	D	E	F
46	A	B	C	D	E	F
47	A	B	C	D	E	F
48	A	B	C	D	E	F
49	A	B	C	D	E	F
50	A	B	C	D	E	F
51	A	B	C	D	E	F
52	A	B	C	D	E	F

OFFICE USE ONLY - DO NOT WRITE OR MAKE ANY MARK BELOW THIS LINE

Page 2 of 2

38926

20512

OFFICE USE ONLY - DO NOT WRITE OR MAKE ANY MARK ABOVE THIS LINE

Cambridge Assessment English

Candidate Name		Candidate Number	
Centre Name		Centre Number	
Examination Title		Examination Details	
Candidate Signature		Assessment Date	

Supervisor: If the candidate is ABSENT or has WITHDRAWN shade here ○

First Listening Candidate Answer Sheet

Instructions

Use a PENCIL (B or HB).
Rub out any answer you want to change using an eraser.

Parts 1, 3 and **4:**
Mark ONE letter for each question.

For example, if you think **A** is the right answer to the question, mark your answer sheet like this:

Part 2:
Write your answer clearly in CAPITAL LETTERS.

Write one letter or number in each box.
If the answer has more than one word, leave one box empty between words.

For example:

Turn this sheet over to start.

OFFICE USE ONLY - DO NOT WRITE OR MAKE ANY MARK BELOW THIS LINE

Page 1 of 2

20512

Listening

20512

Part 1

1	A	B	C
2	A	B	C
3	A	B	C
4	A	B	C
5	A	B	C
6	A	B	C
7	A	B	C
8	A	B	C

Part 2 (Remember to write in CAPITAL LETTERS or numbers)

		Do not write below here
9		9 1 0
10		10 1 0
11		11 1 0
12		12 1 0
13		13 1 0
14		14 1 0
15		15 1 0
16		16 1 0
17		17 1 0
18		18 1 0

Part 3

19	A	B	C	D	E	F	G	H
20	A	B	C	D	E	F	G	H
21	A	B	C	D	E	F	G	H
22	A	B	C	D	E	F	G	H
23	A	B	C	D	E	F	G	H

Part 4

24	A	B	C
25	A	B	C
26	A	B	C
27	A	B	C
28	A	B	C
29	A	B	C
30	A	B	C

Writing

Answer Sheet Page 1

Part One Answer You must write within the grey lines.

Speaking Part 2

- **Why might people choose to do exercise in these different ways?**

A

B

Speaking Part 2

- **How do you think the people feel about their achievements?**

A

B

Test 1 Exam practice Speaking • Part 2

- What do you think these people are enjoying about being at home?

A

B

Test 1 Exam practice Speaking • Part 2

- Why do you think these people are busy?

A

B

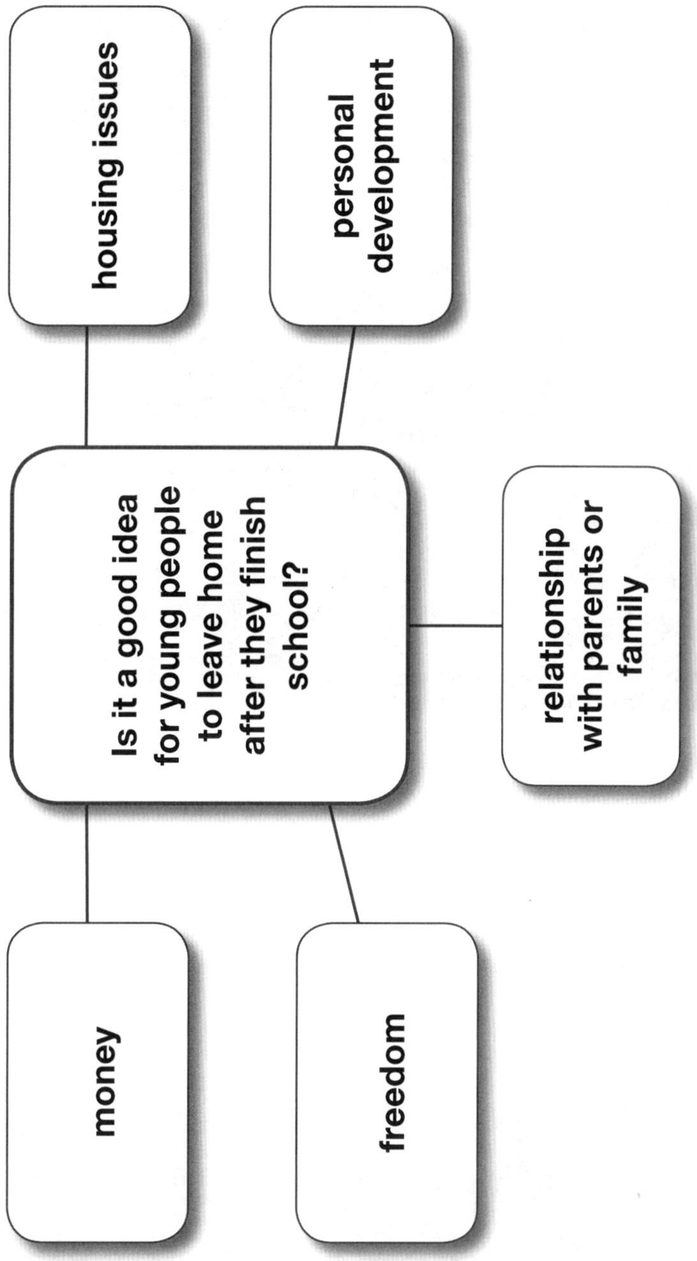
Is it a good idea for young people to leave home after they finish school?
housing issues
personal development
relationship with parents or family
money
freedom

Test 2 Training Speaking Part 2

- How do you think the people feel about the photos they are taking?

A

B

Speaking Part 2

- Why are the people playing music?

A

B

Speaking • Part 2

- Why do you think the people are using the laptops?

A

B

Speaking • Part 2

- What do you think the people are enjoying about eating together?

A

B

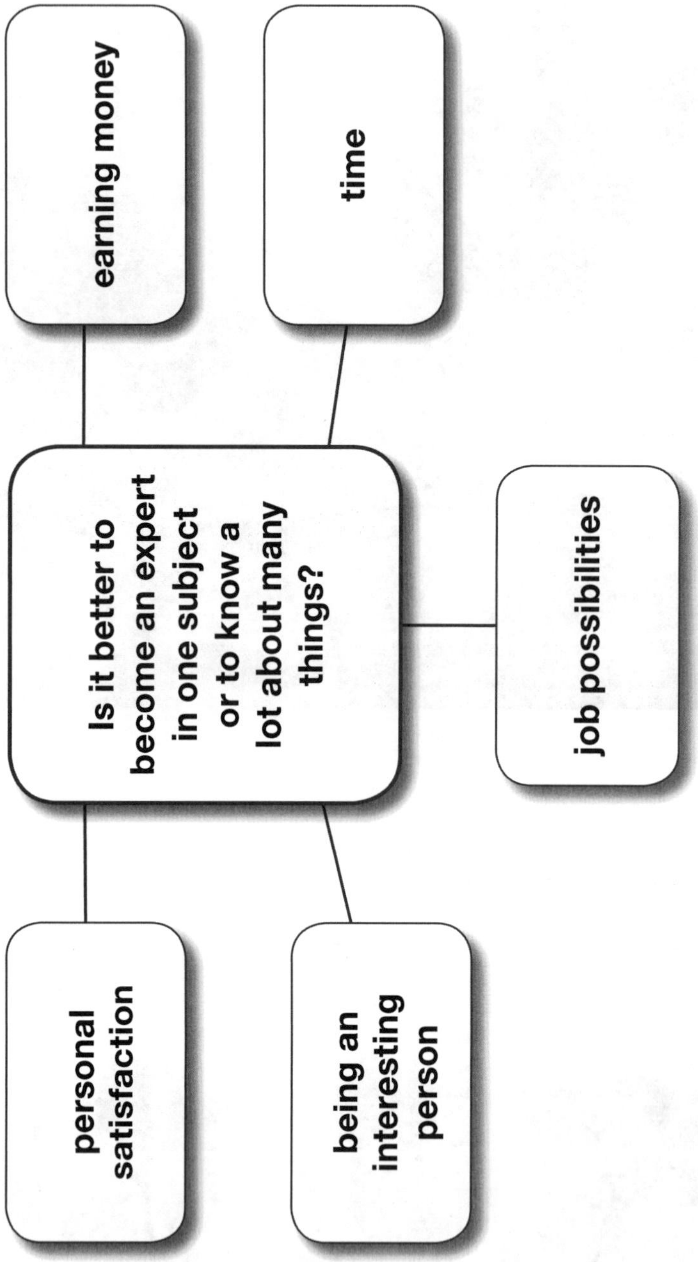
Is it better to become an expert in one subject or to know a lot about many things?
earning money
time
job possibilities
personal satisfaction
being an interesting person

Speaking • Part 2

- Why do you think these people are taking exercise in these ways?

A

B

Test 3 Speaking • Part 2

- What are these people enjoying about listening to music in the different places?

A

B

Speaking • Part 3

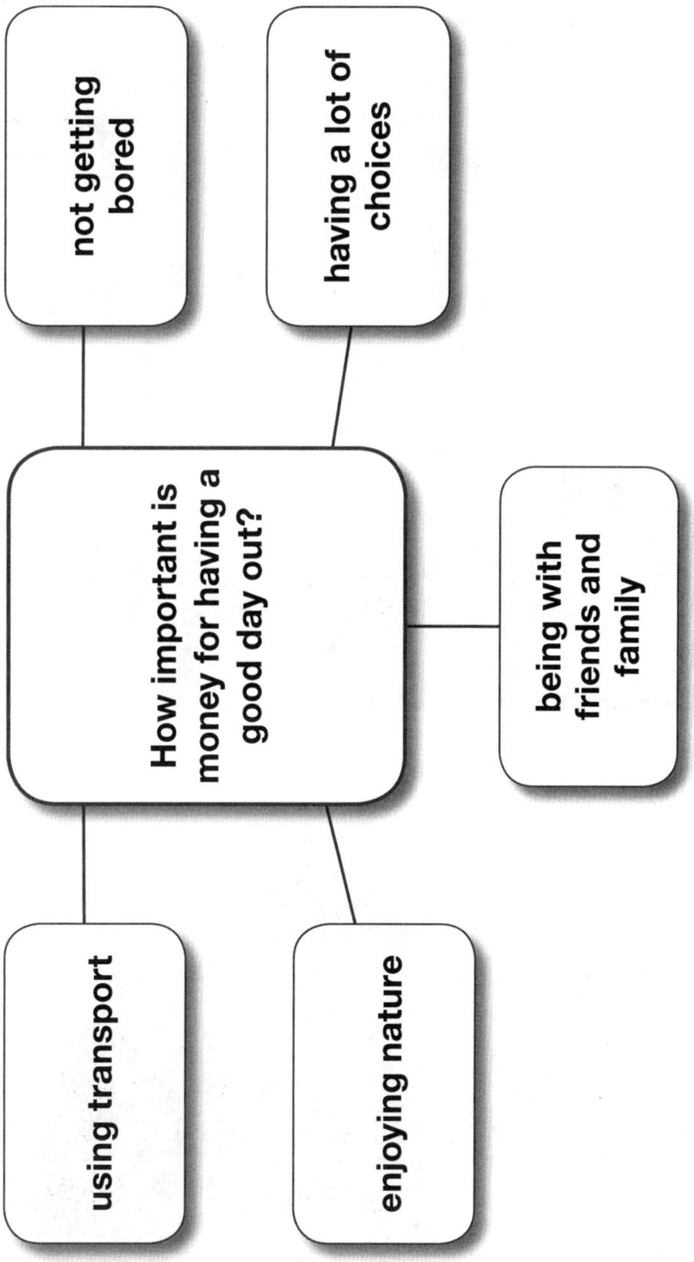

Speaking • Part 2

- **Why do you think the people are reading?**

A

B

Speaking • Part 2

- Why do you think the people are dancing in these places?

A

B

Speaking • Part 3

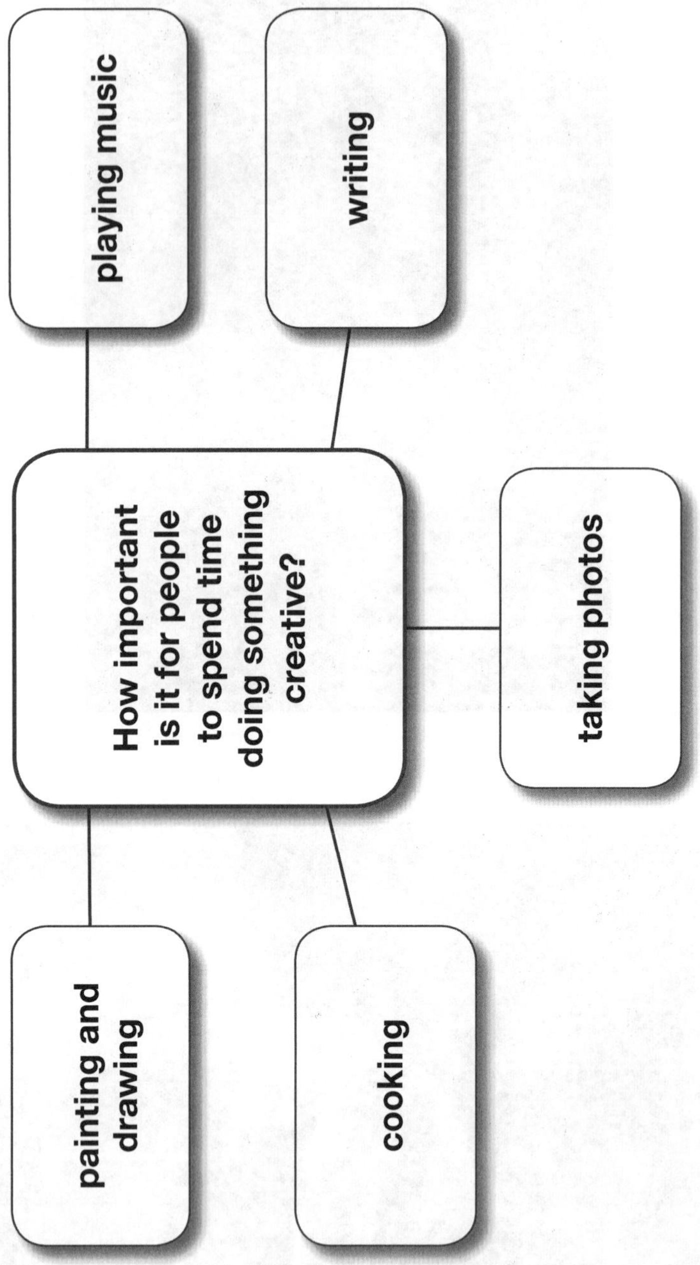

Speaking • Part 2

- Why do you think the people are doing these things?

A

B

Test 5 Speaking • Part 2

- How do you think the weather is affecting the people in these situations?

A

B

Test 5 Speaking • Part 3

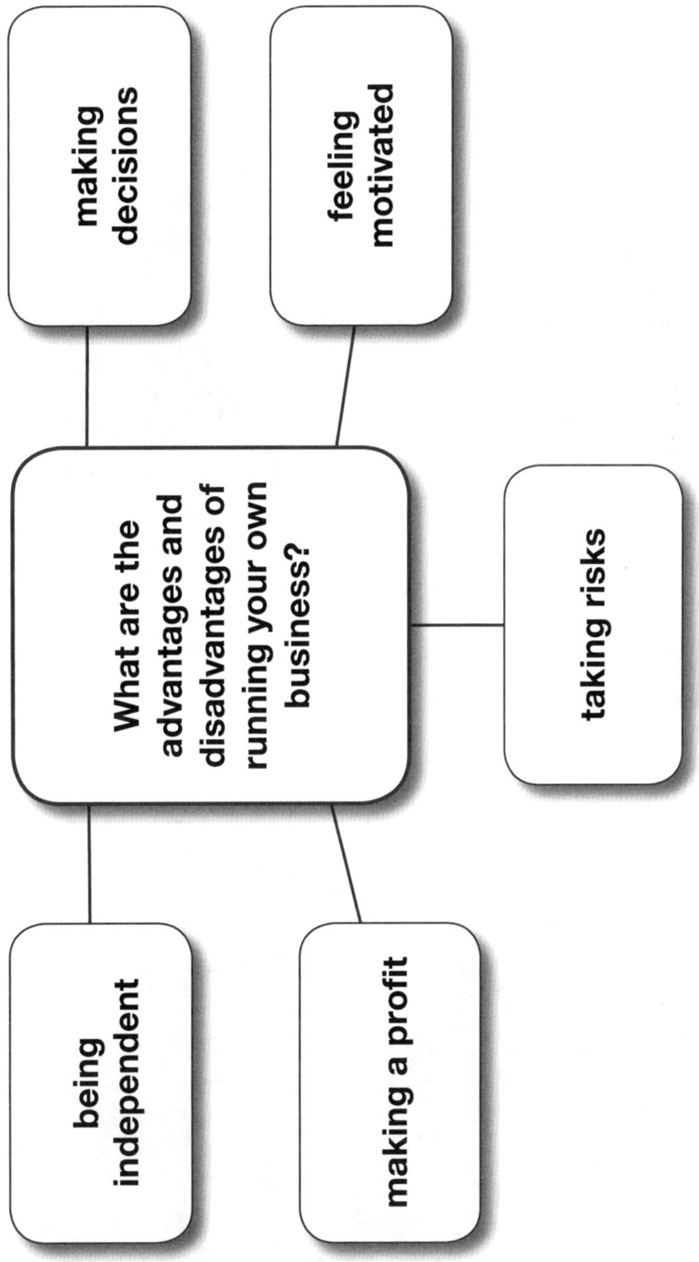

Test 6 Speaking • Part 2

- Why do you think these people are working together?

A

B

Speaking • Part 2

- How do you think the people are feeling about growing things?

A

B

Speaking • Part 3

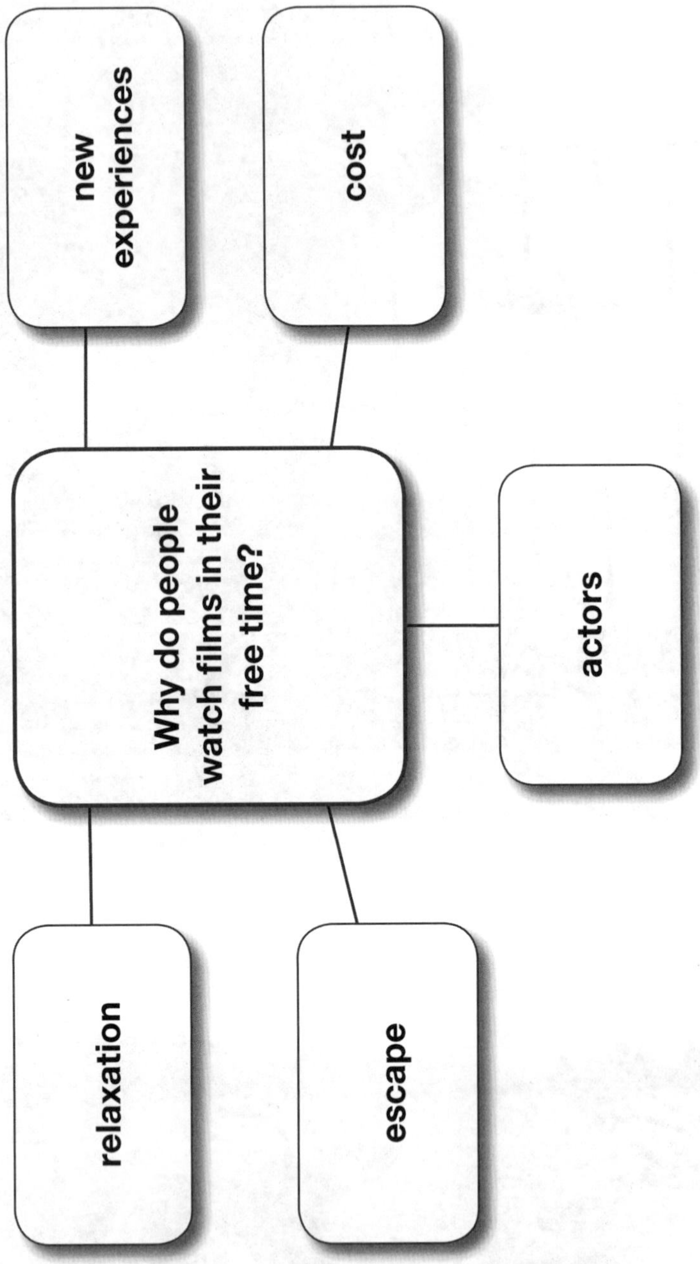

Acknowledgements

Our highly experienced team of Trainer writers, in collaboration with Cambridge English Language Assessment reviewers, have worked together to bring you *First Trainer 2*. We would like to thank Carole Allsop (writer), Anthony Cosgrove (writer), Sheila Dignen (writer), Matthew Duffy (writer), Sue Elliott (writer), Peter Sunderland (writer), Helen Tiliouine (writer), Sarah Dymond (writer and reviewer) and Wendy Sharp (reviewer) for their work on the material.

The authors and publishers acknowledge the following sources of copyright material and are grateful for the permissions granted. While every effort has been made, it has not always been possible to identify the sources of all the material used, or to trace all copyright holders. If any omissions are brought to our notice, we will be happy to include the appropriate Acknowledgements on reprinting and in the next update to the digital edition, as applicable.

Text Acknowledgements:
Immediate Media Company Ltd. for the text on pp. 28–29 from 'There are no silver medals: how it feels to row – and lose – the Boat Race' by Tom Ransley, Radio Times website, 02.04.2017. Copyright © 2017 Immediate Media Company. Reproduced with permission; Bloomsbury Publishing Plc for the text on p. 33 from *Polar Bears: The Natural History of a Threatened Species* by Stirling Ian, November 2012. Copyright © 2012 Bloomsbury Publishing Plc. Reproduced with permission; Fitzhenry and Whiteside Limited for the text on p. 33 from 'Polar Bears: The natural history of a threatened species' by Stirling Ian, 2011. Copyright © 2011 Fitzhenry and Whiteside Limited. Reproduced with permission; Immediate Media Company Ltd. for the text on p. 36 from 'TV turns 80 today! The inside story of how it all started' by Joe Moran, Radio Times website, 04.08.2016. Copyright © 2016 Immediate Media Company. Reproduced with permission of Immediate Media; Times Newspapers Limited for the text on pp. 84–85 from 'Gregory Porter: music is more than popularity, more than being cool. It's deeply emotional' by John Bungey, *Times Newspapers,* 29.05.2017. Copyright © 2017 Times Newspapers Limited. Reproduced with permission of News Syndication; Telegraph Media Group Limited for the text on pp. 87–88 from 'Rock star: how Chopard turned the 342-carat Queen of Kalahari rough diamond into an entire high jewellery collection' by Sarah Royce-Greensill, *The Telegraph*, 21.01.2017. Copyright © 2017 Telegraph Group Media Limited. Reproduced with permission; Times Newspapers Limited for the text on p. 91 from 'Dion Leonard: I decided I was bringing Gobi the dog back to the UK ', *Times Newspapers*, 27.05.2017. Copyright © 2017 Times Newspapers Limited. Reproduced with permission of News Syndication; The Financial Times Ltd. for the text on p. 125 from 'No travelling isn't character-building — it's just' by Janan Ganesh, *Financial Times*, 02.06.2017. Copyright © 2017 Financial Times. Reproduced with permission; Telegraph Media Group Limited for the text on pp. 127–128 from 'Northern Lights: Celestial Dancers, or the souls of fallen warriors' by Adrian Bridge, *The Telegraph*, 16.08.2014. Copyright © 2014 Telegraph Media Group Limited. Reproduced with permission; Times Newspapers Limited for the text on p. 130 from 'Film composer's music for the common man (and woman)' by David Waller, Times Newspapers Limited, June 2017. Copyright © 2017 Times Newspapers Limited. Reproduced with permission of News Syndication; Telegraph Media Group Limited for the text on pp. 143–144 from 'Chain gang' by Jeremy Wilson, *The Telegraph*, 26.06.2015. Copyright © 2015 Telegraph Media Group Limited. Reproduced with permission; Rough Guides Limited for the text on pp. 145–146 from '*Rough Guide to Weather*' by Robert Henson, pp. ix–x. Copyright © 2007 *Rough Guides Limited*. Reproduced with permission; Immediate Media Company Ltd. for the text on p. 148 from 'Wild things: the Springwatch team reveal what inspired their love of nature' by The Springwatch Team, Radio Times website. Copyright © 2017 Immediate Media Company. Reproduced with permission; Guardian News and Media Limited for the text on p. 161 from 'Looking sharp! How the cactus became the planet's most-wanted plant' by Paula Cocozza, 31.05.2017. Copyright © 2017 Guardian News & Media Ltd. Reproduced with permission; Telegraph Media Group Limited for the text on pp. 163–164 from 'Flight of imagination: human swan completes 7,000 mile journey to save the Bewick's' by Sacha Dench and Olivia Parke, *The Telegraph*, 17.12.2016. Copyright © 2016 Telegraph Media Group Limited. Reproduced with permission; Guardian News and Media Limited for the text on p. 166 from 'Massimo Bottura and his global movement to feed the hungry' by Tim Adams, 21.05.2017. Copyright © 2017 Guardian News & Media Ltd. Reproduced with permission; Times Newspapers Limited for the text on p. 179 from 'What beautiful writing you have: the rise of modern calligraphy' by Fiona Wilson, *Times Newspapers*, 22.06.2017. Copyright © 2017 Times Newspapers Limited. Reproduced with permission of News Syndication; Times Newspapers Limited for the text on pp. 181–182 from 'How blue whale evolved to size of a Boeing 737' by Ben Webster, *Times Newspapers*, 24.05.2017. Copyright © 2017 Times Newspapers Limited. Reproduced with permission of News Syndication; Times Newspapers Limited for the text on p. 184 from 'Want to look like this? The answer is as much in your mind as in the gym' by Matthew Syed, *Times Newspapers*, 29.05.2017. Copyright © 2017 Times Newspapers Limited. Reproduced with permission of News Syndication.

Photo Acknowledgements:
All the photographs are sourced from Getty Images:

p. 15: Mats Silvan/Moment Open; p. 22: DEA/A. DAGLI ORTI/De Agostini Picture Library; p. 26: FatCamera/E+; p. 27: Topic Images Inc.; p. 29: Chris Williamson/Getty Images News; p. 33: AGF/Universal Images Group; p. 44: Peter Muller/Cultura; p. 55: David Williams/Corbis Documentary; p. 56: Planet Observer/Universal Images Group; p. 58: Caiaimage/Chris Ryan/Caiaimage; p. 59: Michael Dodge/Getty Images Sport; p. 78: Tim Platt/ Photographer's Choice; p. 79: Anik Messier/Moment; p. 85: Tabatha Fireman/Redferns; p. 86: Media for Medical/Universal Images Group; p. 94: Johnnie Davis/Moment; p. 101: DEA/W. BUSS/De Agostini; p. 104, 107: AFP; p. 108: RIEGER Bertrand/hemis.fr; p. 110: Hinterhaus Productions/DigitalVision; p. 111: ullstein bild; p. 122: LeoPatrizi/E+; p. 123: Bettmann; p. 126: Austin Bush/Lonely Planet Images; p. 128: JONATHAN NACKSTRAND/AFP; p. 131: Roy Mehta/DigitalVision; p. 134: T.T./Stone; p. 135: sturti/E+; p. 141: Lisa Wiltse/Corbis News; p. 144: Denis Doyle/Getty Images Sport; p. 146: Sergei Savostyanov/TASS; 147: JUSTIN TALLIS/AFP; p. 149: Tetra Images; p. 153: Erik Isakson/Tetra images; p. 154: Chau Doan/LightRocket; p. 158: KOEN VAN WEEL/AFP/Getty Images; p. 159: Mike Hewitt - FIFA/FIFA; p. 162: JOEL MERINO/AFP/Getty Images; p. 164: Anagr/iStock/Getty Images Plus; p. 165: Michael Loccisano/Getty Images Entertainment; p. 167: Anne Dirkse/Moment; p. 170: Michael Thornton/Perspectives; p. 171: Hero Images; p. 176: Education Images/Universal Images Group; p. 177: Simon McGil/Moment; p. 182: Barcroft Media; p. 185: Megan Maloy/Image Source; p. 189: Thomas Barwick/Stone; p. 190: Flavia Morlachetti/Moment; C1 (T): Jeff Greenberg/Universal Images Group; C1 (B): Keith Getter/Moment Mobile; C2 (T): Paula Bronstein/Getty Images News; C2 (B): Patrick McDermott/Getty Images Sport; C3 (T): Robert Daly/Caiaimage; C3 (B): Oscar Wong/Moment; C4 (T): Caiaimage/Martin Barraud; p. C4 (B): Bashir Osman's Photography/Moment; C6 (T): LIONEL BONAVENTURE/AFP; C6 (B): Digital Camera Magazine/Future; C7 (T): PETER PARKS/AFP; C7 (B): KENZO TRIBOUILLARD/AFP; C8 (T): Hill Street Studios/Blend Images; C8 (B): Hisayoshi Osawa/DigitalVision; C9 (T): Moretti/Viant/Caiaimage; C9 (B): skynesher/E+; C11 (T), C11 (B), C12 (T), C14(B): Hero Images; C12 (B): Chuck Savage/Corbis; C14 (T): Jean Glueck/F1online; C15 (T): Ingolf Pompe/LOOK-foto; C15 (B): DreamPictures/Jensen Walker/Blend Images; C17 (T): Ariel Skelley/DigitalVision; C17 (B): B2M Productions/DigitalVision; C18 (T): Bob Thomas/Photographer's Choice; C18 (B): Himanshu Khagta/Photolibrary; C20 (T): Gary Burchell/Taxi; C20 (B): John Elk III/Lonely Planet Images; C21 (T): Helen Marsden #christmassowhite/DigitalVision; C21 (B): Thomas Barwick/Stone.

Audio recordings by DN and AE Strauss Ltd. Engineer: Neil Rogers; Editor: James Miller; Producer: Dan Strauss. Recorded at Half Ton Studios, Cambridge.